# TODDLERS, PARENTS, AND CULTURE: FINDINGS FROM THE JOINT EFFORT TODDLER TEMPERAMENT CONSORTIUM

One doesn't have to travel extensively to realize that there are intriguing differences in the ways in which people from different cultures tend to behave. Gartstein and Putnam explore whether these differences are shaped during the early years of life, at the moment when children are just beginning to understand how, when, and why they should express some emotions, and not others.

Based on the findings of the Joint Effort Toddler Temperament Consortium (JETTC), which asked parents from 14 different countries multiple questions regarding their main goals and techniques for raising children to be successful in their culture, Gartstein and Putnam analyze how children's characteristics (both normative and problematic) are shaped by different cultural environments. Drawing from insights in anthropology, sociology, and developmental psychology, the book explores the full spectrum of human experience, from broad sets of values and concerns that differentiate populations down to the intimate details of parent–child relationships. The results reveal a complex web of interrelations among societal ideals, parental attempts to fulfill them, and the ways their children manifest these efforts. In doing so, they provide a revealing look at how families raise their young children around the world.

*Toddlers, Parents, and Culture* will be of great interest to students and scholars in temperament, cross-cultural psychology, parenting, and socioemotional development in early childhood, as well as professionals in early education, child mental health, and behavioral pediatrics.

**Maria A. Gartstein** is professor at Washington State University (WSU) Department of Psychology and Director of ADVANCE at WSU. Dr. Gartstein has been studying temperament and cross-cultural differences for the past 20 years. The cross-cultural emphasis in part reflects her own experience as an immigrant, arriving in the US with her family as a child.

**Samuel P. Putnam** is professor and chair of the Psychology Department at Bowdoin College, and Co-Chair of Undergraduate Research for the International Congress of Infant Studies (ICIS). His research concerns the measurement and structure of temperament, and how nature interacts with nurture to shape individual differences in children.

# TODDLERS, PARENTS, AND CULTURE

## Findings from the Joint Effort Toddler Temperament Consortium

*Edited by*
*Maria A. Gartstein and*
*Samuel P. Putnam*

Routledge
Taylor & Francis Group
LONDON AND NEW YORK

First published 2019
by Routledge
2 Park Square, Milton Park, Abingdon, Oxon OX14 4RN

and by Routledge
52 Vanderbilt Avenue, New York, NY 10017

*Routledge is an imprint of the Taylor & Francis Group, an informa business*



*British Library Cataloguing-in-Publication Data*
A catalogue record for this book is available from the British Library

*Library of Congress Cataloging-in-Publication Data*
Names: Gartstein, Maria A., editor. | Putnam, Samuel P., editor.
Title: Toddlers, parents, and culture : findings from the joint effort toddler temperament consortium / edited by Maria A. Gartstein and Samuel P. Putnam.
Description: 1 Edition. | New York : Routledge, 2019.
Identifiers: LCCN 2018033529 (print) | LCCN 2018037266 (ebook) |
ISBN 9781351788847 (ePub) | ISBN 9781351788854 (Adobe) |
ISBN 9781351788830 (Mobipocket) | ISBN 9781138702301 (hardback) |
ISBN 9781138388130 (pbk.) | ISBN 9781315203713 (ebook)
Subjects: LCSH: Child development—Social aspects—Case studies. |
Parenting—Social aspects—Case studies.
Classification: LCC HQ767.9 (ebook) | LCC HQ767.9 .T63 2019 (print) |
DDC 305.231—dc23
LC record available at https://lccn.loc.gov/2018033529

ISBN: 978-1-138-70230-1 (hbk)
ISBN: 978-1-138-38813-0 (pbk)
ISBN: 978-1-315-20371-3 (ebk)

Typeset in Bembo and Stone Sans
by Florence Production Ltd, Stoodleigh, Devon, UK

MIX
Paper from responsible sources
FSC® C013056

Printed and bound in Great Britain by
TJ International Ltd, Padstow, Cornwall

# DEDICATION

This book is dedicated to Dr. Mary Klevjord Rothbart, who fundamentally shaped the way we think about temperament. She also introduced us to each other and to our first international colleague, Dr. Carmen González-Salinas. Dr. Rothbart has continued to guide our efforts, inspiring us with her clarity of mind and strength of spirit.

# CONTENTS

# FIGURES

# TABLES

# CONTRIBUTORS

## JETTC contributor list

### *Belgium*

**Sara Casalin**, Department of Psychology, University of Leuven

### *Brazil*

**Maria Beatriz Martins Linhares**, Department of Neurosciences and Behavior, Ribeirão Preto Medical School, University São Paulo

### *Chile*

**Felipe Lecannelier**, Facultad de Medicina, Universidad de Santiago de Chile

### *China*

**Zhengyan Wang**, College of Psychology, Capital Normal University

### *Finland*

**Soile Tuovinen**, **Kati Heinonen**, and **Katri Räikkönen**, University of Helsinki

## *Italy*

**Rosario Montirosso**, **Lorenzo Giusti**, **Niccolò Butti**, and **Livio Provenzi**, *0–3 Centre for the at-Risk Infant*, Scientific Institute, IRCCCS "E. Medea", Bisisio Parini, Lecco

## *Korea*

**Sae-Young Han** and **Seong-Yeon Park**, Department of Child Development, Ewha Womans University

**Eun Gyoung Lee**, Ewha Social Science Research Institute, Ewha Womans University

## *Mexico*

**Blanca Huitron** and **Guadalupe Domínguez-Sandoval**, Department of Psychology, National Autonomous University of Mexico

## *The Netherlands*

**Carolina de Weerth** and **Roseriet Beijers**, Behavioural Science Institute, Radboud University

**Mirjana Majdandžić**, Research Institute of Child Development and Education, University of Amsterdam

## *Romania*

**Oana Benga** and **Georgiana Susa-Erdogan**, Department of Psychology, Babes Bolyai University

## *Russia*

**Helena Slobodskaya**, Research Institute of Physiology and Basic Medicine, Novosibirsk State University

**Elena Kozlova**, Research Institute of Physiology and Basic Medicine

## *Spain*

**Carmen González-Salinas**, **Noelia Sánchez-Pérez**, and **Luis J. Fuentes**, Faculty of Psychology, University of Murcia

**Emine Ahmetoglu**, Faculty of Education, Trakya University, Department of Early Childhood Education

## *Turkey*

***Ibrahim Acar***, Özyeğin University, Faculty of Social Sciences, Department of Psychology

## *The US*

**Maria A. Gartstein**, **Eric Desmarais**, and **Marlis Cornelia Kirchhoff**, Department of Psychology, Washington State University

**Amanda Prokasky**, Center for Research on Children, Youth, Families and Schools, University of Nebraska—Lincoln

**Samuel P. Putnam** and **Hannah Broos**, Psychology Department, Bowdoin College

# ACKNOWLEDGMENTS

We acknowledge the contribution of all participating families who made this work possible and are grateful for the funding provided by the Washington State University College of Arts and Sciences 2014 Berry Family Faculty Excellence Award to the first author (MAG). Also, we credit Manuel Veas Porlán and Vanesa García Peñas as the artists responsible for the JETTC logo below.

# 1

# INTRODUCTION TO THE JOINT EFFORT TODDLER TEMPERAMENT CONSORTIUM (JETTC)

*Maria A. Gartstein, Samuel P. Putnam, Helena Slobodskaya, and Carolina de Weerth*

Those who travel beyond their own borders are frequently struck by the differences in how people around the world conduct themselves. These differences have been long acknowledged, however, to this day, such observations typically concern adult behavior, scarcely paying attention to the youngest members of societies. Temperament, defined as early appearing and relatively stable individual differences in reactivity and regulation, is a useful construct for exploring such differences in infants and children. The primary purpose of this book is to conduct such comparative work, considering a range of cultures, as well a variety of contextual effects expected to contribute to temperament development, and often associated behavior problems.

We have pursued the study of temperament, largely influenced by the psychobiological model proposed by Dr. Mary Rothbart, with whom the directors of the current project were fortunate to work as post-doctoral fellows at the University of Oregon. This research focused largely on instrument development, with measures designed to assess multiple fine-grained indicators of temperament shown to form three overarching factors: Negative Affectivity (NEG)—tendencies to experience and display fear, anger, sadness, and physical discomfort, Surgency (SUR)—activity level, approach to novel stimuli, and expression of positive affect in contexts of high-intensity stimulation, and Regulatory Capacity/Effortful

Control (EFF)—attentional attributes, behavioral control, and enjoyment of calm activities. According to the psychobiological definition of temperament, individual differences in reactivity and regulation are viewed as constitutionally based, and influenced over time by heredity, maturation, and environment (Rothbart & Derryberry, 1981). Although the biological underpinnings of temperament are often stressed, the openness to environment suggests possible cultural effects.

Culture can be viewed as "a dynamic distribution of meanings, practices, and artifacts throughout a linguistic community" (Mascolo, 2004, p. 83). Culture embodies a system of categories and values, as well as emotions, providing a largely shared approach to family life, as parents are motivated to raise their children so that offspring characteristics, including temperament, are aligned with their values and those of their cultural group (Kohnstamm, 1989). Ubiquitous in nature, culture represents a constant backdrop molding the environment of a developing individual. "Multiple trials" of exposure provided within a cultural context can be even more consequential in early childhood due to the rapid development of the central nervous system (Panksepp, 2001). Thus, culture is a powerful force, shaping how emotions are experienced, evaluated, and regulated, influencing behavior of individuals and likely the underlying neural bases. Moreover, culture is not contained or defined by national boundaries, but rather is reflective of less clearly delineated geographic regions. Multiple differentiated cultures are often contained within the same nation, and conversely, cultural groups often span across borders. For the sake of brevity, our descriptions in this book refer to differences between countries, but it should be recognized that we are more precisely referring to variability among distinct cultural groups represented by samples recruited from different countries.

As we considered pathways through which culture could "get inside the brain," ultimately impacting temperament development, we were influenced by the work of Charlie Super and Sara Harkness, as well as Heidi Keller. The construct of "developmental niche," described as a function of (1) customs (especially those related to child rearing), (2) settings available to the child, and (3) caregiver psychosocial characteristics (Super & Harkness, 1986), became central to our thinking about the multifaceted influence that broader cultural distinctions, such as Individualism/Collectivism, have on child development. Parental ethnotheories (belief systems held by parents regarding children and how they are to be treated; Harkness & Super, 1996) and socialization goals (qualities parents expect that a child should develop early in life;

Keller et al., 2006) represent key caregiver characteristics, especially in the cross-cultural context. Parental ethnotheories and socialization goals have been conceptualized in terms of relational and autonomy-focused domains, which parallel Individualism/Collectivism used to describe cultures as a whole. Instruments developed by Keller to measure these orientations discriminated among samples from different cultures, and were consequential to child social-emotional outcomes, including those relevant to temperament (Keller & Otto, 2009; Keller et al., 2004).

The conceptual basis of the study described in this book integrates the psychobiological theory of temperament with the framework of the developmental niche as the context in which temperament development unfolds, impacting the risk for symptoms of psychopathology (see Figure 1.1). That is, our approach to defining and measuring temperament is consistent with the psychobiological framework, which casts temperament development as "open" to experience. In our model, this experience is defined primarily in terms of the developmental niche, focusing on the caregiving/socialization context. In this overarching model, the philosophies inherent to different cultures govern the goals and presumptions regarding optimal growth held by parents, which are translated into specific parenting behaviors and elements of daily routine that shape individual differences in children's early emotional tendencies and capacity for regulation. Relations between parenting and child behaviors in this book are largely interpreted as parent-driven in the direction of influence, consistent with our expectations regarding cultural influences.

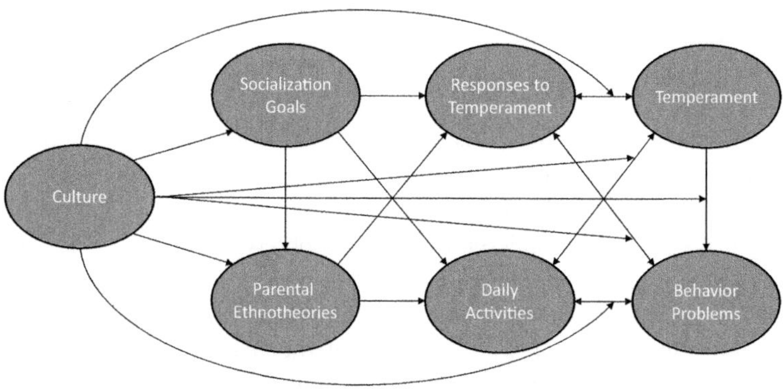


**FIGURE 1.1** Model of culturally driven influences on child behavioral outcomes: Mediation by parents' psychology and children's environment, moderation by culture

However, the perspective that individual differences in children can have a substantial influence on the environments they inhabit, including parenting to which they are exposed (Bell, 1968; Scarr & McCartney, 1983), is important as well, and is acknowledged by the bidirectional arrows connecting parenting behaviors and child characteristics in Figure 1.1.

Investigating both child characteristics and parental behaviors across multiple cultures provides insight regarding the relative universality, or lack thereof, of links between the two. In developmental science, connections between parenting to child behavior are often regarded as evidence of relations that would hold true in all contexts. This consistency is unlikely, however, as both child characteristics and parental behaviors may hold different meanings across cultures (Bornstein, 1995; Bornstein & Lansford, 2010). Given differences in the acceptability of emotional expression, for instance, certain traits may be discouraged in some cultures but rewarded and unrelated to behavior problems in others. In the same vein, certain parenting behaviors and cognitions may have different connotations in different cultures, leading to inconsistencies regarding the type of child behaviors that may elicit them. We also view culture as capable of modulating biological inputs embodied by temperament, altering the nature of links between these attributes and behavior problems. This moderation has not been widely examined, yet in one example, falling reactivity (infants' ability to lower level of arousal) was linked with behavior problems in the United States (US), but not Russia (Gartstein, Slobodskaya, Putnam, & Kirchhoff, 2013). Given recent demonstrations of such cultural specificity (e.g., Gartstein et al., 2013; Lansford et al., 2005), it was anticipated that culture would moderate relations between parenting and child outcomes, a process represented by arrows from culture that intercept the connecting lines between parenting and child constructs, and from temperament to behavior problems, in Figure 1.1.

Over the past several years, we have completed a number of small-scale studies documenting cross-cultural differences in the temperament of infants, toddlers, children, and adults. In these efforts, we have only speculated about the underpinnings of the observed differences in temperament, arguing that they are the product of various components of the developmental niche. The Joint Effort Toddler Temperament Consortium (JETTC) was born out of the need to address social-emotional development through a cross-cultural lens in a more systematic manner, directly measuring developmental niche constructs in an attempt to discern contextual foundations of cross-cultural differences in child reactivity/regulation and emerging behavior problems. The JETTC is also in large part a product of our collaborative work on the Rothbart instruments. That is, in the process of disseminating our scales based on the psychobiological model of temperament we developed professional relationships with a number of international colleagues. The idea of reaching out to this group in an attempt to establish collaborations first presented itself at the International Conference on Infant Studies, Vancouver, BC, Canada, in 2008. Now, we have our first set of findings to report that includes all of the JETTC research sites: The US, Brazil, Spain, Mexico, Italy, Russia, Finland, Romania, Belgium, the Netherlands, China, South Korea, Turkey, and Chile.

In addition to directly focusing on aspects of the family environment to help explain early appearing individual differences, the JETTC surpasses earlier cross-cultural work on temperament in its scope. Unlike large-scale personality research that has captured an extensive body of cultures around the world (e.g., McCrae, 2001), the majority of studies examining individual differences in children have focused on only two to four cultures (e.g., the US and Netherlands; Sung, Beijers, Gartstein, de Weerth, & Putnam, 2015) or single narrow dimensions (e.g., shyness; Chen et al., 1998). The current investigation spans three broad components of temperament, examining these in 14 cultures, in order to address these limitations. The array of JETTC cultures also makes it possible to examine geographically and culturally proximal settings expected to be more similar to each other, for example sites in northern Europe (e.g., Finland and the Netherlands), and those distant in terms of geography and cultural orientation (e.g., The US and China). At the same time, sites selected for this research are not characterized by gross differences in the standard of living. That is, all of the countries are categorized as either "very high" (nine countries) or "high" (Romania, Turkey, Mexico, Brazil, and China) on the Human Development Index (HDI; United Nations Development Programme, 2014). As such, samples included in this work all represent relatively developed cultures, reducing potential for confounding of culture and socioeconomic status (see Lansford, 2012).

The JETTC cultures do, however, differ substantially in terms of broad constructs that have proven useful in characterizing the thoughts, values, and behaviors of adults around the world. The dimensional model developed by Hofstede and colleagues (e.g., Hofstede, Hofstede, & Minkov, 2010) comprises six "dimensions of national cultures" reflecting the goals and attitudes of societies. Four original dimensions were developed based on multi-national corporate (IBM) employee data:

Individualism/Collectivism (contrasting an emphasis on caring for oneself versus the wellbeing of the larger group), Power Distance (the acceptance of inequality in power among members of a society), Masculinity/Femininity (the extent to which a society is driven by competition, achievement, and success, rather than cooperation, modesty, nurturance, and a focus on consensus), and Uncertainty Avoidance (the degree to which society members are threatened by unstructured or unusual situations). Later, a dimension labeled Long- versus Short-Term Orientation (an emphasis on thrift and the usefulness of shame versus protecting one's esteem) resulted from Hofstede's collaboration with Bond (Hofstede & Bond, 1988), and Indulgence/Restraint (allowance of gratification of desires versus expectations of restraint) was developed in collaboration with Minkov (Hofstede et al., 2010). We recently connected these dimensions to temperament in a meta-analysis (Putnam & Gartstein, 2017). The JETTC sample offers the opportunity to replicate these findings, as well as examine the ways in which cultural beliefs are transmitted across generations through parental understandings, goals, and actions.

The participating sites provide sufficient variability in terms of the developmental niche parameters to evaluate a model linking cultural influences to child outcomes. Some of these locations have been previously compared in terms of the niche components, typically parental socialization goals, ethnotheories, and/or daily routine (Carra, Lavelli, Keller, & Kärtner, 2013; Harkness et al., 2011; Keller et al., 2006). Others, wherein such comparisons were yet to be performed (e.g., Chile and Turkey), are associated with considerable contrasts in the cultural milieu, expected to translate into developmental niche differences. Cross-cultural differences in relational vs. autonomy-oriented socialization goals and parental ethnotheories have not been widely investigated to date (e.g., Keller et al., 2006). The daily routine element of the niche is multifaceted in nature, including play, sleep/bedtime, and discipline dimensions. A number of these components have been addressed (e.g., sleep; Super et al., 1996), yet have not been studied together, as they were in this investigation. Other aspects of the developmental niche received even less attention. Parental responses to child temperament have not been studied widely, and their importance in the context of the developmental niche supports inclusion in our conceptual model (Figure 1.1). That is, parental behaviors and socialization practices around child displays of reactivity/regulation are consequential for social-emotional development (Eisenberg, Cumberland, & Spinrad, 1998), with some indication of cross-cultural differences (Camras, Kolmodin, & Chen, 2008; Chen et al., 1998).

We studied these processes during toddlerhood, a period during which the consolidation of temperament traits is profound. NEG and SUR attributes undergo rapid development throughout infancy, typically stabilizing in the toddler period (Lemery, Goldsmith, Klinnert, & Mrazek, 1999). A transition to reliance on the frontally mediated attentional network facilitating executive functions results in rapid development of EFF (Posner, Rothbart, Sheese, & Voelker, 2012). This regulation-related set of attributes enables toddlers to modulate their behaviors and emotions more effectively, with socialization strongly contributing to this improved and more flexible regulation (e.g., Spinrad et al., 2012).

In conjunction with biological maturation, this developmental period marks an important transition in terms of societal expectations for self-regulation and the emergence of clinically significant behavioral/emotional concerns. Toddlerhood can be viewed as a critical window for translation of temperament risk and protective factors into symptoms/disorders via interactions with elements of the developmental niche (e.g., approaches to discipline). Early-appearing behavioral problems represent an important public health concern, as these often continue, exacerbating into identifiable disorders (Briggs-Gowan et al., 2003), with only a fraction of affected youngsters receiving adequate care. Thus, efforts that elucidate etiological factors, which may differ cross-culturally (Gartstein et al., 2013), are particularly important because of preventative/early intervention implications.

## Looking Forward . . . Organizational Structure

As our approach is developmentally focused, after describing our measures and data collection sites, we begin by addressing child temperament and behavior problems (Part 1)—the dependent variables in the overarching conceptual model. Elements of the developmental niche, starting with caregiver psychology, are addressed in Part 2, which also begins to address their interrelations. All aspects of the proposed model are examined in Part 3, devoted to integration across broad cultural orientation, the developmental niche and child behavioral outcomes. Thus, the progression of the book will involve increasing complexity, with earlier chapters discerning patterns of differences between aspects of parents and children from different cultures, and later chapters expanding to focus on interrelations between these aspects. We hope that the journey through our findings will be of interest to others who view cross-cultural developmental research as essential to discerning universality vs. specialization of processes involved in development.

## References

Bell, R. Q. (1968). A reinterpretation of the direction of effects in studies of socialization. *Psychological Review, 75*, 81–95.

Bornstein, M. H. (1995). Form and function: Implications for studies of culture and human development. *Culture and Psychology, 1*, 123–137.

Bornstein, M. H., & Lansford, J. E. (2010). Parenting. In M. H. Bornstein (Ed.), *The handbook of cross-cultural developmental science* (pp. 259–277). New York, NY: Taylor & Francis.

Briggs-Gowan, M. J., Owens, P. L., Schwab-Stone, M. E., Leventhal, J. M., Leaf, P. J., & Horwitz, S. M. (2003). Persistence of psychiatric disorders in pediatric settings. *Journal of American Academy of Child and Adolescent Psychiatry, 42*, 1360–1369.

Camras, L., Kolmodin, K., & Chen, Y. (2008). Mothers' self-reported emotional expression in Mainland Chinese, Chinese American and European American families. *International Journal of Behavioral Development, 32*, 459–463.

Carra, C., Lavelli, M., Keller, H., & Kärtner, J. (2013). Parenting infants: Socialization goals and behaviors of Italian mothers and immigrant mothers from West Africa. *Journal of Cross-Cultural Psychology, 44*, 1304–1320.

Chen, X., Hastings, P. D., Rubin, K. H., Chen, H., Cen, G., & Stewart, S. L. (1998). Child-rearing attitudes and behavioral inhibition in Chinese and Canadian toddlers: A cross-cultural study. *Developmental Psychology, 34*, 677–686.

Eisenberg, N., Cumberland, A., & Spinrad, T. L. (1998). Parental socialization of emotion. *Psychological Inquiry, 9*, 317–333.

Gartstein, M. A., Putnam, S. P., & Rothbart, M. K. (2012). Etiology of preschool behavior problems: Contributions of temperament attributes in early childhood. *Infant Mental Health Journal, 33*, 197–211.

Gartstein, M. A., Slobodskaya, H. R., Putnam, S. P., & Kirchhoff, C. (2013). Cross-cultural differences in the development of behavior problems: Contributions of infant temperament in Russia and U.S. *International Journal of Developmental Science, 7*, 95–104.

Harkness, S., & Super, C. M. (1996). *Parents' cultural belief systems: Their origins, expressions, and consequences*. New York: Guilford.

Harkness, S., Zylicz, P. O., Super, C., Welles-Nystrom, B., Bermudez, M. R., Bonichini, S., Mavridis, C. J. (2011). Children's activities and their meanings for parents: A mixed-methods study in six Western cultures. *Journal of Family Psychology, 25*, 799–813.

Hofstede, G., & Bond, M. H. (1988). The Confucius connection: From cultural roots to economic growth. *Organizational Dynamics, 16*, 4–21.

Hofstede, G., Hofstede, G. J., & Minkov, M. (2010). *Cultures and organizations: Software of the Mind* (Rev. 3rd ed.). New York, NY: McGraw-Hill.

Keller, H., Lamm, B., Abels, M., Yovsi, R., Borke, J., Jensen, H., Chaudhary, N. (2006). Cultural models, socialization goals, and parenting ethnotheories: A multicultural analysis. *Journal of Cross-Cultural Psychology, 37*, 155–172.

Keller, H., & Otto, H. (2009). The cultural socialization of emotion regulation during infancy. *Journal of Cross-Cultural Psychology, 40*, 996–1011.

Keller, H., Yovsi, R., Borke, J., Kartner, J. H., Jensen, H., & Papaligoura, Z. (2004). Developmental consequences of early parenting experiences: Self-recognition and self-regulation in three cultural communities. *Child Development, 75*, 1745–1760.

Kohnstamm, G. A., Halverson, C. F., Jr., Mervielde, I., & Havill, V. L. (1998). Analyzing parental free descriptions of child personality. In G. A. Kohnstamm, C. F. Halverson, Jr., I. Mervielde, & V. L. Havill (Eds.), *Parental descriptions of child personality: Developmental antecedents of the Big Five?* (pp. 1–19). Mahwah, NJ: Lawrence Erlbaum Associates.

Lansford, J. E. (2012). Cross-cultural and cross-national parenting perspectives. In V. Maholmes & R. King (Eds.), *The Oxford handbook of poverty and child development* (pp. 656–677). New York, NY: Oxford University Press.

Lansford, J. E., Chang, L., Dodge, K. A., Malone, P. S., Oburo, P., Palmerus, K., . . . Quinn, N. (2005). Cultural normativeness as a moderator of the link between physical discipline and children's adjustment: A comparison of China, India, Italy, Kenya, Philippines, and Thailand. *Child Development, 76*, 1234–1246.

Lemery, K. S., Goldsmith, H. H., Klinnert, M. D., & Mrazek, D. A. (1999). Developmental models of infant and childhood temperament. *Developmental Psychology, 35*, 189–204.

McCrae, R. R. (2001). Trait psychology and culture: Exploring intercultural comparisons. *Journal of Personality, 69*, 819–846.

Mascolo, M. F. (2004). The coactive construction of selves in cultures. *New Directions for Child and Adolescent Development, 104*, 79–90.

Panksepp, J. (2001). The long-term psychobiological consequences of infant emotions: Prescriptions for the twenty-first century. *Infant Mental Health Journal, 22*, 132–173.

Posner, M. I., Rothbart, M. K., Sheese, B. E., & Voelker, P. (2012). Control networks and neuromodulators of early development. *Developmental Psychology, 48*, 827–835.

Putnam, S. P. & Gartstein, M. A. (2017). Aggregate temperament scores from multiple countries: Associations with aggregate personality traits, cultural dimensions, and allelic frequency. *Journal of Research in Personality, 67*, 157–170.

Rothbart, M. K., & Derryberry, D. (1981). Development of individual differences in temperament. In M. E. Lamb & A. L. Brown (Eds.), *Advances in developmental psychology* (Vol. 1, pp. 37–86). Hillsdale, NJ: Lawrence Erlbaum Associates.

Scarr, S., & McCartney, K. (1983). How people make their own environments: A theory of genotype greater than environment effects. *Child Development, 54*, 424–435.

Spinrad, T. L., Eisenberg, N., Silva, K. M., Eggum, N. D., Reiser, M., Edwards, A., Gaertner, B. M. (2012). Longitudinal relations among maternal behaviors, effortful control and young children's committed compliance. *Developmental Psychology, 48*, 552–566.

Sung, J., Beijers, R., Gartstein, M.A., de Weerth, C., & Putnam, S. (2015). Exploring temperamental differences in infants from the United States of America (US) and the Netherlands. *European Journal of Developmental Psychology, 12*, 15–28.

Super, C. M., & Harkness, S. (1986). The developmental niche: A conceptualization at the interface of child and culture. *International Journal of Behavioral Development, 9*, 545–569.

Super, C. M., Harkness, S., van Tijen, N., van der Vlugt, E., Dykstra, J., & Fintelman, M. (1996). The three R's of Dutch child rearing and the socialization of infant arousal. In S. Harkness & C. M. Super (Eds.), *Parents' cultural belief systems: Their origins, expressions, and consequences* (pp. 447–466). New York, NY: Guilford Press.

United Nations Development Programme. (2014). *Human development report 2014—Sustaining human progress: Reducing vulnerabilities and building resilience.* New York, NY: Author.

# 2

# METHODOLOGY OF THE JOINT EFFORT TODDLER TEMPERAMENT CONSORTIUM (JETTC)

*Samuel P. Putnam, Maria A. Gartstein, Sara Casalin, Carmen González-Salinas, Blanca Huitron, Sae-Young Han, Mirjana Majdandžić, Rosario Montirosso, Oana Benga, Ibrahim Acar, Maria Beatriz Martins Linhares, Katri Räikkönen, Zhengyan Wang, Felipe Lecannelier, Roseriet Beijers, and Elena Kozlova*

## Participants

Researchers at all sites recruited samples of about 50 families of toddlers who were roughly between 18 and 36 months of age. A total of 865 families were recruited, although only the 853 indicating the sex of their child were included in analyses. Only one child was selected per family, and children with clinical diagnoses were excluded. For all but two countries, data were collected in a single site. In the Netherlands and the United States (US), data from two locations were combined. Our recruitment approaches necessarily differed by site, as is common with cross-cultural research (Keller, 2007), because identical techniques are not viable in all locations. At the same time, our samples can be thought of as similarly representative of communities from which they were recruited. There was some variability in demographic characteristics among the 14 sites (Table 2.1), as a function of the samples reflecting the circumstances predominant in each country/community. Overall, families in this study represent a range of occupations, primarily reflecting mid socioeconomic status (Revised Duncan Sociometric Index, RDSI [Stevens & Featherman, 1981] $M = 55.64$, SD = 25.82).

## US

US participants were recruited primarily in Brunswick, Maine. Brunswick is a large town located in the northeast US, near the small city of Portland. The population is primarily employed in the manufacturing, fishing, and service industries. Participants were largely Caucasian (97 percent), and were recruited through flyers placed at child-care centers, and in person by undergraduate research assistants at weekly farmer's markets and other community events.

A number of participants were additionally recruited in Pullman, Washington, a large town in a rural area of the northwestern US. Pullman is also primarily a median income community, with service, manufacturing, and farming economic opportunities. This sample was primarily Caucasian (91 percent), recruited by research assistants at a local farmer's market and through a Facebook advertisement.

A number of mothers were not working outside the home (13–20 percent), with most common occupations involving service-oriented positions.

## Belgium

Belgian participants were recruited primarily in the Flemish region, occupying the northern part of the country, with an economy based largely in trade, transport, and government services. This sample was also largely Caucasian (96 percent), recruited through a Facebook advertisement, several websites for new parents, flyers dispersed by mailings to child-care centers, and in person by undergraduate research assistants at child-care centers. Mothers reported primarily sales and administrative support occupations.

## Brazil

Brazilian participants were recruited in Ribeirão Preto city, located in the southeast of São Paulo State. This is a city that relies primarily on a farming economy (i.e., sugar cane plantation). Participating mothers were

**TABLE 2.1** Demographic characteristics of the JETTC cultures

| *Culture* | *Child gender* | | *Child age (in months)* | | | *Family socioeconomic status (RDSI)*[1] | | | *Marital status (in percent)*[2] | | | | *Maternal education (in years)* | | | *Number of children in the household* | | |
|---|---|---|---|---|---|---|---|---|---|---|---|---|---|---|---|---|---|---|
| | *F* | *M* | *Range* | *M* | *SD* | *Range* | *M* | *SD* | *Ma* | *Lt* | *Di* | *Si* | *Range* | *M* | *SD* | *Max* | *M* | *SD* |
| US | 49 | 39 | 17–36 | 25.6 | 5.8 | 10–97 | 50.3 | 26.2 | 92 | 7 | 1 | 0 | 9–24 | 17.2 | 2.3 | 1–6 | 1.7 | 1 |
| Belgium | 21 | 27 | 17–41 | 25.7 | 5.3 | 10–97 | 63.8 | 21.1 | 56 | 38 | 12 | 4 | 10–32 | 18.0 | 2.9 | 1–5 | 1.9 | 1 |
| Brazil | 23 | 28 | 18–38 | 29.4 | 5.6 | 15–96 | 56.9 | 24.2 | 82 | 12 | 0 | 6 | 11–37 | 18.3 | 4.9 | 1–3 | 1.4 | 1 |
| Chile | 21 | 28 | 17–41 | 27.3 | 7.2 | 10–97 | 49.7 | 28.3 | 62 | 15 | 2 | 21 | 12–28 | 18.1 | 4.9 | 1–4 | 1.8 | 1 |
| China | 30 | 24 | 19–36 | 26.4 | 4.7 | 15–97 | 58.7 | 29.9 | 87 | 13 | 0 | 0 | 8–23 | 15.6 | 3.6 | 1–2 | 1.2 | 1 |
| Finland | 24 | 31 | 18–40 | 27.6 | 5.7 | 10–97 | 61.6 | 20.8 | 62 | 30 | 2 | 6 | 12–26 | 17.7 | 2.6 | 1–4 | 1.5 | 1 |
| Italy | 24 | 28 | 17–36 | 26.6 | 4.9 | 15–97 | 61.9 | 20.6 | 77 | 23 | 0 | 0 | 11–25 | 17.2 | 3.1 | 1–5 | 1.7 | 1 |
| Mexico | 25 | 29 | 18–36 | 26.4 | 5.6 | 10–97 | 38.3 | 29.8 | 69 | 24 | 6 | 1 | 9–25 | 16.8 | 3.8 | 1–5 | 1.6 | 1 |
| Netherlands | 55 | 64 | 16–40 | 26.6 | 5.8 | 10–87 | 56.6 | 22.3 | 53 | 40 | 2 | 5 | 5–25 | 17.7 | 3.7 | 1–3 | 1.6 | 1 |
| Romania | 30 | 28 | 17–38 | 21.2 | 6.4 | 15–97 | 72.4 | 19.4 | 98 | 2 | 0 | 0 | 12–29 | 18.1 | 6.4 | 1–3 | 1.4 | 1 |
| Russia | 26 | 25 | 17–36 | 27.0 | 5.6 | 15–93 | 62.8 | 19.0 | 77 | 21 | 2 | 0 | 10–22 | 14.9 | 2.1 | 1–8 | 1.6 | 1 |
| Spain | 27 | 35 | 18–35 | 26.1 | 5.1 | 10–97 | 58.2 | 27.3 | 74 | 18 | 1 | 7 | 8–21 | 15.6 | 4.2 | 1–4 | 1.8 | 1 |
| S. Korea | 26 | 27 | 17–35 | 28.0 | 4.8 | 15–96 | 51.6 | 24.5 | 100 | 0 | 0 | 0 | 7–18 | 15.3 | 2.2 | 1–3 | 1.9 | 1 |
| Turkey | 25 | 34 | 16–36 | 27.7 | 5.6 | 10–97 | 50.5 | 26.1 | 92 | 7 | 1 | 0 | 9–24 | 14.4 | 3.9 | 1–4 | 1.4 | 1 |

1 RDSI: Revised Duncan Sociometric Index—an occupation based measure of social prestige, based on maternal occupations (Stevens & Featherman, 1981)

2 Ma = married, Lt = living together, Di = divorced, Si = single

predominantly Caucasian (82 percent), and parents were invited into the study through written information distributed via directors of child-care centers. A number of mothers (10 percent) did not work outside the home, with service-oriented occupations most commonly reported.

### Chile

Chilean participants were recruited in Santiago, the capital. This large city in the central mountains has an economy based in industry, trade, and finance. Participants self-identified as primarily Hispanic/Latino (71 percent) or Caucasian (23 percent). Families were recruited from a private school in the context of a larger intervention effort and were connected via meeting groups and telephone. The women in this sample were frequently employed in industrial jobs, operating equipment (e.g., textile industry/sewing machine).

### China

Chinese participants were recruited from 13 provinces across China, but mainly from Beijing city, resulting in an ethnically homogeneous sample. Participants were recruited via internet advertisement (official account of Wechat), and in person by research assistants during the Spring Festival holidays. A notable portion of participating mothers were not employed outside the home (22 percent), with another sizable portion working in a variety of professional positions (e.g., engineers, teachers).

### Finland

Finnish participants were recruited in the Helsinki Metropolitan Area, home to a quarter of all Finns. The Helsinki economy is diversified; however, the majority of employees work in the service sector. All families in this sample were Caucasian and were recruited through day-care centers by directly contacting parents. Most common occupations were sales and administrative support-oriented.

### Italy

Participants were recruited in three Italian northwest cities that are part of Lombardia: Milano, Lecco, and Como. Lombardia's economy represents a spectrum of industrial activities and services. Participants were all Caucasian, and recruited in person by a senior researcher, made possible by collaborative relationships with several child-care centers. Italian mothers reported technical support (e.g., health technician) and sales occupations most frequently.

## Mexico

Mexican participants were recruited in the Metropolitan Area of the Valley of Mexico, in the center of the country. The majority of the population engages in trade, professional, financial and corporate services, and manufacturing. Most mothers (94 percent) self-identified as Hispanic/ Latina and were recruited in person by a research coordinator at an early childhood education center in the State of Mexico. Half of the mothers were not employed outside the home, with the remainder often reporting professional occupations (e.g., physician).

## The Netherlands

The first Dutch sample was recruited around the city of Amsterdam, the capital, located in the west of the country, with finance, shipping, and tourism contributing to its economy. Mothers of this sample were mostly Caucasian (96 percent), recruited through flyers distributed in child-care centers and kindergartens, and through Facebook advertisements targeting a larger portion of the Netherlands.

The second Dutch sample was recruited around the city of Nijmegen located in the mid-east of the Netherlands, with economy revolving around education, health care, and technology. Families in this sample were all Caucasian and recruited through Facebook advertisements and flyers dispersed in child-care centers and well-baby clinics.

Whereas mothers not working outside the home were more common in the Amsterdam subsample (20 percent), in the Nijmegen subsample the most common occupations were sales and administrative support-oriented in nature.

## Romania

The Romanian sample was recruited in Cluj-Napoca, in the northwestern Transylvania region of the country. This is a university city, as well as a medical and educational center, with a significant industrial component. Primarily Caucasian (96 percent) participants were recruited through flyers distributed in child-care and play centers, in-person invitations by research assistants, and written information distributed through child-care staff. Romanian mothers frequently reported professional occupations (e.g., economist).

### Russia

Russian participants were recruited primarily in Novosibirsk, Russia's third largest city. Novosibirsk is considered the economic and academic capital of Siberia, whose population is primarily employed in industries, education, health services, and trade. This sample was largely Caucasian (96.2 percent), recruited in person by research assistants, and through references by current participants. Technical and administrative support, as well as sales occupations, were frequently reported in this sample.

### Spain

Spanish participants were living in the Region of Murcia, near the Mediterranean Sea. Murcia's economy is mostly based in service, manufacturing, and agriculture. The Spanish sample was ethnically homogeneous, contacted through day-care centers and Psychology Faculty (University of Murcia) Facebook page. A small portion of these mothers did not work outside the home (8 percent), with a number reporting professional occupations (e.g., professor).

### South Korea

Korean participants were recruited in Seoul and Gyeonggi areas in northwestern South Korea. Seoul is the capital of South Korea, and Gyeonggi Province is a region including large satellite cities south of Seoul. The main industries include trade, service, and manufacturing. All participants self-identified as Asian and were invited through written information distributed by child-care center directors. A number of mothers did not work outside the home (19 percent), with another sizable portion reporting administrative and service occupations.

### Turkey

Turkish participants were recruited in and near the city of Edirne, which is located in the northwestern region of Turkey on the borders of

Greece and Bulgaria. Agriculture and civil service represent the main sources of income. The sample was ethnically homogeneous, with families recruited through advertisements in pediatric offices, and by "word of mouth" through college students and their acquaintances. Almost half (47 percent) of this sample did not work outside the home, with a number reporting technical support occupations.

## Measures

Multiple constructs were measured: children's temperament and behavior problems; parents' goals for socialization and the parental ethnotheories regarding proper parenting behavior; parental responses to temperament-related behaviors; information regarding the daily routines of families and children; parental strategies regarding the challenges of child sleep and misbehavior; and demographic profiles. The majority of the utilized instruments were translated for the purposes of this study, adhering to the recommended procedures that include translation followed by back-translation and analyses of discrepancies, completed by native speakers/bilingual individuals (Peña, 2007). At all sites, the project was explained to the mothers, who were asked to complete various forms after providing informed consent.

An initial measurement challenge concerned arrival at questionnaire scales that were psychometrically sound in all countries. Prior to creating scale scores, Cronbach's alphas and item-total correlations were calculated for all scales and items for all countries. Items were then deleted one-by-one from scales to maximize the number of countries for which alpha >0.60 (considered to be a threshold for adequate internal consistency; DeVellis, 1991), and to minimize the number of items which diminished alpha for multiple countries. Because alpha is strongly determined by the number of items in a scale, and because some scales were composed of only 4 or 5 items, it was not possible to achieve alphas >0.60 for all scales in all countries. Scales for which this ideal was not met are indicated in the descriptions below. These occasional shortcomings represent a limitation, yet because poor internal consistency is a product of random, not systematic, error, it does not raise the likelihood of spurious effects, instead limiting the chance of identifying true associations.

Descriptions of the scales and their development are provided in the following paragraphs. Please see Table 2.2 for internal consistency statistics.

*Early Childhood Behavior Questionnaire* (ECBQ; Putnam, Gartstein, & Rothbart, 2006) was designed to assess temperament between 18 and 36

**TABLE 2.2** Internal consistency of JETTC scales

| *Scale* | *Number of items* | *Internal consistency* | | | |
|---|---|---|---|---|---|
| | | *Statistic* | *Country-specific range* | *Country-specific average* | *Combined dataset* |
| ECBQ | | | | | |
| Negative Affectivity | 77[a] | α | 0.84–0.93 | 0.89 | 0.91 |
| Surgency | 48[a] | α | 0.80–0.88 | 0.85 | 0.86 |
| Effortful Control | 57[a] | α | 0.82–0.93 | 0.88 | 0.88 |
| CBCL | | | | | |
| Internalizing | 36 | α | 0.72–0.94 | 0.82 | 0.86 |
| Externalizing | 24 | α | 0.83–0.94 | 0.89 | 0.89 |
| Total problems | 99 | α | 0.89–0.97 | 0.93 | 0.94 |
| Socialization goals | | α | | | |
| Autonomy | 4 | α | 0.61–0.86 | 0.75 | 0.76 |
| Relatedness | 5 | α | 0.54–0.81 | 0.72 | 0.73 |
| Parental ethnotheories | | | | | |
| Autonomy | 4 | α | 0.35–0.68 | 0.55 | 0.58 |
| Relational | 5 | α | 0.64–0.78 | 0.72 | 0.73 |
| DAQ-leisure activities | | | | | |
| Low-INT toy play | 4 | α | 0.48–0.79 | 0.65 | 0.67 |
| High-INT toy play | 4 | α | 0.45–0.74 | 0.61 | 0.65 |
| Play with purpose | 2 | *r* | 0.10–0.71 | 0.46 | 0.50 |
| Engage with parent | 6 | α | 0.48–0.73 | 0.63 | 0.67 |
| DAQ-sleep | | | | | |
| Active techniques | 4 | α | 0.42–0.79 | 0.61 | 0.65 |
| Gentle techniques | 4 | α | 0.47–0.68 | 0.54 | 0.60 |
| Parent remains | 2 | *r* | 0.14–0.60 | 0.31 | 0.38 |
| DAQ-discipline | | | | | |
| Inductive | 3[b] | α | 0.46–0.73 | 0.61 | 0.61 |
| Power assertion | 4[b] | α | 0.46–0.67 | 0.56 | 0.55 |
| PRTD | | | | | |
| Encourage NEG | 9 | α | 0.61–0.88 | 0.79 | 0.82 |
| Encourage SUR | 4 | α | 0.40–0.81 | 0.63 | 0.66 |
| Punish low EFF | 4 | α | 0.44–0.75 | 0.64 | 0.66 |
| Reward high EFF | 4 | α | 0.66–0.92 | 0.82 | 0.85 |

a ECBQ scales were calculated as the average of subscale scores, not item scores

b Substantive analyses of discipline used individual items. Scales used only to organize discussion months of age. This parent-report instrument consists of 201 items, distributed over 18 scales and three factors: *Negative Affectivity* (NEG)—Discomfort, Fear, Sadness, Frustration, Motor Activation, Perceptual Sensitivity, Shyness, and Soothability, loading negatively; *Surgency* (SUR)—Impulsivity, Activity Level, High-intensity Pleasure, Sociability, and Positive Anticipation; and *Effortful Control* (EFF)–Inhibitory Control, Attention Shifting, Low-intensity Pleasure, Cuddliness, and Attention Focusing. Items are rated on a 1–7 Likert-type scale reflecting frequency. Scale scores are calculated as the average of ratings for all applicable items, and factor scores are the averages of relevant scale scores. Prior studies supported the longitudinal stability and inter-parent agreement of the measure (Putnam et al., 2006), as well as predictive validity from and to similar infant and childhood measures (Putnam, Rothbart, & Gartstein, 2008), construct validity via connections to behavior problems (Gartstein, Putnam, & Rothbart, 2012), and convergence with laboratory measures (Stepien-Nycz, Rostek, Bialecka-Pikul, & Bialek, 2017).

For 13 scales, no items were deleted for internal consistency considerations. Three items from Activity Level, two each from Attention Focusing and Impulsivity, and one each from Attention Shifting, Low-Intensity Pleasure, and Shyness were removed. Internal consistency for one scale, Impulsivity, remained below 0.60 in eight countries, but was retained in creation of the Surgency factor score to enhance comparability of our findings to those obtained in other studies.

*The Child Behavior Checklist* (CBCL; Achenbach & Rescorla, 2000) for ages 18 months to 5 years, containing 100 items, was administered to assess behavior problems. The *Internalizing* scale consists of the sum of items measuring anxious/depressed, emotionally reactive, withdrawn, and somatic complaint behaviors, and the *Externalizing* score includes items relevant to attention problems and aggressive behavior. A total problems score is the sum of all CBCL item scores. Reliability and validity of this measure are well established, with adequate criterion-related validity, inter-rater, and test-retest reliability (Achenbach & Rescorla, 2000). This instrument has been used extensively in prior cross-cultural research (Achenbach et al., 2008). Because alphas were >0.60 in all countries, no refinement was necessary.

*Socialization Goals (SG)/Parental Ethnotheories* (PE; Keller et al., 2006) questionnaires provide autonomy and relational orientation indicators. Caregivers indicated their agreement to 10 statements concerning qualities a child should learn or develop in early childhood, using a five-point Likert-type scale. The five-item Autonomous *Socialization Goals* scale includes items such as "develop self-confidence" or "develop independence," and relational socialization goals are addressed by items such as "obey elderly people" or "learn to care for the wellbeing of others." In scale refinement analyses of the *Autonomous* scale, item 3, referring to development of competitiveness, lowered alpha in eight countries and was eliminated. The resulting four-item scale generated alphas >0.60 for all 14 countries. The *Relational* scale generated alphas >0.60 for all countries but Mexico.

Parental Ethnotheories were also assessed with a list of 10 statements, this time describing opinions regarding parenting practices, also designated as Autonomous (five items) or Relational (five items). As with socialization goals, a five-point Likert-type scale is used to ascertain agreement with these statements. The Autonomous subscale includes items focusing on independence (e.g., "it is good for the child to sleep alone"). The Relational scale emphasizes body contact/proximity and prompt satisfaction of physical needs (e.g., "it is important to physically comfort a crying child with a hug or kiss in order to console him/her". In scale refinement analyses, the *Autonomous* scale demonstrated poor internal consistency, with alphas <0.60 for all 14 countries. Item 10, referring to caregivers being in constant contact with the child, lowered alpha in 12 countries and was eliminated. This led to improved internal consistency; however, internal consistency remained very poor in China, and alpha remained <0.60 in all but four countries. The *Relational* scale generated alphas >0.60 for all countries.

*Daily Activities Questionnaire* was designed for the purposes of this study to address leisure activities, sleeping practices, and discipline routines. This parent-report instrument includes 46 items regarding how often parents or children engage in certain behaviors, using a five-item Likert-type scale ranging from 0 = never to 5 = very often.

For leisure activities, exploratory factor analyses on the items concerning play and engagement with parents was performed upon the entire sample to derive potential scales. Analyses resulted in four factors, requiring further scale refinement. A four-item scale reflecting amount of *Play with Low-intensity Toys* (i.e., books, cuddly toys such as stuffed animals, role-playing toys such as dolls, and learning toys such as crayons) yielded alphas >0.60 in 12 of 14 countries. A four-item scale reflecting *Play with High-intensity Toys* (i.e., push or pull toys such as cars, musical toys, riding toys, and household items) demonstrated alpha >0.60 in nine countries. A two-item scale representing *Play with Purpose* (i.e., have the child engage in play with main purpose of advancing the child's development, or to prepare child for future responsibilities). Correlations between these two items were >0.45 in 11 countries. A single item, "Have the child engage in play for the main purpose of entertaining the child" was labeled *Play for Entertainment*. The child's *Engagement with Parent* was measured with six items regarding involvement in housework, taking the child out of the home, and playing with him/her, demonstrating alphas >0.60 in 10 countries. Two questions asked how many hours per day the child *Watched Television* and *Used a Computer* or other electronic device(s).

Questions regarding sleep included those regarding techniques used by parents to calm children and assist their sleeping, whether they woke the child, and items assessing children's sleep patterns. Regarding parental techniques, exploratory factor analyses suggested three primary factors. A four-item scale reflecting *Active Sleep Techniques* (i.e., walking while holding, walking in stroller, car ride, special play activity) generated alphas >0.60 in 9 of 14 countries. A four-item scale reflecting *Gentle Sleep Techniques* (i.e., talking softly, reading stories, cuddling, singing) performed poorly in Spain and Romania, and alphas were >0.60 in only six countries. Two items assessed whether the *Parent Remained* with the child, either staying near their bed or lying with the child. Although correlations between these items were low ($r_s < 0.25$ in six countries), they were combined due to their conceptual similarity. A single item asked whether the parent left the child *Alone to Cry*, so they could learn to soothe themselves. A single item asked whether the child *Napped* for 2 or more hours per day. Finally, the timing and *Amount of Night Sleep* was measured by asking parents what time the child went to *Bed at Night* and *Woke in the Morning*.

Seven items asked parents to indicate how frequently they used different discipline techniques in response to child misbehavior. Exploratory factor analyses suggested two factors. The first included three techniques consistent with an *Inductive Discipline* approach (ask child to repair the damage, talk the problem over, tell child to think about what they did). Alphas >0.60 for this three-item scale were observed in eight countries. A second scale reflected *Power Assertion* (shout or swear, spank or hit, withdraw privileges or separate child from others). Results indicated alphas >0.60 in only five countries. Due to relatively low alphas, and because distinctions among the strategies were expected to be meaningful (e.g., previous research suggests corporal punishment is more closely linked to child problems than are other power-assertive strategies such as withdrawing privileges), these strategies were analyzed independently.

*Parental Responses to Temperament Displays (PRTD)* were assessed using a questionnaire designed for this study. Items comprising the scales for Encouraging NEG and Encouraging SUR concerned behaviors reflecting these temperament factors (e.g., "When your child becomes frustrated or angry"; "When your child is playing very actively"), asking parents to rate the likelihood that they would encourage or discourage the behavior using a seven-point Likert-type scales ranging from "extremely likely" to "extremely unlikely." It was deemed improbable that parents in any culture would actively discourage EFF; yet, caregivers could encourage manifestations of regulation both by rewarding behaviors indicative of high EFF and punishing behaviors associated with low EFF. As such, items described contexts associated with EFF (e.g., "When you offer your child calm or quiet games to play"), asking the likelihood the parent would reward (e.g., "praise or give her or him a reward if they play appropriately?") or punish (e.g., "punish her or him if they do not play quietly?") to promote the behavior. Scale refinement analyses resulted in an *Encouraging NEG* scale containing nine items, for which alphas were >0.60 for all sites. The *Encouraging SUR* scale contains four items reflecting parent responses to risky and active play. Alphas were >0.60 for nine sites. The *Punishing Low EFF* and *Rewarding High EFF* scales each contained four items regarding attention shifting, attention focusing, inhibitory control, and low-intensity pleasure contexts. Alphas for Punishing Low EFF were >0.60 for nine countries. Alphas for Rewarding High EFF were >0.60 for all sites.

*Cultural Orientation Scores* represent country-level values for Hofstede's six dimensions (Hofstede, Hofstede, & Minkov, 2010), obtained from www.geerthofstede.nl/research--vsm on July 22, 2015. High (Individualist) scores on *Individualism/Collectivism* indicate values emphasizing concern for one's self and immediate family, with low (Collectivist) scores reflecting greater investment in the group as a whole. High scores on *Power Distance* define countries whose citizens accept imbalances of power, whereas low scores characterize societies that discourage such inequalities. High (Masculine) scores on *Masculinity/Femininity* reflect valuing competition and achievement, with low (Feminine) scores indicating a societal emphasis on caring for others and quality of life. Countries with high scores on *Uncertainty Avoidance* hold values suggesting strong discomfort regarding ambiguous situations, along with relatively rigid codes of conduct to minimize such discomfort, whereas low scores on this dimension indicate ease with uncertainty and a more flexible approach to rules. On the dimension of

*Long-versus Short-Term Orientation*, high (Long-Term) scores reflect thrift and perseverance, along with a willingness to adapt societal norms to achieve long-term goals, whereas low (Short-Term) scores indicate a focus on immediate results and maintenance of tradition. High scores on *Indulgence* are found in cultures in which citizens are allowed to gratify their desires and pursue enjoyment, whereas cultures with low scores on this dimension are expected to exercise restraint.

## Research Goals and Data Analyses

Two broad goals are addressed through our analyses. The first is to explore cross-cultural commonalities and differences in child characteristics and aspects of the developmental niche, relating these differences to cultural orientation, rarely incorporated within developmental psychology. In Chapters 3, 4, and 6–10, we first address this goal using Analyses of Variance (ANOVA), with Bonferroni adjustments applied to subsequent pairwise comparisons; child age and sex controlled. In our previous papers, we have investigated the interaction between culture and these child variables in relation to temperament (e.g., Sung, Beijers, Gartstein, de Weerth, & Putnam, 2015), but in the interest of brevity rarely do so in the current text. In order to maintain adequate statistical power for our analyses, we did not control for demographic variables, such as income, family size, or ethnicity. These variables reflect aspects of the cultural context in the communities being studied, with relatively inconsequential contributions to cross-cultural differences in temperament and related constructs (Super et al., 2008). The cross-cultural goal is further addressed by correlating country-average scores for JETTC variables with Hofstede cultural orientation scores, enabling interpretation of distinctions among children and parents from around the world in terms of these established dimensions.

Our second goal was to examine relations within and between variables representing aspects of the developmental niche and the developing child (Chapters 5 and 11–16). Importantly, the correlational analyses used in service of this goal are organized to test both between- and within-culture relations. Between-culture relations represent paths through which cultural differences are transmitted from generation to generation. Tested by calculating correlations between the country-average scores obtained for the 14 JETTC sites, these relations enable us to determine how differences between cultures in ways parents think and act are associated with one another and with differences in typical child behaviors.

Examination of within-culture correlations between scores from individual families, and the extent to which the magnitude and direction of these correlations differ across cultures, offers the opportunity to ascertain the degree to which relations between parent and child variables are universal or culture-specific. Findings of consistent relations across all or most cultures suggest developmental processes that are largely invariant worldwide. In contrast, inconsistencies reveal distinctions in the perceptions and values ascribed to certain behaviors in parents or children in different cultures. In our final empirical chapter (17), we attempt to "bring it all together," using regression analyses to investigate the degree to which relations between broad aspects of culture and child outcomes are explained by more discrete elements of the niche. In doing so, we hope to further elucidate mechanisms through which culture shapes the developing individual.

## References

Achenbach, T. M., & Rescorla, L. A. (2000). Manual for ASEBA preschool forms & profiles. Burlington: Department of Psychiatry, University of Vermont.

Achenbach, T. M., Becker, A., Döpfner, M., Heiervang, E., Roessner, V., Steinhausen, H. C., & Rothenberger, A. (2008). Multicultural assessment of child and adolescent psychopathology with ASEBA and SDQ instruments: Research findings, applications, and future directions. *Journal of Child Psychology and Psychiatry*, *49*(3), 237–250.

DeVellis, R. R. (1991). *Scale development: Theory and applications*. Thousand Oaks, CA: Sage.

Gartstein, M. A., Putnam, S. P., & Rothbart, M. K. (2012). Etiology of preschool behavior problems: Contributions of temperament attributes in early childhood. *Infant Mental Health Journal*, *33*, 197–211.

Hofstede, G., Hofstede, G. J., & Minkov, M. (2010). *Cultures and organizations: Software of the mind* (Rev. 3rd ed.). New York, NY: McGraw-Hill.

Keller, H. (2007). *Cultures of infancy*. Mahwah, NJ: Lawrence Erlbaum Associates.

Keller, H., Lamm, B., Abels, M., Yovsi, R., Borke, J., Jensen, H., . . . Chaudhary, N. (2006). Cultural models, socialization goals, and parenting ethnotheories: A multicultural analysis. *Journal of Cross-Cultural Psychology*, *37*, 155–172.

Peña, E. D. (2007). Lost in translation: Methodological considerations in cross-cultural research. *Child Development*, *78*, 1255–1264.

Putnam, S. P., Gartstein, M. A., & Rothbart, M. K. (2006). Measurement of fine-grained aspects of toddler temperament: The early childhood behavior questionnaire. *Infant Behavior and Development*, *29*, 386–401.

Putnam, S. P., Rothbart, M. K., & Gartstein, M. A. (2008). Homotypic and heterotypic continuity of fine-grained temperament during infancy, toddlerhood, and early childhood. *Infant and Child Development*, *17*, 387–405.

Stepien-Nycz, M., Rostek, I., Bialecka-Pikul, M., & Bialek, A. (2017). The Polish adaptation of the Early Childhood Behavior Questionnaire (ECBQ): Psychometric properties, age and gender differences and convergence between the questionnaire and the observational data. *European Journal of Developmental Psychology*, *15*, 192–213.

Stevens, G., & Featherman, D. L. (1981). A revised socioeconomic index of occupational status. *Social Science Research*, *10*, 365–395.

Sung, J., Beijers, R., Gartstein, M. A., de Weerth, C., & Putnam, S. (2015). Exploring temperamental differences in infants from the United States of America (US) and the Netherlands. *European Journal of Developmental Psychology*, *12*, 15–28.

Super, C. M., Axia, G., Harkness, S., Welles-Nystrom, B., Zylicz, P. O., Parmar, P., . . . McGurk, H. (2008). Culture, temperament, and the "Difficult Child": A study in seven Western cultures. *International Journal of Developmental Science*, *2*, 136–157.

# PART 1

# Temperament and Emerging Symptoms/ Behavior Problems

# 3

# CROSS-CULTURAL DIFFERENCES IN TEMPERAMENT

*Helena Slobodskaya, Elena Kozlova, Sae-Young Han, Maria A. Gartstein, and Samuel P. Putnam*

The Early Childhood Behavior Questionnaire (ECBQ; Putnam, Gartstein, & Rothbart, 2006) has been translated into multiple languages. Prior studies have largely supported the three-factor structure of the ECBQ, including Surgency (SUR), Negative Affectivity (NEG), and Effortful Control (EFF), in different countries (Casalin, Luyten, Vliegen, & Meurs, 2012; Maller et al., 2009; Nakagawa, Sukigara, & Mizuno, 2007). The replicability of the trait structure makes it possible to compare mean scores on the ECBQ factors across cultures. In this chapter, we explore

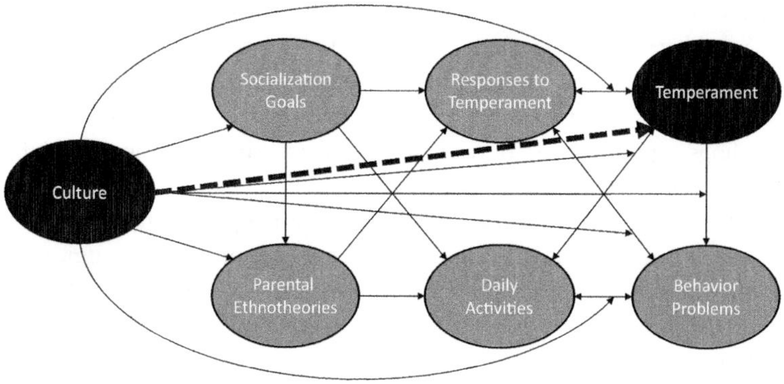


**FIGURE 3.1** ECBQ temperament in the JETTC Conceptual Model

differences between the 14 JETTC cultures in mean levels of NEG, SUR, and EFF, and examine how ECBQ culture-level factor scores relate to Hofstede's cultural dimensions (see Figure 3.1).

Cross-cultural research addressing temperament in toddlerhood has not been widespread. Using observational techniques, Chen et al. (1998) found that Chinese toddlers were more behaviorally inhibited than Canadian toddlers. More recently, Rubin et al. (2006) examined behavioral inhibition in toddlers from five countries, Australia, Canada, China, Italy, and Korea, using structured observational methods. The findings suggest differences between eastern and western cultures: Chinese and South Korean toddlers were more inhibited than toddlers from the other countries, whereas Italian and Australian toddlers were less inhibited.

Using parent report instruments developed in the psychobiological tradition, Cozzi et al. (2013) did not report cultural differences in the ECBQ factors between Italian and American toddlers, although there were a number of significant differences in fine-grained traits. Another study of early temperament in Japan, Russia, and the US revealed cultural differences: US toddlers were rated highest on SUR, whereas Japanese toddlers were rated highest on NEG and lowest on EFF (Slobodskaya, Gartstein, Nakagawa, & Putnam, 2013). Comparisons of the ECBQ factors across six cultures indicated that US and Chilean toddlers were rated highest on SUR; Chileans and Koreans were rated highest on NEG; whereas EFF scores were lowest in Japanese and highest in Korean toddlers (Maller et al., 2009).

More recently, a study of toddler temperament in four countries, Chile, Poland, South Korea, and the US, also found significant culture effects for all three ECBQ factors (Krassner et al., 2017). For NEG, Chilean toddlers were rated highest, followed by Korean, Polish, and US toddlers. For SUR, American toddlers were rated higher than Polish and Korean toddlers. South Korean toddlers were rated highest in EFF, followed by American and Polish toddlers. Overall, Krassner et al.'s findings supported an Individualism/Collectivism distinction for NEG and an east-west distinction for SUR.

A number of studies have now examined temperament traits around the world using translations of Rothbart questionnaires. A longitudinal study of infant temperament (Gartstein et al., 2006) showed that Spanish and US infants were more similar to one another and different from Chinese infants, suggesting that eastern/western distinction, rather than Individualism/Collectivism, plays a major role in predicting cross-cultural differences. Another study found differences in temperament for children from Curacao, Germany, the Netherlands, Suriname, Taiwan, and the US that could not be easily explained by Individualism/Collectivism (Majdandžić et al., 2009).

A meta-analysis of temperament data from 18 countries (Putnam & Gartstein, 2016) showed a consistent pattern of cross-cultural differences in mean levels of three overarching factors: East Asian cultures were higher in NEG and lower in SUR and EFF than northern European cultures. Similar to adult personality research (Hofstede & McCrae, 2004), temperament factors were linked to dimensions of cultural orientation outlined by Hofstede, Hofstede, & Minkov (2010). NEG was related to Uncertainty Avoidance, Masculinity, and Collectivism; SUR to low Power Distance; and EFF to low Power Distance and Femininity.

Hypotheses regarding comparisons of the ECBQ factors in the JETTC cultures are based on prior cross-cultural temperament research, along with implications of Hofstede's cultural dimensions for individual differences. We anticipate multiple significant mean-level differences and expect that NEG will be higher in East Asia and in cultures high on Uncertainty Avoidance, Masculinity, and Collectivism. SUR is expected to be higher in the west and cultures low on Power Distance, with lower EFF hypothesized for the east and cultures low on Power Distance and Masculinity, and higher EFF in northern Europe.

## Results

As shown in Table 3.1, substantial cross-cultural effects for all three factors were revealed through 2 (sex) by 14 (country) Analyses of Variance (ANOVAs), with age as a covariate. Significant age effects indicated higher NEG and EFF in older children. Sex differences were also indicated, with females rated significantly lower in SUR and higher in NA and EC than males.

Figures 3.2–3.4 reflect marginal means for each country on the three temperament factors, with darker shading indicative of higher values (descriptive statistics available upon request from the volume editors). Regarding NEG, main effects comparisons (Bonferroni adjustment) indicated that children from China, Korea, Brazil, Turkey, and Chile were rated higher than those from the six lowest-scoring countries: US, Finland, Netherlands, Italy, Mexico, and Belgium. Those from China, Korea, and Brazil additionally scored higher than those from Russia and Romania, with Chinese children also rated higher than Spanish toddlers.

**TABLE 3.1** Effects of culture, age, and sex on ECBQ temperament factors

| *ECBQ factor* | *Age* | *Culture* | *Sex* | *Culture × Sex* |
|---|---|---|---|---|
| Negative Affectivity | 5.22* | 16.03** | 5.03* | 0.98 |
| Surgency | 1.40 | 5.89* | 7.37* | 1.05 |
| Effortful Control | 72.92** | 3.12** | 9.18* | 1.58# |

Note: ANOVAs, with age as covariate, gender and country as factors. Dfs for age and sex = 1,836. Dfs for culture and culture × sex = 13,836
**$p < 0.001$, *$p < 0.05$. #$p < 0.10$

Children from Finland, Chile, and Belgium were rated higher on SUR than those from South Korea and Turkey, with Finnish and Chilean children also rated higher than those from Mexico, China, and the US, and Finnish toddlers receiving higher ratings than their Russian and Romanian counterparts. Children from South Korea received higher ratings for EFF than children from China and Turkey. Ratings for Spanish and Romanian children were also higher than those for youth from China.

## Relations to Cultural Orientation Dimensions

To explore connections between temperament and established cultural distinctions, Pearson's correlations were calculated between average country scores on the three temperament factors and Hofstede's cultural orientation dimensions. High NEG was found to be associated with low scores on Individualism, $r(14) = -0.77$, $p < 0.05$.

## Discussion

Results are partly in line with expectations, for example, confirming well-documented differences between eastern and western cultures on NEG. Toddlers from Asian countries: China, Korea, and Turkey, were rated higher than those from the US and four European countries (i.e., Finland, Netherlands, Italy, and Belgium), whereas children from eastern European countries, Russia and Romania, scored mid-range on NEG. The picture is much less clear for Latin America, as toddlers from Brazil and Chile scored significantly higher than those from Mexico. While we should be cautious about generalizing from this study, it is worth noting that the Personality Profiles of Cultures Project showed that adult

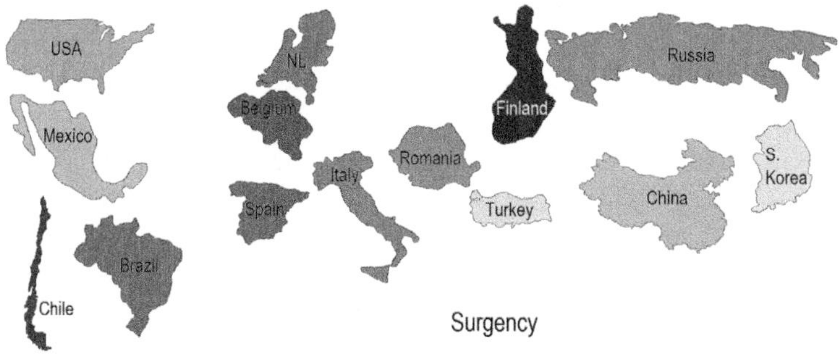


FIGURE 3.2 Map of Surgency marginal means. Darker shading indicates higher scores

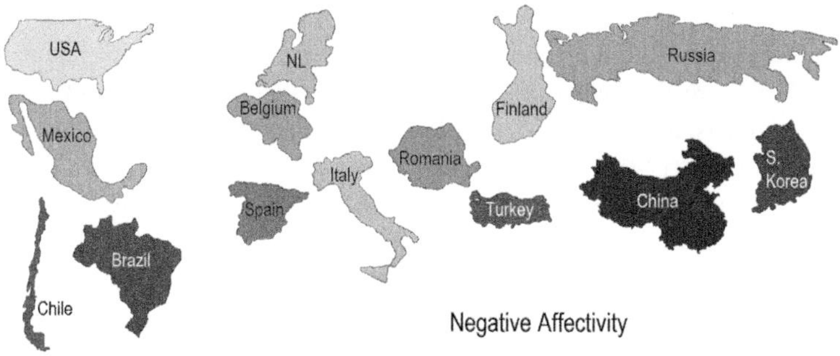


FIGURE 3.3 Map of Negative Affectivity marginal means. Darker shading indicates higher scores

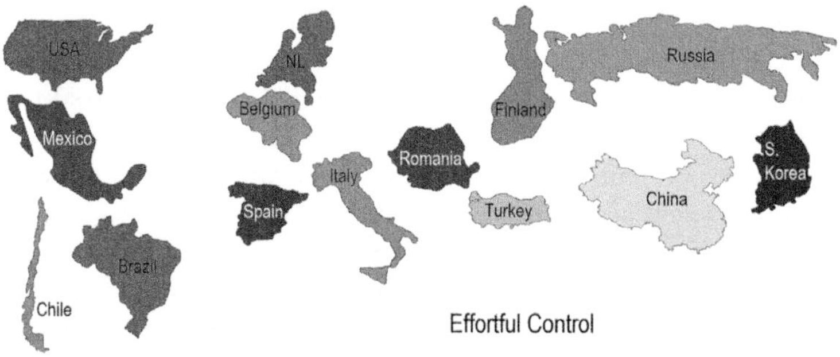


FIGURE 3.4 Map of Effortful Control marginal means. Darker shading indicates higher scores

Brazilians were rated highest in Neuroticism among 51 cultures around the world, whereas Mexicans were rated lowest (McCrae et al., 2005).

For SUR, the findings also point to east-west cultural differences, showing that Finnish and Belgium toddlers were among the highest-scoring, South Korean, Turkish, and Chinese toddlers were among the lowest-scoring, whereas Russian and Romanian toddlers scored in between. Overall, both reactivity dimensions of toddler temperament demonstrated a consistent pattern of cultural differences, confirming expectations that individuals from east Asian cultures would be higher in NEG and lower in SUR, relative to western European counterparts. In Latin America, our findings are consistent with earlier studies of toddler temperament, wherein Chileans received high NEG and SUR ratings (Krassner et al., 2017; Maller et al., 2009).

For EFF, the largest differences were found between Asian cultures, with South Korean toddlers scoring highest among the 14 JETTC countries and Chinese toddlers scoring lowest. Spanish and Romanian toddlers were the next two highest-scoring, whereas Turkish and Russian toddlers were the next two lowest-scoring. Based on the Putnam and Gartstein (2016) meta-analysis, lower EFF scores in the east and higher EFF in northern Europe were anticipated. Although two JETTC eastern cultures scored lowest, the third—South Korea, scored highest, and northern European cultures did not tend to score high on EFF.

The difference in parental ratings for toddler EFF between the two east Asian countries, China and South Korea, deserves closer attention, as it is usually assumed that geographically close cultures will have similar trait profiles. While large-scale personality studies have generally found support for this assumption, there is also evidence that some neighboring countries differ considerably in aggregate trait levels (McCrae et al., 2005). Why? This is not yet known, though it is reasonable to suppose that culture-level factors may play a role in the development of traits. China and South Korea differ strongly in terms of Uncertainty Avoidance, a dimension that describes culture's tolerance for ambiguity, and Masculinity/Femininity, referring to the degree to which a culture values assertiveness and achievement or caring for others and social support. China is quite low on Uncertainty Avoidance and fairly Masculine, whereas South Korea is high on both Uncertainty Avoidance and Femininity. In addition, China is higher than South Korea on Power Distance, referring to the extent to which the younger and less powerful members of society expect and accept hierarchy and status differences. Given that these three cultural dimensions were the most important predictors of EFF in a meta-analysis by Putnam and Gartstein (2017), the difference between China and South Korea should perhaps come as no surprise.

Overall, the effect of culture on toddler temperament factors in our study (11 percent of the variance) was larger than in large-scale studies of Big Five personality factors in adolescence (McCrae et al., 2010) and adulthood (McCrae & Terracciano, 2008), where culture accounted for 3.5–4 percent of the total variance. It remains unclear at this stage whether these differences in cultural effect size are artefactual, reflecting sampling biases or method effects, or whether cultural effects differ at different developmental stages. One study that conducted such comparisons with infants and toddlers from Japan, Russia, and the US showed that cross-cultural differences in SUR significantly decreased with age (Slobodskaya et al., 2013).

In the current study, the largest cross-cultural differences were for NEG. This temperament factor was closely aligned with the cultural dimension of Individualism/Collectivism, suggesting that toddlers from more collectivist cultures (Korea, China, and Chile) were more frequently distressed than those from more individualist cultures (The US, Finland, Italy, and the Netherlands). This finding was consistent with our expectations; however, NEG was not related to other cultural dimensions, and there were no significant correlations between SUR, EFF, and Hofstede's dimensions.

## Note

Preparation of this chapter was supported by grants of the Russian Scientific Foundation # 16–18–00003 and Russian Foundation for Basic Research # 16–06–00022.

## References

Casalin, S., Luyten, P., Vliegen, N., & Meurs, P. (2012). The structure and stability of temperament from infancy to toddlerhood: A one-year prospective study. *Infant Behavior and Development, 35*, 94–108.

Chen, X., Hastings, P. D., Rubin, K. H., Chen, H., Cen, G., & Stewart, S. L. (1998). Child-rearing attitudes and behavioral inhibition in Chinese and Canadian toddlers: A cross-cultural study. *Developmental Psychology, 34*, 677–686.

Cozzi, P., Putnam, S. P., Menesini, E., Gartstein, M. A., Aureli, T., Calussi, P., & Montirosso, R. (2013). Studying cross-cultural differences in temperament in toddlerhood: United States of America (US) and Italy. *Infant Behavior and Development, 36*, 480–483.

Gartstein, M. A., Gonzalez, C., Carranza, J. A., Ahadi, S. A., Ye, R., Rothbart, M. K., & Yang, S. W. (2006). Studying cross-cultural differences in the development of infant temperament: People's Republic of China, the United States of America, and Spain. *Child Psychiatry and Human Development, 37*, 145–161.

Hofstede, G., & McCrae, R. R. (2004). Personality and culture revisited: Linking traits and dimensions of culture. *Cross-Cultural Research, 38*, 52–88.

Hofstede, G., Hofstede, G. J., & Minkov, M. (2010). *Cultures and organizations: Software of the mind* (Rev. 3rd ed.). New York, NY: McGraw-Hill.

Krassner, A. M., Gartstein, M. A., Park, C., Dragan, W. L., Lecannelier, F., & Putnam, S. P. (2017). East–west, collectivist-individualist: A cross-cultural examination of temperament in toddlers from Chile, Poland, South Korea, and the US. *European Journal of Developmental Psychology, 14*, 449–464.

McCrae, R. R., & Terracciano, A. (2008). The five-factor model and its correlates in individuals and cultures. In F. J. R. van de Vijver, D. A. van Hemert, & Y. H. Poortinga (Eds.), *Multilevel analysis of individuals and cultures* (pp. 249–283). Mahwah, NJ: Lawrence Erlbaum Associates.

McCrae, R. R., Terracciano, A., & 79 Members of the Personality Profiles of Cultures Project. (2005). Personality profiles of cultures: Aggregate personality traits. *Journal of Personality and Social Psychology, 89*, 407–425.

McCrae, R. R., Terracciano, A., De Fruyt, F., De Bolle, M., Gelfand, M. J., Costa Jr, P. T., . . . Yik, M. (2010). The validity and structure of culture-level personality scores: Data from ratings of young adolescents. *Journal of Personality, 78*, 815–838.

Majdandžić, M., Putnam, S. P., Siib, F., Kung, J-F., Lay, K.-L., van Liempt, I., Gartstein, M. A. (2009, April). *Cross-cultural investigation of temperament in early childhood using the Children's Behavior Questionnaire*. Paper presented at the Society for Research in Child Development Biennial Meeting, Denver, CO.

Maller, R. D., Nakagawa, A., Slobodskaya, H. R., Ogura, T., Lee., J., Park, C., Dragan, W., and LeCannelier, F. (2009, April). *Mean-level and structural comparisons of fine-grained temperament attributes in toddlers from multiple countries*. Paper presented at the Society for Research in Child Development Biennial Meeting, Denver, CO.

Nakagawa, A., Sukigara, M., & Mizuno, R. (2007, April). *Cultural effects reflected in the early childhood behavior questionnaire for Japanese toddlers: Psychometrics and factor structure*. Paper presented at the Society for Research in Child Development Biennial Meeting, Boston, MA.

Putnam, S. P., & Gartstein, M. A. (2017). Aggregate temperament scores from multiple countries: Associations with aggregate personality traits, cultural dimensions, and allelic frequency. *Journal of Research in Personality, 67*, 157–170.

Putnam, S. P., Gartstein, M. A., & Rothbart, M. K. (2006). Measurement of fine-grained aspects of toddler temperament: The Early Childhood Behavior Questionnaire. *Infant Behavior and Development, 29*, 386–401.

Rubin, K. H., Hemphill, S. A., Chen, X., Hastings, P., Sanson, A., Coco, A. L., . . . Cui, L. (2006). A cross-cultural study of behavioral inhibition in toddlers: East–West–North–South. *International Journal of Behavioral Development, 30*, 219–226.

Slobodskaya, H. R., Gartstein, M. A., Nakagawa, A., & Putnam, S. P. (2013). Early temperament in Japan, the United States, and Russia: Do cross-cultural differences decrease with age? *Journal of Cross-Cultural Psychology*, *44*, 438–460.

# 4

# CROSS-CULTURAL DIFFERENCES IN BEHAVIOR PROBLEMS

*Samuel P. Putnam, Sara Casalin, Blanca Huitron, Mirjana Majdandžić, and Maria Beatriz Martins Linhares*

Identifying cross-cultural differences in early appearing emotional and behavior problems is important, as understanding cultural variability can be informative with respect to etiology, trajectory, and potential therapeutic targets. In this chapter, we explore differences between the 14 JETTC cultures with regard to parent reports of emotional and behavior problems in toddlers.

Analyses carried out in multiple cultures suggest that childhood emotional/behavioral difficulties can be organized under primary domains (e.g., Achenbach, Edelbrock, & Howell, 1987), with internalizing

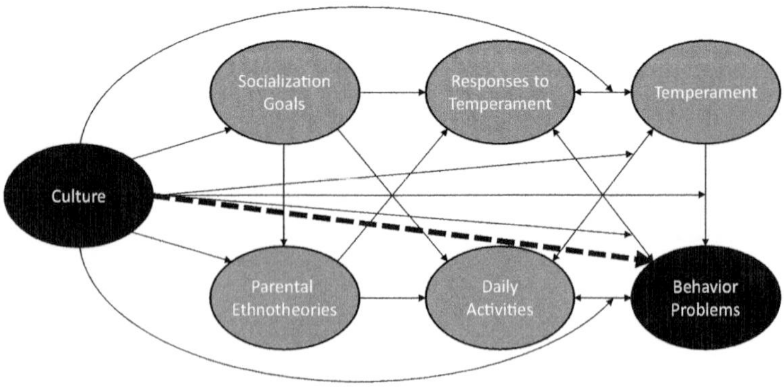


**FIGURE 4.1** CBCL behavior problems in the JETTC Conceptual Model

problems (INT) involving one's experience of distressful emotions, such as anxiety and sadness, and externalizing (EXT) including aggressive, noncompliant, and destructive behaviors, directed outward. Cross-cultural comparisons of behavior problems have been conducted primarily with older children, typically in the context of bi-cultural designs. Bergeron and Schneider (2005) provided a quantitative review of the literature with respect to peer-directed aggression. In this summary of 36 studies involving 22 nations, JETTC countries in which children and/or adults demonstrated relatively high levels of aggression included Mexico, Finland, the US, and Spain. Belgium and China were near the median of the distribution, and the Netherlands and South Korea were low. A meta-analysis by Polanczyk, deLima, Horta, Beiderman, and Rohde (2007) suggested very high rates of attention problems in children from South America, moderate rates in North America and Europe, and low levels in Asia. Regarding internalizing-type disorders, a comparison of lifetime prevalence of disorders in 17 countries by the World Health Organization suggested high rates of anxiety and mood disorders in the US, with moderate rates in Mexico and in Europe (including the JETTC countries of Belgium, Italy, Netherlands, and Spain), and low levels in China (Kessler et al., 2007). Importantly, both Bergeron and Schneider (2005) and Polanczyk et al. (2007) noted a large degree of variability in the results of the studies they reviewed, and implicated methodological factors, including age and measurement tools, as important influences on findings of cross-cultural differences.

Recently, Rescorla and colleagues have conducted multicultural comparisons of behavioral and emotional problems measured by the Child Behavior Checklist (CBCL), used in the current study. Rescorla et al. (2007) reported on children ages 6–16 years in 31 societies (including 10 JETTC countries), and Rescorla et al. (2011) compared children ages 1.5–5 from 24 societies (including 11 JETTC countries). Preschoolers and older children from Spain, South Korean preschoolers (but not older children), and Chinese older children (but not preschoolers) scored low, whereas preschoolers from Chile, Turkey, and Russia scored high on total behavior problems (i.e., INT and EXT combined). Rescorla et al. (2011) reported that Spain was low in EXT and INT, Chile high in both, South Korea low in EXT, and Romania and Turkey high in INT. Although not significantly lower than the omnicultural mean, scores from northern European cultures (Belgium, Finland, and the Netherlands) were below the mean in both studies; and US, Italy, and Romania had scores near or slightly above the mean in both reports.

Bergeron and Schneider (2005) noted that value placed on competition and hierarchy leads to higher aggression in individualistic countries and countries high on Power Distance, with values emphasizing nurturance potentially diminishing aggression in feminine cultures. Bergeron and Schneider (2005) also found aggression to be linked to high Uncertainty Avoidance. Negative Affectivity (NEG), particularly fearfulness, was reported to be higher in collectivist countries (Chen et al., 1998; Krassner et al., 2017; Putnam & Gartstein, 2017), and given the strong relation between NEG and INT (e.g., Gartstein, Putnam, & Rothbart, 2012), we expect higher INT problems in collectivist cultures as well.

As there is a considerable degree of inconsistency among existing multi-national studies of disorder rates (e.g., Finland demonstrated high rates of aggression in Bergeron and Schneider (2005), low attention problems in Polanczyk et al. (2007), low problem levels in Rescorla et al. (2007), and moderate problems in Rescorla et al. (2011)), our hypotheses are tentative. Because our methods align most closely with Rescorla et al. (2011), we anticipated children from Spain would be rated low in both INT and EXT, with South Korean children demonstrating low EXT, Chilean children rated high in both types of problems, and Turkish and Romanian toddlers particularly high in INT. Consistent with Bergeron and Schneider (2005), we expected higher EXT in countries characterized as high in Individualism, Power Distance, Masculinity and Uncertainty Avoidance, and higher INT in collectivist cultures.

## Results

As shown in Table 4.1, substantial cross-cultural effects for INT, EXT, and total problems were revealed through 2 (sex) by 14 (country) Analyses of Variance (ANOVAs), with age as a covariate. No effects were significant for age, sex, or the interaction between culture and sex.

**TABLE 4.1** Effects of culture, age, and sex on CBCL behavior problems

| *CBCL score* | *Age* | *Culture* | *Sex* | *Culture × Sex* |
|---|---|---|---|---|
| Internalizing | 1.23 | 7.66** | 1.68 | 0.69 |
| Externalizing | 0.95 | 6.07** | 1.03 | 0.30 |
| Total problems | 0.37 | 6.82** | 0.09 | 0.40 |

Note: ANOVAs, with age as covariate, gender and country as factors. Dfs for age and sex = 1,810. Dfs for culture and culture × sex = 13,810

$^{**}p < 0.001$. $^{*}p < 0.05$. $^{\#}p < 0.10$

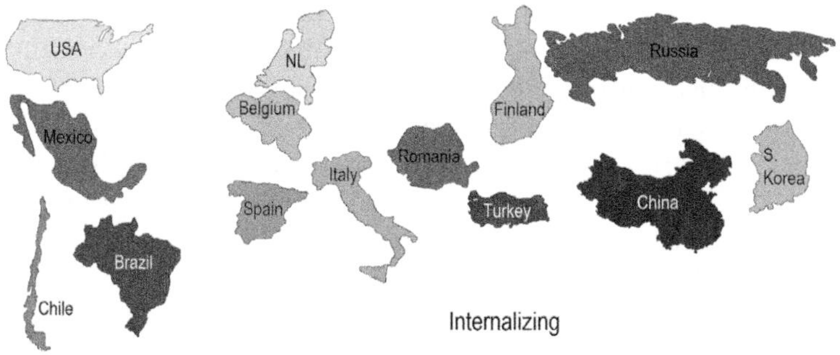


FIGURE 4.2 Map of Internalizing marginal means. Darker shading indicates higher scores

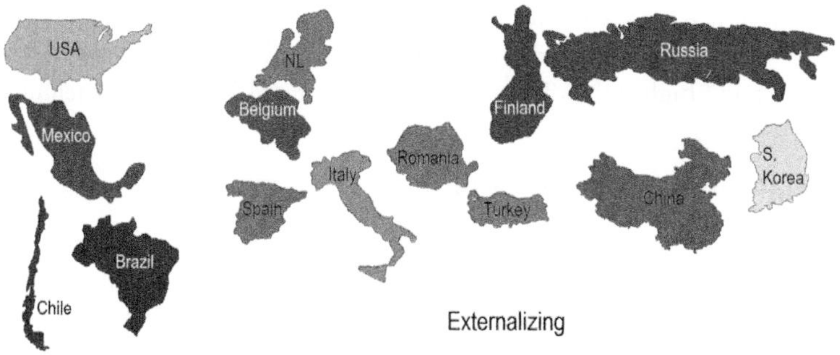


FIGURE 4.3 Map of Externalizing marginal means. Darker shading indicates higher scores

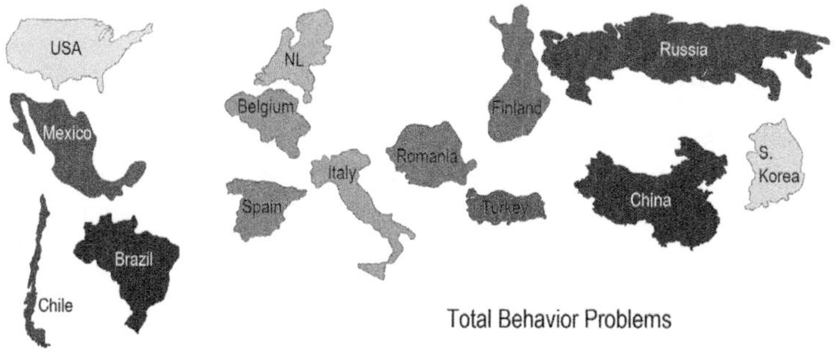


FIGURE 4.4 Map of total behavior problems marginal means. Darker shading indicates higher scores

Main effects comparisons with Bonferroni adjustments indicated children from China, Turkey, and Brazil were all rated higher in INT than the five lowest-scoring countries (Figure 4.2): US, Netherlands, Belgium, South Korea, and Finland. Children from China and Turkey were additionally rated higher than those from Italy, with those from China rated higher than Spain. Children from the US and Netherlands were also rated lower than those from Romania and Russia, with those from the US also lower than Mexico.

Children from Brazil, Chile, Finland, Russia, Mexico, and Belgium were all rated higher in EXT (Figure 4.3) than those from the US and South Korea. Brazil was rated higher than Italy, and China was rated higher than South Korea.

In total problems (Figure 4.4), children from Brazil, China, Russia, Chile, Mexico, and Turkey were all rated higher than those from the US and South Korea. Children from Chile, Russia, China, and Brazil were also rated higher than those from the Netherlands; China and Brazil were rated higher than Italy; and Brazil was rated higher than Belgium.

## Relations to Cultural Orientation Dimensions

To explore connections between behavior problems and established cultural distinctions, Pearson's correlations were calculated between average country scores on the three CBCL variables and Hofstede's six cultural orientation dimensions. High levels of both INT and total problems were associated with Collectivism, $r_s$ (14) = –0.70, $p < 0.01$, and –0.60, $p < 0.05$, respectively. INT and total problems were also linked to high Power Distance, $r_s$ (14) = 0.74, $p < 0.01$ and 0.60, $p < 0.05$.

## Discussion

Our results converge with those from other multicultural investigations in demonstrating culture exerts a powerful influence on indices of emotional and behavioral problems. Furthermore, the comparisons between JETTC sites were roughly consistent with, and extend, those obtained in the only previous study to examine parent reports of symptomology in young children from multiple countries. Of the 11 countries included in Rescorla et al. (2011) and the current study, children from Chile, Turkey, and Romania were near or at the top of the distribution for total problems, South Korea was near the bottom, and

Belgium and the Netherlands were near the middle in both studies. Modest exceptions to the agreement between the two studies include Spain, which demonstrated very low levels in Rescorla et al. (2011) but moderate levels in the JETTC; the US, rated low in the current study but moderately in Rescorla et al. (2011); and China—moderate in Rescorla et al. (2011) but high in the current study. Results were also consistent insofar as South Korea was particularly low in EXT and Turkey high in INT.

It is of note that correspondence between our findings and those obtained by Rescorla et al. (2011) is greater than that between these two studies and a similar investigation by Rescorla et al. (2007) focused on older children and adolescents. For example, South Korean preschoolers obtained low scores in our study and Rescorla et al. (2011), but older Korean youth were rated relatively high in problems (Rescorla et al., 2007).

The present findings and those of Rescorla et al. (2007, 2011) contrast considerably with reports of worldwide diagnostic rates of Attention Deficit Hyperactivity Disorder (ADHD) in children and lifetime prevalence of disorders (e.g., Kessler et al., 2007; Polanczyk et al., 2007). Polanczyk et al. (2007), in reference to their metaregression of worldwide ADHD rates, suggested that the role of culture paled in comparison to variability explained by differing methodology across studies. Cultural bias may play a stronger role in clinical diagnoses than responses to a questionnaire checklist. Whereas clinical judgments require a professional to determine whether behaviors violate expected norms, thus meeting criteria for a diagnosis, items of the CBCL (e.g., "Cries a lot," "Defiant," and "Unusually loud") only ask parents to report on the degree to which their children exhibit certain behaviors. Achenbach et al. (2008) have argued convincingly in support of the validity of the CBCL and associated measures in multiple cultures. Additional research is necessary, however, to illuminate the degree to which between-culture comparisons of the CBCL represent differences in child behavior versus parental interpretations.

Recognition of coherence in terms of geographical patterns and cultural orientation correlates of CBCL scores can be useful in deciphering their meaning. Geographically, trends are apparent suggesting high scores on EXT in Latin America, high INT in Asia (with the exception of South Korea), and generally low INT for Europe. Among JETTC cultures, the highest homicide rates were reported in Brazil, Mexico, and Russia (United Nations Office on Drugs and Crime, 2013), where children were rated high on EXT, and these scores may represent early manifestations of aggression that is relatively normative in these cultures. Higher behavioral inhibition, a predisposition linked with INT, was observed for Chinese children, relative to those from western cultures (Chen et al., 1998). In this study, countries where children were perceived as demonstrating elevated INT and total problems were united by endorsement of collectivism and an acceptance of inequality (Power Distance). Regarding the latter, Bergeron and Schneider (2005) contended that individuals residing in countries in which power is distributed unequally may experience frustration manifesting high levels of aggression. JETTC data suggest that social conditions of this nature may manifest themselves in higher perceptions of problematic anxiety and sadness in families' young children.

## References

Achenbach, T. M., Becker, A., Döpfner, M., Heiervang, E., Roessner, V., Steinhausen, H. C., & Rothenberger, A. (2008). Multicultural assessment of child and adolescent psychopathology with ASEBA and SDQ instruments: Research findings, applications, and future directions. *Journal of Child Psychology and Psychiatry*, *49*(3), 237–250.

Achenbach, T. M., Edelbrock, C., & Howell, C. T. (1987). Empirically based assessment of the behavioral/emotional problems of 2- and 3-year-old children. *Journal of Abnormal Child Psychology*, *15*(4), 629–650.

Bergeron, N., & Schneider, B. H. (2005). Explaining cross-national differences in peer-directed aggression: A quantitative synthesis. *Aggressive Behavior*, *31*, 116–137.

Chen, X., Hastings, P. D., Rubin, K. H., Chen, H., Cen, G., & Stewart, S. L. (1998). Child-rearing attitudes and behavioral inhibition in Chinese and Canadian toddlers: A cross-cultural study. *Developmental Psychology*, *34*, 677–686.

Gartstein, M. A., Putnam, S. P., & Rothbart, M. K. (2012). Etiology of preschool behavior problems: Contributions of temperament attributes in early childhood. *Infant Mental Health Journal*, *33*, 197–211.

Kessler, R. C., Angermeyer, M., Anthony, J. C., DeGraaf, R., Demyttenaere, K., Gasquet, I., . . . Ustün, T. B. (2007). Lifetime prevalence and age-of-onset distributions of mental disorders in the World Health Organization's World Mental Health Survey Initiative. *World Psychiatry*, *6*, 168–176.

Krassner, A., Gartstein, M. A., Park, C., Dragan, W. L., Lecannelier, F., & Putnam, S. P. (2017). East-West, collectivist-individualist: A cross-cultural examination of temperament in toddlers from Chile, Poland, South Korea, and the U.S. *European Journal of Developmental Psychology*, *14*(4), 449–464.

Polanczyk, G., deLima, M. S., Horta, B. L., Beiderman, J., & Rohde, L. A. (2007). The worldwide prevalence of ADHD: A systematic review and metaregression analysis. *American Journal of Psychiatry*, *164*, 942–948.

Putnam, S. P., & Gartstein, M. A. (2017). Aggregate temperament scores from 18 countries: Associations with aggregate personality traits, cultural dimensions, and allelic frequency. *Journal of Research in Personality*, *67*, 157–170.

Rescorla, L. A., Achenbach, T. M., Ivanova, M. Y., Dumenci, L., Almqvist, F., Bilenberg, N., Verhulst, F. (2007). Behavioural and emotional problems reported by parent of children ages 6 to 16 in 31 societies. *Journal of Emotional and Behavioural Disorders*, *15*, 130–142.

Rescorla, L. A., Achenbach, T. M., Ivanova, M. Y., Harder, V. S., Otten, L., Bilenberg, N., Verhulst, F. C. (2011). International comparisons of behavioral and emotional problems in preschool children: Parents' reports from 24 societies. *Journal of Clinical Child & Adolescent Psychology*, *40*(3), 456–467.

United Nations Office on Drugs and Crime. (2013). UNODC Global Study on Homicide 2013. *United Nations Publication*, Sales No. 14.IV.1.

# 5

# CROSS-CULTURAL DIFFERENCES IN ASSOCIATIONS BETWEEN TEMPERAMENT AND BEHAVIOR PROBLEMS

*Carmen González-Salinas, Noelia Sánchez-Pérez, Luis J. Fuentes, Rosario Montirosso, and Kati Heinonen*

Children's behavior problems are considered a major risk for future maladaptation and mental health problems. There is consensus that studying links between temperament and behavior problems early in childhood is valuable because it may provide means to identify at-risk individuals who could benefit from prevention and early intervention efforts (Kovacs & Lopez-Duran, 2010). In this chapter we analyze

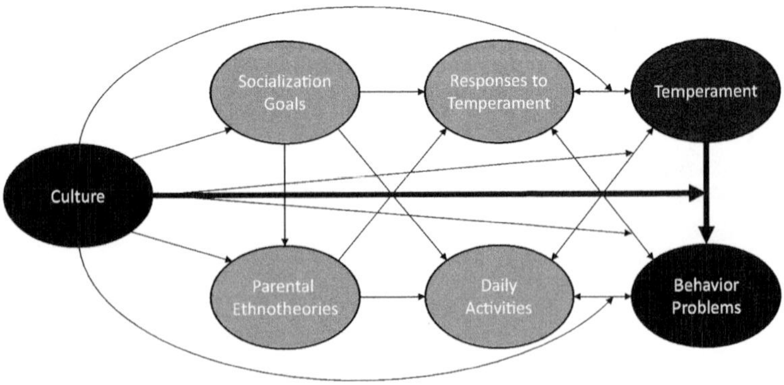


**FIGURE 5.1** ECBQ–CBCL associations in the JETTC Conceptual Model

associations between temperament and first signs of behavioral problems in toddlers from the 14 JETTC countries (see Figure 5.1).

In studying connections between temperament/personality and psychopathology, a large body of research has associated higher temperamental Negative Affectivity (NEG) with internalizing problems (INT; Gartstein, Putnam, & Rothbart, 2012; Slobodskaya & Akhmetova, 2010). Observational measures in young childhood have mainly focused on behavioral inhibition, characterized by fearful affect, social withdrawal, and vigilance, consistently associated with anxiety disorders (Chronis-Tuscano et al., 2009; Kagan, Snidman, Kahn, & Towsley, 2007). Higher levels of NEG in infancy and toddlerhood have also been associated with externalizing problems (EXT) in early childhood (e.g., Lipscomb et al., 2012).

Effortful Control (EFF) is the primary higher-order trait most often linked to EXT (Eisenberg, Spinrad, & Eggum, 2010; Nigg, 2006). Low self-regulation, expressed in the form of impulsive behavior and disinhibition, has been related to EXT throughout childhood (Eisenberg et al., 2010; Rubin, Burgess, Kennedy, & Stewart, 2003), with lower EFF particularly predictive of disruptive behavior for children who are less guilt prone (Kochanska, Barry, Jimenez, Hollatz, & Woodard, 2009). Low EFF was also associated with depression and anxiety in children, especially in the context of high NEG (Gartstein et al., 2012; Lonigan, Phillips, & Hooe, 2003). However, in some cases associations with INT were weak (e.g., Gartstein et al., 2012).

Higher levels of Surgency (SUR) were positively associated with EXT, longitudinally (Gartstein et al., 2012; Rothbart, Ahadi, Hershey, & Fisher, 2001) and concurrently (Slobodskaya & Akhmetova, 2010). Exuberance in infancy predicted EXT (Stifter, Putnam, & Jahromi, 2008) and propensity for risk-taking, associated with sensation seeking and antisocial behaviors (Lahat et al., 2012). Concerning connections between SUR and INT, the literature is mixed; for instance, Gartstein et al. (2012) found only a negative concurrent association between preschool SUR and INT, and no prediction was found for infant and toddler SUR in connection to preschool INT.

Two alternative models aimed at explaining temperament-psychopathology connections have received considerable attention (Tackett, 2006). The *spectrum* model hypothesizes that many disorders represent extremes of temperament (Rettew & McKee, 2005), with Martel, Gremillion, Roberts, Zastrow, and Tackett (2014), for example, supporting this interpretation. Higher SUR and NEG, along with lower EFF, were associated with initial Attention Deficit Hyperactivity Disorder

(ADHD) symptoms; however, these traits did not predict a 1-year course of ADHD symptoms. The authors concluded that the identified temperament profile and ADHD symptoms were different expressions of the same underlying continuum. In our study, if behavioral problems were extreme manifestations of temperament traits, their association would *not* be highly influenced by culture, and a consistent trend of associations would emerge across countries.

On the other hand, the *risk* or *vulnerability* model establishes that temperament and psychopathology are qualitatively distinct entities, and that certain temperament dimensions in combination with given environmental conditions will contribute to a higher probability of developing a particular disorder (Tackett, 2006). In line with this interpretation, Mian, Wainwright, Briggs-Gowan, and Carter (2011) found that children's behavioral inhibition, negative affectivity, and anxiety symptoms in the toddler/preschool period acted in confluence with maternal anxiety/depression and violence exposure to predict school-aged anxiety symptoms. From this perspective, the association between temperament and psychopathology will be affected by environmental factors such as parental practices, which are highly influenced by culture. Thus, significant variability in the strength of associations across cultures would support this model.

Cross-cultural research models view cultural beliefs as moderating the contribution of children's temperament to developmental outcomes (Chen, Yang, & Fu, 2015), presumably through mechanisms related to parental psychology, as well as approaches to child-rearing (Bornstein, 2010; Super & Harkness, 1986). Chen et al. (2015) demonstrated that shyness/inhibition was related to socioemotional difficulties in western societies, where there is an emphasis on autonomy and assertiveness. In contrast, less deviant and maladaptive behaviors have been associated with shyness in societies with no such emphasis. Gartstein, Slobodskaya, Kirchhoff, and Putnam (2013) compared the contribution of infant temperament to preschool behavioral problems in Russia and the United States (US), reporting that a greater propensity toward experiencing NEG, and lower levels of emerging self-regulation, were associated with behavioral difficulties for the US but not Russian children.

In this chapter we examine associations between temperament and behavioral problems for toddlers in 14 countries, considering commonalities and differences. Due to a dearth of relevant cross-cultural literature, our analyses are largely exploratory, but we expect some moderation by culture.

## Results

Correlations were calculated first using the entire sample of individual families, which conflate within-country and between-country differences, as shown in Table 5.1. They indicate that NEG was positively correlated, and EFF negatively correlated, with INT, EXT, and total problems. SUR was positively correlated with EXT and total problems, but not INT.

Table 5.2 contains correlations between the countries' marginal means for the temperament and behavior problem variables. The results of these

**TABLE 5.1** Correlations between temperament and behavior problems for the entire sample

| | *Internalizing* | *Externalizing* | *Total problems* |
|---|---|---|---|
| Negative Affectivity | 0.52** | 32** | 0.47** |
| Surgency | −0.04 | 0.26** | 0.13** |
| Effortful Control | −0.22** | −0.44** | −0.37** |

Note: $N = 839$, $^{**}p < 0.001$

**TABLE 5.2** Between-country correlations between countries' marginal means of temperament and behavior problems

| | *Internalizing* | *Externalizing* | *Total problems* |
|---|---|---|---|
| Negative Affectivity | 0.63* | 0.07 | 0.47# |
| Surgency | −0.32 | 0.59* | 0.14 |
| Effortful Control | −0.44 | −0.38 | −0.47# |

Note: $N = 14$, $^{*}p < 0.05$, $\#p < 0.10$

**TABLE 5.3** Average within-country correlations between temperament and behavior problems

| | *Internalizing* | *Externalizing* | *Total problems* |
|---|---|---|---|
| Negative Affectivity | $0.50^{14}$ | $0.36^{12}$ | $0.47^{14}$ |
| Surgency | $0.01^{0}$ | $0.23^{5}$ | $0.14^{4}$ |
| Effortful Control | $-0.23^{5}$ | $-0.46^{14}$ | $-0.38^{14}$ |

Note: Superscripts indicate the number of countries (out of 14) for which the correlation was significant to $p < 0.05$

between-country correlations indicate that countries with high NEG also rated children high in INT, whereas countries for which SUR was high also reported high EXT.

Results of within-country correlations demonstrated both universal trends and culture-based variations. The average within-culture correlations are shown in Table 5.3, with the graphs in Figure 5.2 indicating the correlation coefficients for all 14 sites.

Country-specific correlations between NEG, INT, and total problems were positive and significant in all countries. Positive correlations with EXT were significant in all countries but Italy and Belgium; associations were highest in Brazil, Chile, and South Korea. Low associations were apparent in Italy, Belgium (especially for EXT), the Netherlands, and Finland (especially for INT).

For SUR, no country-specific correlations with INT were significant. Positive correlations with EXT reached significance in Russia, Chile, Brazil, Romania, and the Netherlands; and with total problems for Chile, Russia, Brazil, and Spain.

Country-specific correlations for EFF, EXT, and total problems were negative and significant in all countries. Negative correlations with INT reached significance for Brazil, Chile, the Netherlands, Belgium, and the US. The strongest correlations were obtained in Chile and Brazil, with Belgium, the US, and Russia also showing high associations. The lowest associations were apparent in Italy, Romania, Turkey (especially for EXT), and South Korea (especially for INT).

## Discussion

In this chapter, we aimed to analyze the relation between temperament and symptoms of behavioral problems in toddlers, focusing on the role of culture. Correlations computed with the entire sample were consistent with previous studies, wherein higher NEG and lower EFF were associated with greater expression of behavioral problems; and SUR was associated positively with EXT, but not INT. However, the association between NEG and EXT was significant in only 12 of the 14 countries studied. Moreover, the correlations of EFF with INT, and SUR with EXT, were only significant for 5 of the 14 countries considered. Additionally, even when countries showed similar directions of associations, differences were found in the strength of the relations. Thus, both universal trends and culture-based variations were apparent.

In line with previous literature (e.g., Gartstein, Putnam & Rothbart, 2012; Slobodskaya & Akhmetova, 2010), our study supports an early link between a higher tendency to experience and express negative emotions with the expression of anxiety and/or depression symptoms. The present study is unique in extending this finding to toddlers from diverse countries.

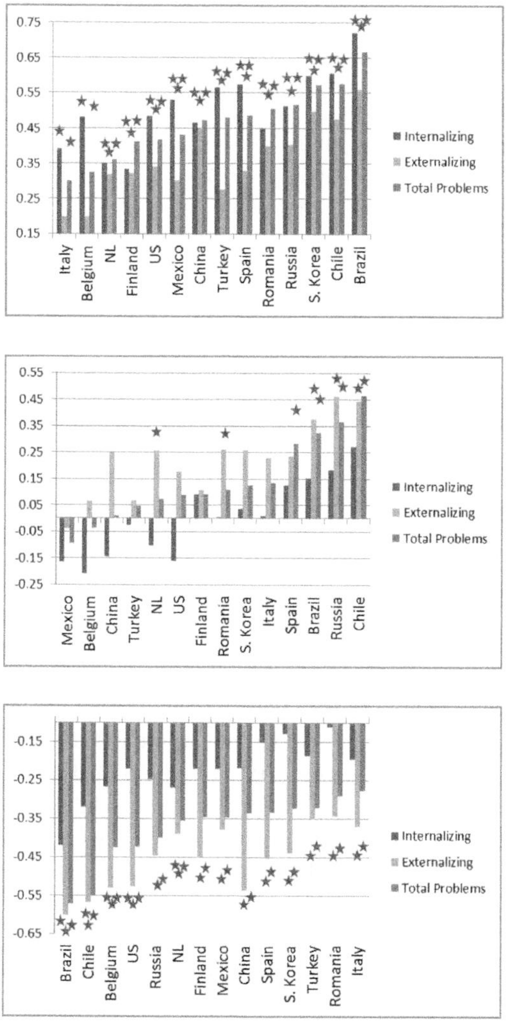


Negative Affectivity predicting Behavior Problems

Surgency predicting Behavior Problems

Effortful Control predicting Behavior Problems

**FIGURE 5.2** ECBQ–CBCL correlations for JETTC countries

★ indicates significant correlation

NEG was also positively associated with EXT; however, the correlation did not reach significance in Belgium and Italy. These two countries, located in western Europe, are geographically proximate and have experienced similar recent historical events. Moreover, these countries are both characterized by high Uncertainty Avoidance, which reflects the extent to which members of a culture feel threatened by ambiguous or unknown situations and may thus value structure (Hofstede, Hofstede, & Minkov, 2010). Parents in these cultures may tend to provide a more structured environment, offering support for children high in NEG, possibly preventing exacerbation of EXT.

In all countries, toddlers exhibiting poorer EFF tended toward EXT, consistent with the literature (Gartstein et al., 2012; Rothbart et al., 2001). EFF protects children from behavioral problems by enabling them to inhibit tendencies toward expressing anger and avoidance, relying on positive alternatives, such as compliance, empathy, and social competence in challenging situations instead (Rothbart, 2011). EFF exhibited negative correlations with INT in many countries, as previously reported (Gartstein et al., 2012; Lonigan et al., 2003; Oldehinkel, Hartman, DeWinter, Veenstra, & Ormel, 2004). According to Eisenberg and Morris (2002), the use of attentional strategies such as redirecting focus away from distressing stimuli plays an essential role in dampening negative emotions culminating in INT. Notably, the five countries for which this relation was significant (Brazil, Belgium, Netherlands, US, and Chile) can be characterized as indulgent, allowing members to be unrestrained and pursue self-gratification (Hofstede et al., 2010). Indulgently oriented parents may put less emphasis on control over their toddlers' behavior and, as a consequence, regulation of negative emotions (e.g., sadness and anxiety) relies more on children's dispositional tendencies than on contextual factors. Alternatively, for those countries where EFF failed to show a direct association with INT problems, EFF may interact with NEG, such that EFF primarily led to INT in highly negative children, as found by Gartstein et al. (2012). Exploring this possibility goes beyond the scope of this chapter and will be addressed in continuing analyses of the present data.

In five samples, SUR was positively associated with EXT, in line with existing research (Gartstein et al., 2012). High SUR could indicate control deficits that lead to manifestation of EXT behaviors (Eisenberg & Morris, 2002). We were not able to discern a coherent pattern to explain why the correlation was positive and significant for some countries (Brazil, Russia, Netherlands, Romania, and Chile), modest and not significant for others (South Korea, Spain, China, Italy, Finland, and US), and even close to zero in a few (Mexico, Turkey, and Belgium). We speculate that inconsistency could be in part explained by differences in parents' standards for their children's behaviors across countries.

Between-country correlations implicate cultural patterns of temperament as contributors to cross-cultural differences in behavior problems. In countries where children had higher average NEG, children were rated higher in INT as well. This pattern was also apparent in the within-country correlations, suggesting a universal nature. If the same processes underlie the propensity to experience and express negative affectivity and the development of problems such as anxiety or depression, the differences between this temperament predisposition and psychopathology are likely a matter of quantity (degree, intensity) rather than quality (nature), supporting the spectrum model. Between-country correlations also indicated that countries rating children high in SUR were those in which children showed more EXT. However, in this case, the within-country correlations provided inconsistent results across cultures. Consequently, the vulnerability model may be more appropriate, as the propensity for SUR would be better understood as a risk factor acting in confluence with contextual risk/protection in contributing to the development of problems such as ADHD or Oppositional Defiant Disorder.

## References

Bornstein, M. H. (2010). From measurement to meaning in Caregiving and Culture; current challenges and future prospects. In C. M. Worthman, P. M. Plotsky, D. S. Schechter, & C. A. Cummings (Eds.), *Formative experiences: The interaction of caregiving, culture and developmental psychobiology* (pp. 36–50). New York, NY: Cambridge University Press.

Chen, X., Yang, F., & Fu, R. (2015). Culture and temperament. In M. Zentner & R. L. Shiner (Eds.), *Handbook of temperament* (pp. 462–478). New York, NY: Guildford.

Chronis-Tuscano, A., Degnan, K. A., Pine, D. S., Pérez-Edgar, K., Henderson, H. A., Diaz, Y., . . . Fox, N. A. (2009). Stable early maternal report of behavioral inhibition predicts lifetime social anxiety disorder in adolescence. *Journal of the American Academy of Child and Adolescent Psychiatry, 48*, 928–935.

Eisenberg, N., & Morris, A. S. (2002). Children's emotion-related regulation. In R. V. Kail (Ed.), *Advances in child development and behavior* (Vol. 30, pp. 189–229). San Diego, CA: Academic Press.

Eisenberg, N., Spinrad, T. L., & Eggum, N. D. (2010). Emotion-related self-regulation and its relation to children's maladjustment. *Annual Review of Clinical Psychology, 6*, 495–525.

Gartstein, M. A., Putnam, S. P., & Rothbart, M. K. (2012). Etiology of preschool behavior problems: Contributions of temperament attributes in early childhood. *Infant Mental Health Journal, 33*(2), 197–211.

Gartstein, M. A., Slobodskaya, H. R., Kirchhoff, C., & Putnam, S. (2013). Cross-cultural differences in the development of behavior problems: Contributions of infant temperament in Russia and U.S. *International Journal of Developmental Science,* 7, 95–104.

Hofstede, G., Hofstede, G. J., & Minkov, M. (2010). *Cultures and organizations: Software of the mind* (Rev. 3rd ed.). New York, NY: McGraw-Hill.

Kagan, J., Snidman, N., Kahn, V., & Towsley, S. (2007). The preservation of two infant temperaments into adolescence. *Monographs of the Society for Research on Child Development, 72,* 1–95.

Kochanska, G., Barry, R. A., Jimenez, A. L., Hollatz, A. L., & Woodard, J. (2009). Guilt and effortful control: Two mechanisms to prevent disruptive developmental trajectories. *Journal of Personality and Social Psychology, 97*(2), 322–333.

Kovacs, M., & Lopez-Duran, N. (2010). Prodromal symptoms and atypical affectivity as predictors of major depression in juveniles: Implications for prevention. *Journal of Child Psychology and Psychiatry, 51,* 472–496.

Lahat, A., Degnan, K. A., White, L. K., McDermott, J. M., Henderson, H. A., Lejuez, C. W., & Fox, N. A. (2012). Temperamental exuberance and executive function predict propensity for risk taking in childhood. *Development and Psychopathology, 24,* 847–856.

Lipscomb, S. T., Leve, L. D., Shaw, D. S., Neiderhiser, J. M., Scaramella, L. V., Ge, X., . . . Reiss, D. (2012). Negative emotionality and externalizing problems in toddlerhood: Overreactive parenting as a moderator of genetic influences. *Development and Psychopathology, 24*(1), 167–179.

Lonigan, C. J., Phillips, B. M., & Hooe, E. S. (2003). Relations of positive and negative affectivity to anxiety and depression in children: Evidence from a latent variable longitudinal study. *Journal of Consulting and Clinical Psychology, 71,* 465–481.

Martel, M. M., Gremillion, M. L., Roberts, B. A., Zastrow, B. L., & Tackett, J. L. (2014). Longitudinal prediction of the one-year course of preschool ADHD symptoms: Implications for models of temperament-ADHD associations. *Personality and Individual Differences, 64,* 58–61.

Mian, N. D., Godoy, L., Briggs-Gowan, M. J., & Carter, A. S. (2012). Patterns of anxiety symptoms in toddlers and preschool-age children: Evidence of early differentiation. *Journal of Anxiety Disorders, 26*(1), 102–110.

Nigg, J. T. (2006). Temperament and developmental psychopathology. *Journal of Child Psychology and Psychiatry, 47*(3–4), 395–422.

Oldehinkel, A. J., Hartman, C. A., DeWinter, A. F., Veenstra, R., & Ormel, J. (2004). Temperament profiles associated with internalizing and externalizing problems in preadolescence. *Development and Psychopathology, 16,* 421–440.

Rettew, D. C., & McKee, L. (2005). Temperament and its role in developmental psychopathology. *Harvard Review of Psychiatry, 13*(1), 14–27.

Rothbart, M. K. (2011). *Becoming who we are: Temperament and personality in development.* New York, NY: Guildford.

Rothbart, M. K., Ahadi, S. A., Hershey, K. L., & Fisher, P. (2001). Investigations of temperament at three to seven years: The Children's Behavior Questionnaire. *Child Development, 72,* 1394–1408.

Rubin, K. H., Burgess, K., Kennedy, A. E., & Stewart, S. (2003). Social withdrawal and inhibition in childhood. In E. Mash & R. Barkley (Eds.), *Child psychopathology* (pp. 372–406). New York, NY: Guilford.

Slobodskaya, H. R., & Akhmetova, O. A. (2010). Personality development and problem behavior in Russian children and adolescents. *International Journal of Behavioral Development, 34*(5), 441–451.

Stifter, C. A., Putnam, S., & Jahromi, L. (2008). Exuberant and inhibited toddlers: Stability of temperament and risk for problem behavior. *Development and Psychopathology, 20,* 401–421.

Super, C., & Harkness, S. (1986). The developmental niche: A conceptualization at the interface of child and culture. *International Journal of Behavioral Development, 9,* 545–569.

Tackett, J. L. (2006). Evaluating models of the personality-psychopathology relationship. *Clinical Psychology Review, 26,* 584–599.

# PART 2

# The Developmental Niche

# 6

# CROSS-CULTURAL DIFFERENCES IN SOCIALIZATION GOALS AND PARENTAL ETHNOTHEORIES

*Samuel P. Putnam, Maria A. Gartstein, Hannah Broos, Sara Casalin, and Felipe Lecannelier*

The psychology of parents is central to the transmission of culture across generations. The values, practices, and understandings shared among members of a community shape parents' views and practices used to guide children to meet cultural ideals. Building on the work of Kagitçibasi (2005), Keller (e.g., Keller & Kartner, 2013; Keller et al., 2006)

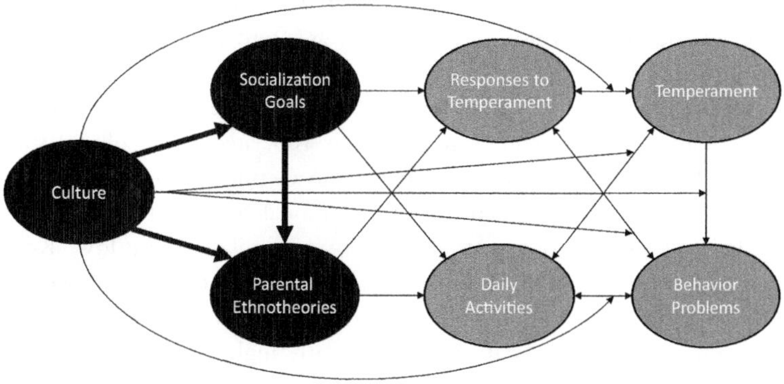


**FIGURE 6.1** Goals and parental ethnotheories in the JETTC Conceptual Model

emphasized two independent dimensions: autonomy and relational orientation. Fundamental in shaping socialization goals (SG)—norms and values shared in a culture that parents aim to transmit to their children—autonomy and relational orientations also influence parental ethnotheories (PE), defined as culture-specific understandings of what constitutes proper parenting and optimal child development. These dimensions form the basis of three cultural models: independence, interdependence, and autonomous–relational (Kagitçibasi, 2005). Cultures bound in the independence model prioritize autonomy over relational, with SG promoting the development of self-esteem and independence (i.e., Autonomous SG), and PE that value providing children with opportunities and time to play alone (i.e., Autonomous PE). Interdependent cultures, in contrast, de-emphasize autonomy, but prize relational orientation, holding SG that concern helping others and obedience to elders (i.e., Relational SG), and PE including the importance of body contact and prompt responding to children's signals (i.e., Relational PE). Autonomous–relational cultures combine an emphasis on autonomous functioning with value placed on interpersonal/relational.

In this chapter, we explore differences between the 14 JETTC cultures in their Autonomous and Relational SG and PE (see Figure 6.1), using a version of Keller's questionnaires modified for use with toddlers, rather than infants. Keller et al. (2006) found support for the three cultural models, using the original instruments, as parents in cultures assumed to be independent (Germany, US, and Greece) and autonomous-related (China, Costa Rica, Mexico, and urban India) scored higher on Autonomous SG and Relational PE than parents from groups deemed interdependent (Cameroon and rural India). However, autonomous-related countries did not score as highly as interdependent countries on relational goals and PE.

Keller et al.'s (2006) findings inform hypotheses for the current study, insofar as geographic proximity is associated with cultural similarity. For example, because mothers from Germany scored lower than other countries in these groups on Relational SG and PE, we expect JETTC countries from northern Europe to similarly score low. Keller et al. (2006) also reported: (1) relational goals were highest in Costa Rica (Latin America); (2) Chinese mothers demonstrated high Relational PE; (3) autonomy-related goals were particularly high in China and low in Mexico; and (4) Autonomous PE were lowest in Germany and highest in Greece. We anticipated similar results in overlapping cultures, as well as regions geographically close to those studied by Keller et al. (2006).

Collectivism/Individualism is the most thoroughly studied cultural dimension also linked to parenting (e.g., Triandis, 1988; Triandis & Suh, 2002), with autonomous goals and PE consistent with individualist ethos, and relational orientation consistent with Collectivism. However, the existence of autonomous-related cultures, in which both relational and autonomous goals are salient, has led to questions regarding the limits of Individualism/Collectivism as an influence on PE (e.g., Harkness, Super, & van Tijen, 2000). Halberstadt and Lozada (2011) argued for the importance of Power Distance, a cultural dimension addressing the acceptance of differences in the relative power of some individuals over others, as useful in a developmental context. For example, in Latin American cultures the ideal of respeto leads to expectations of obedience and respect to elders, values consistent with relational SG. We also expand the exploration of cultural dimensions in relation to parenting psychology to include additional constructs identified by Hofstede, Hofstede, and Minkov (2010).

Regarding Masculinity/Femininity, which contrasts preferences for assertive, competitive, and heroic behavior with modest, caring, and cooperative conduct, the masculine pole appears to be consistent with SG of high autonomy and low relation orientation. The implications of Uncertainty Avoidance, concerning the degree to which members of a culture experience ambiguity as threatening, for SG are less clearly defined. However, firm and clear rules characteristic of societies high in Uncertainty Avoidance are reminiscent of relational SG emphasizing obedience, and fear of the unknown may lead to discouragement of autonomous action in such cultures. Long-Term/Short-Term Orientation concerns the degree to which cultures foster virtues based in perseverance and thrift in comparison to more immediate benefits, including saving face and fulfilling social obligations. Short-term goals can be considered consistent with the ideals of self-esteem enhancement associated with autonomous SG, whereas an emphasis on treating others well, inherent to relational goals, appears to be more aligned with the Long-Term Orientation pole of this dimension. Similarly, Indulgence/Restraint concerns the extent to which a society allows its members to gratify their desires. High Indulgence appears to be consistent with philosophies endorsing autonomous action, but low on caring for others (i.e., high autonomous and low relational goals).

It was anticipated that relational goals and PE would be high in Latin American and Asian cultures, low in northern Europe, and demonstrated by societies characterized by Collectivism, high Power Distance, Femininity, high Uncertainty Avoidance, Long-Term Orientation, and Restraint. Autonomous goals were expected to be high in Asia and low in Latin America. Autonomous PE were hypothesized to be low in northern Europe and high in southern Europe and southwest Asia, with relations expected for autonomous parenting and Individualism, low Power Distance, Masculinity, low Uncertainty Avoidance, Short-Term Orientation, and Indulgence.

Not central to the overall aims of this book, interrelations between aggregate scores for PE and SG were also examined. Keller's model presumes connections between these components of parent psychology, yet previous studies (e.g., Keller et al., 2006) have not explicitly tested this proposition. Although some consistency between Autonomous SG and PE, as well as Relational SG and PE, can be expected (i.e., a country can be expected to score high on both, low on both, or in between on both), PE and SG represent relatively independent aspects of caregiver psychology.

## Results

As shown in Table 6.1, substantial cross-cultural effects for all four scales were revealed through 2 (Sex) by 14 (Culture) Analyses of Variance (ANOVAs), with age as a covariate. The culture × sex interaction was significant for autonomous SG and discussed below. Figures 6.2–6.5 reflect marginal means for each country on the four dimensions of parental psychology, available from volume editors upon request. Main effects

**TABLE 6.1** Effects of culture, age, and sex on socialization goals and parental ethnotheories

| *SG and PE scales* | *Age* | *Culture* | *Sex* | *Culture × Sex* |
|---|---|---|---|---|
| Relational Socialization Goals | 0.79 | 10.65** | 3.06# | 0.41 |
| Autonomous Socialization Goals | 1.02 | 3.36** | 2.13 | 2.14* |
| Relational Parental Ethnotheories | 0.44 | 9.27** | 2.93# | 0.896 |
| Autonomous Parental Ethnotheories | 0.22 | 7.47** | 0.41 | 0.64 |

Note: ANOVAs, with age as covariate, gender and country as factors. Socialization Goals Dfs for age and sex = 1,806; Dfs for culture and culture × sex = 13,806. Parental Ethnotheories Dfs for age and sex = 1,808; Dfs for culture and culture × sex = 13,808. $^{**}p < 0.001$, $^{*}p < 0.05$, $^{\#}p < 0.10$

comparisons (Bonferroni adjusted) of Relational SG indicated that mothers from Mexico, Brazil, Russia, Spain, the Netherlands, Chile, and the US reported higher relational goals than mothers in Italy, Finland, and Romania. Mothers from South Korea also reported higher relational goals than those from Italy and Finland. In addition, Belgian, Turkish, and Chinese mothers held relational goals lower than those from at least one other country.

Higher Autonomous goals were reported by mothers from Mexico and the Netherlands, relative to those from Italy and China. Following up the significant sex × country interaction, tests of simple effects indicated higher scores for males than females in Brazil, Romania, and (marginally) Chile.

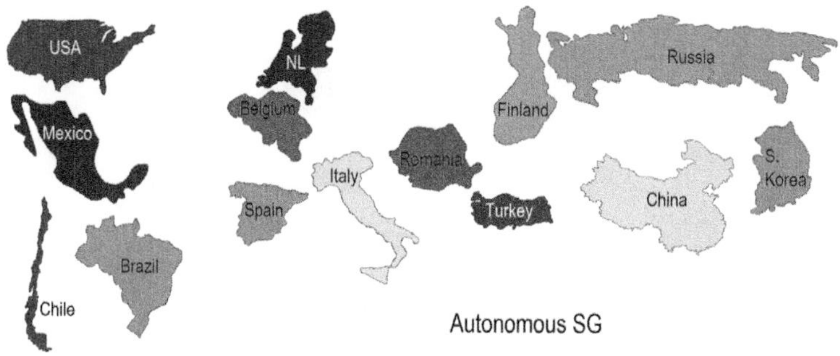


**FIGURE 6.2** Map of Autonomous Socialization Goals marginal means. Darker shading indicates higher scores

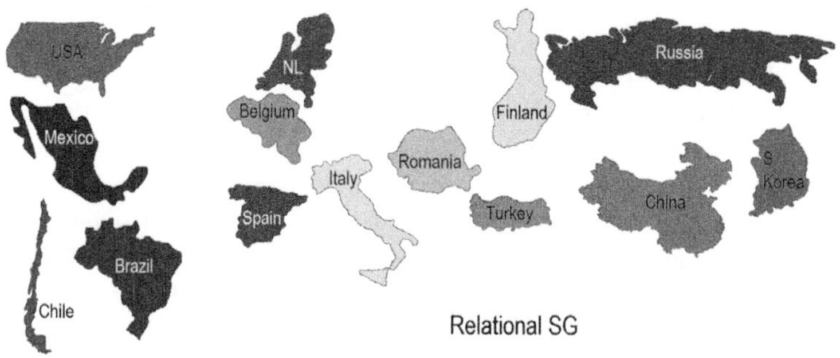


**FIGURE 6.3** Map of Relational Socialization Goals marginal means. Darker shading indicates higher scores

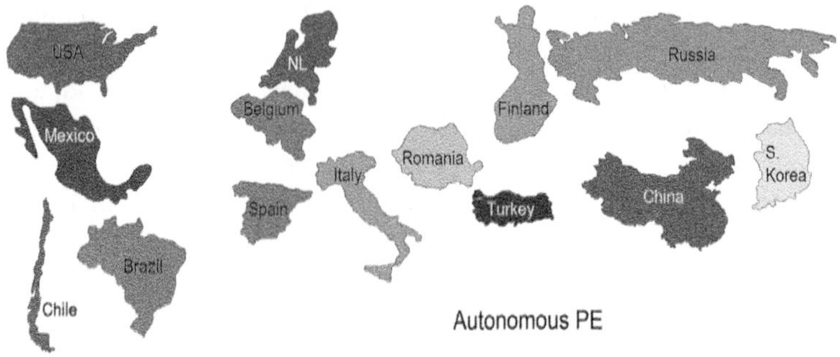


FIGURE 6.4 Map of Autonomous Parental Ethnotheories marginal means. Darker shading indicates higher scores

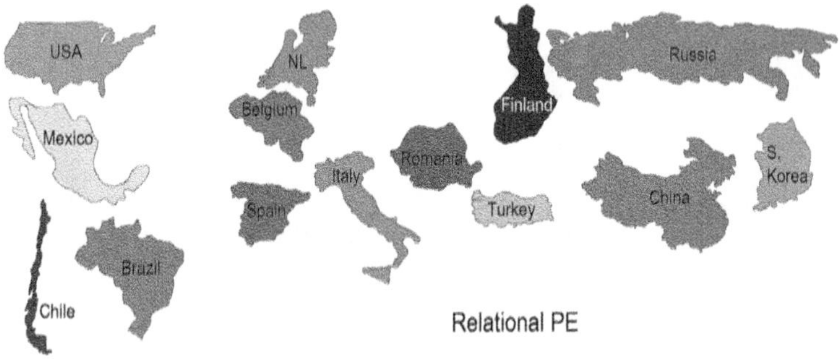


FIGURE 6.5 Map of Relational Parental Ethnotheories marginal means. Darker shading indicates higher scores

Relational PE scores were higher for mothers from Finland relative to those from all countries but Chile and Romania. Chilean mothers in turn scored higher than mothers from Mexico, Turkey, South Korea, the US, Italy, and the Netherlands. Mothers from Spain and Romania scored higher compared to Turkish caregivers. Mexican mothers' scores were significantly lower compared to nine highest-scoring countries.

Regarding Automous PE, mothers from Turkey scored significantly higher than caregivers from South Korea, Romania, Italy, Finland, Russia, Brazil, Belgium, and Spain. Mothers from Mexico, the Netherlands, China, and the US scored higher than their Romanian and Korean counterparts, with Mexican mothers also scoring higher than caregivers from Italy and Finland. Korean mothers demonstrated scores lower than those from the eight lowest-scoring countries.

## Relations to Cultural Orientation Dimensions

To explore connections between PE, SG, and Hofstede's dimensions (Hofstede et al., 2010), Pearson's correlations were calculated between average country scores on the four parent variables and six cultural orientation dimensions. Maternal reports of Autonomous SG were associated with high Indulgence, $r(14) = 0.70$, $p < 0.01$. Autonomous PE were also linked to Indulgence, $r(14) = 0.56$, $p < 0.05$, and marginally associated with Short-Term Orientation, $r(14) = -0.44$, $p < 0.10$. In addition, Relational PE were marginally associated with Femininity, $r(14) = -0.52$, $p < 0.10$.

Correlations among average country scores on the SG and PE dimensions were nonsignificant. A marginal association between Autonomous PE and SG, $r(14) = 0.52$, $p < 0.10$, was observed, along with a nonsignificant negative association between Relational PE and SG, $r(14) = -0.36$, ns.

## Discussion

Our findings are mixed in their consistency with previous investigations, and speak to the complexity of links between culture, development, and parent psychology. Patterns of Relational SG were generally similar to those obtained for parents of infants by Keller et al. (2006), insofar as both studies reported high relational goals among Latin American cultures and low relational goals in northern European sites. The obtained patterns of results for Relational PE, however, were less consistent with expectations. As hypothesized, Chile was high, and Brazil and China moderately high, on this dimension. However, countries from northern Europe were not particularly low in relational ethnotheory tendencies, and South Korea was relatively low.

In the context of the (nonsignificant) negative correlation between Relational PE and goals, it is not surprising that the patterns for SG and PE effects were rather dissimilar. This distinction between the two constructs was especially striking for two countries. Whereas Mexico evinced the highest relational goals, Mexico's Relational PE score was the lowest among the countries included. The opposite pattern was observed for Finland. These contradictions may in part be due to changes between infancy and toddlerhood in the nature of strategies that parents use to enact their SG and PE. Keller's research (Keller et al., 2006) indicates that relationship-oriented goals and PE lead parents of infants to rapidly soothe their crying babies in part to cultivate closeness and dependence. However, it may be the case that toddlers' negative affect is perceived by parents as more of a willful act, representing a failure of the child to respect others' needs and thus less deserving of immediate comforting. This change in caregivers' interventions with toddlers may contribute to altering elements of parental psychology—the manner in which Relational and Autonomous PE and SG are conceptualized. The latter speaks to the importance of the developmental transition between the first year of life and the toddler period, wherein parental expectations concerning improved self-regulation likely contribute to a shift in approaches to child distress, and caregiving more generally.

Keller's suggestion that PE allowing children to spend time in pursuit of their own goals would be most prevalent in countries which emphasize the development of attributes such as self-confidence was marginally supported by the positive correlation between autonomous SG and PE. However, our findings regarding the Autonomous SG of individual countries are contrary to those obtained by Keller et al. (2006), with mothers from Mexico demonstrating greater endorsement of autonomous goals than those from China. As the samples from the two studies were obtained from the same cities (Mexico City and Beijing, although Keller et al. also included some respondents from Taiyuan), and this scale was identical across the two studies, it is possible to directly compare the scores. Doing so reveals a substantial decline (from an average score of 4.6–4.0) between infancy and toddlerhood in autonomous goals of Chinese mothers, but a dramatic increase (from 3.5 to 4.5) for Mexican mothers. Further research using longitudinal samples is needed to replicate and understand this unexpected pattern of results. Our findings regarding Autonomous PE were in part consistent with expectations, as Turkey (geographically proximal to Greece, with high scores in Keller et al., 2006) also scored very high on this dimension. However, hypothesized high scores in southern, in comparison to northern, Europe did not materialize. The latter discrepancy could be a function of variability among northern European countries, or result from our focus on toddlerhood, as mentioned earlier.

The cultural dimension of Indulgence (versus Restraint) was predictive of high parental emphasis on autonomy, in terms of both beliefs regarding desired outcomes for their child (SG) and desired parental behaviors expected to achieve these outcomes (PE). Identified by Minkov (2007, 2009) through analyses of World Values Survey data, Indulgence/Restraint is defined through three core elements consisting of the self-evaluation of happiness, importance placed on leisure, and a perception that one has control over their life, rather than being constrained by social restrictions. A perception of autonomy among adults high in Indulgence is likely to be transmitted to children through prioritizing development of confidence and self-esteem (SG), and expectations that children should experience solitude to develop independence (PE).

## References

Halberstadt, A. G., & Lozada, F. T. (2011). Emotion development in infancy through the lens of culture. *Emotion Review, 3*, 158–168.

Harkness, S., Super, C. M., & Tijen, N. V. (2000). Individualism and the "Western Mind" reconsidered: American and Dutch parents' ethnotheories of the child. *New Directions for Child and Adolescent Development, 2000*, 23–39.

Hofstede, G., Hofstede, G. J., & Minkov, M. (2010). *Cultures and organizations: Software of the mind* (Rev. 3rd ed.). New York, NY: McGraw-Hill.

Kagitçibasi, C. (2005). Autonomy and relational in cultural context: Implications for self and family. *Journal of Cross-Cultural Psychology, 36*(4), 403–422.

Keller, H., & Kartner, J. (2013). Development: The cultural solution of universal developmental tasks. In M. J. Gelfand, C. Chiu, & Y. Hong (Eds.), *Advances in culture and psychology* (Vol. 3, pp. 63–116). New York, NY: Oxford University Press.

Keller, H., Lamm, B., Abels, M., Yovsi, R., Borke, J., Jensen, H., . . . Chaudhary, N. (2006). Cultural models, socialization goals, and parenting ethnotheories: A multicultural analysis. *Journal of Cross-Cultural Psychology, 37*, 155–172.

Minkov, M. (2007). *What makes us different and similar: A new interpretation of the world values survey and other cross-cultural data*. Sofia, Bulgaria: Klasika I Stil.

Minkov, M. (2009). Predictors of differences in subjective well-being across 97 nations. *Cross-Cultural Research, 43*, 152–179.

Triandis, H. C. (1988). Collectivism and development. In S. Durganand & H. S. R. Kao (Eds.), *Social values and development: Asian perspectives* (pp. 285–303). Thousand Oaks, CA: Sage.

Triandis, H. C., & Suh, E. M. (2002). Cultural influences on personality. *Annual Review of Psychology, 53*, 133–160.

# 7

# CROSS-CULTURAL DIFFERENCES IN CHILD ACTIVITIES

*Eric Desmarais, Maria A. Gartstein, Zhengyan Wang, Emine Ahmetoglu, and Roseriet Beijers*

Activities of daily living reflect critical contextual influences, operating via toddlers' exposure to culturally influenced learning over the course of early childhood. Play occupies a unique place among these activities, as its representational nature provides an effective avenue for cultural transmission (Bornstein & Tamis-LeMonda, 1995; Nielsen, Cucchiaro, & Mohamedally, 2012). The type of play in which a child engages,

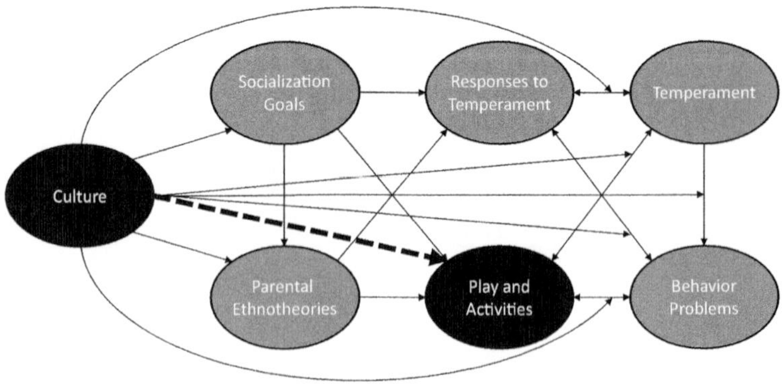


**FIGURE 7.1** Play and activities in the JETTC Conceptual Model

and the contextual (e.g., parental, peer) response to their play, provides the foundation from which more advanced social, emotional, and cognitive abilities develop (Feldman, 2007; Nielsen, 2012). Other daily living activities are consequential (Harkness et al., 2011; White & Brinkerhoff, 1981), although there is a surprising dearth of research concerning parental involvement of children in daily activities (e.g., household chores and activities outside the home). United States (US) access to TV and other media provides the means of exposing youngsters to culturally relevant concepts and has been linked to important outcomes, such as increased aggression and obesity (Manganello & Taylor, 2009; Zimmerman & Bell, 2010). This chapter focuses on differences between the 14 JETTC cultures across the domains of time spent playing, exposure to TV/media, and engagement in activities with parents (see Figure 7.1).

Although play was originally cast as a universal construct (e.g., Piaget, 1951), later research identified cultural variations (Haight, Wang, Fung, Williams, & Mintz, 1999). For example, in a comparison of US and Argentinian mother-child dyadic play, US dyads emphasized play for exploration, whereas Argentinian dyads engaged in more symbolic play (Bornstein, Haynes, Pascual, Painter, & Galperín, 1999). Mothers from Argentina were more likely to verbally praise their children and engage in social play. Thus, parents engage in play activities with differing purposes, with US caregivers likely aiming to foster independence and cognitive development, and Argentinian parents focusing on goals related to sociability and connectedness (Parmar, Harkness, & Super, 2008). Perhaps as a result of caregivers' enactment of these differing purposes, Chessa et al. (2012) found that US children produced more elaborate and imaginative play scenarios, whereas their Italian counterparts were better able to incorporate emotional content. These studies suggest parental structuring of play activities influenced by culture, such as establishing a purpose beyond entertainment, is consequential to child behavior.

A comprehensive review by Roopnarine and Davidson (2015) indicates that high-intensity "rough-and-tumble" play (i.e., chasing, jumping, and play fighting; Pellegrini, 1995), is less common in collectivist societies than individualistic European cultures. Parmar et al. (2004, 2008) compared daily activities of Asian and Euro-American families, indicating that caregivers of collectivistic origin were more likely to engage in play with a purpose (e.g., school readiness or academic enrichment), whereas a more individualistic culture translated into an emphasis on play for entertainment. This research would further suggest that parents in individualistic cultures are more likely to involve their children in household activities (e.g., chores) than their collectivistic counterparts (Parmar et al., 2004). However, it should be noted that the role of Individualism/Collectivism was inferred based on reported differences between the few cultures studied. Moreover, additional domains defined by Hofstede, Hofstede, and Minkov (2010) are likely important for discerning cross-cultural differences in play, despite neglect in developmental studies.

With regard to time spent watching television, Singer, Singer, Agostino, and Delong (2009) assessed TV use across 16 countries, 4 of which are part of the JETTC, finding the highest reported use by parents from Brazil (82 percent of parents), followed by Turkey (69 percent), China (64 percent), and the US (46 percent). For other media use, 35 percent of Brazilian, 30 percent of US, 21 percent of Turkish, and 14 percent of Chinese parents reported their children frequently played with electronic games (Singer et al., 2009). Thus, collectivistic cultures appear to provide more opportunities for TV exposure, relative to their more individualistic counterparts; however, this pattern does not generalize to other electronic media exposure.

Previous research by Harkness et al. (2011) suggests that the amount of time families allocate to different activities often reflects culturally influenced values. Parents determine their children's schedule, particularly during the early developmental period assessed in the JETTC project, and the degree to which caregivers involve their children in household chores, errands, and other activities outside the home, can be expected to reflect cultural and parental concerns. Thus, the exposure to "multiple trials" noted earlier as critical to culturally influenced learning is in fact shaped by caregivers, who prioritize certain experiences for their toddlers over others.

Based on Roopnarine and Davidson (2015), we expected greater frequency of high-intensity play in more individualistic cultures, and an opposite pattern of results for low-intensity play (i.e., more low-intensity play in collectivistic cultures). More specific hypotheses could be formulated for TV/media outcomes, with children from Brazil and the US expected to exhibit more frequent use of electronics (other than TV) relative to their Turkish and Chinese peers. The pattern of results observed by Singer et al. (2009) suggests that caregivers from collectivistic cultures would be more likely to report greater TV exposure relative to their individualistic counterparts. Parents from more collectivistic backgrounds may value child housework participation to a greater extent, because of an emphasis on contributing to the common good of the family.

## Results

### *High and Low-Intensity/Purpose in Play*

Regarding Low-Intensity Play (Figure 7.2), Bonferroni adjusted main effects comparison indicated that children in Spain and the US engaged more in this type of play than those from Turkey, China, South Korea, Russia, Belgium, the Netherlands, and Finland; with the US also significantly higher than Mexico and Italy. In addition, Chile and Romania scored higher than Turkey, with Romania scoring higher than China and South Korea. Children from the US and Spain engaged in most frequent High-Intensity Play (Figure 7.3), compared to children from South Korea, Italy, Belgium, Finland, Turkey, and Russia. Brazilians were also significantly higher than Koreans on this variable. Parents from Romania and Turkey indicated frequent Play with a Purpose (Figure 7.4), significantly higher than 10 lowest-scoring countries. Italy and Brazil scored higher than the Netherlands, Finland, and Belgium. Mexico, Chile, Spain, Russia, and the US were higher than Belgium, with Chile and Mexico also scoring higher than Finland. Regarding play as a means to entertain, Finland, Turkey, South Korea, Italy, Brazil, the US, Romania, and China were significantly higher than Russia, the Netherlands, and Spain (Figure 7.5). Mexico also scored lower than the six highest-scoring countries.

**TABLE 7.1** Effects of culture, age, and sex on play and activities

| *Activity* | *Age* | *Culture* | *Sex* | *Culture × Sex* |
|---|---|---|---|---|
| Play with Low-Intensity Toys | 0.89 | 7.19** | 84.61** | 0.93 |
| Play with High-Intensity Toys | 28.78** | 5.00** | 23.07** | 1.59# |
| Play with Purpose | 3.25# | 13.46** | 3.81# | 1.00 |
| Play to Entertain | 2.12 | 11.05** | 1.00 | 0.47 |
| Activities with Parent | 4.53* | 8.77** | 0.05 | 1.02 |
| Time watching TV | 8.23* | 10.55** | 0.03 | 0.55 |
| Time on other Electronics | 10.48** | 3.67** | 0.64 | 0.43 |

Note: ANOVAs, with age as covariate, gender and country as factors. For Care by Other Relative, Dfs for age and sex = 1,761; Dfs for culture and culture × sex = 13,761. For Care by Other Provider, Dfs for age and sex = 1,805; Dfs for culture and culture × sex = 13,805. For all other tests, Dfs for age and sex = 1,812; Dfs for culture and culture × sex = 13,812.
$^{**}p < 0.001$, $^{*}p < 0.05$, $^{\#}p < 0.10$

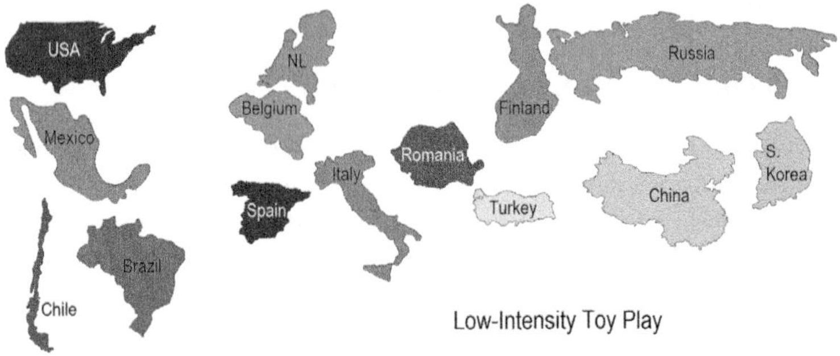


FIGURE 7.2 Map of Low-Intensity Toy Play. Darker shading indicates higher scores

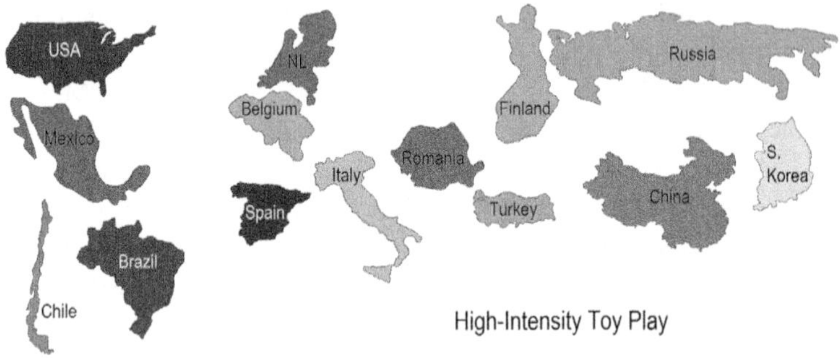


FIGURE 7.3 Map of High-Intensity Toy Play. Darker shading indicates higher scores

## *Activities with Parent*

Reports of parents' engagement with their children during housework, travel, and play (Figure 7.6) were higher among Romanians than Mexicans, Belgians, Russians, Turks, Italians, Chinese, and Koreans. In addition, Spain, Brazil, the Netherlands, Finland, the US, and Chile scored higher than China and Korea, with Spain, Brazil, and the Netherlands also scoring higher than Turkey, Russia, and Belgium.

## *Media (TV and Other Electronics)*

Regarding media exposure (Figures 7.7 and 7.8), parents from Brazil, Mexico, and Russia reported higher levels of children's TV watching

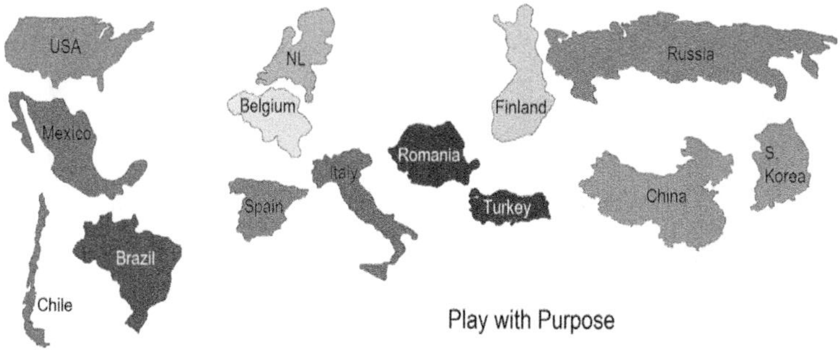


**FIGURE 7.4** Map of Play with Purpose. Darker shading indicates higher scores

**FIGURE 7.5** Map of Play to Entertain. Darker shading indicates higher scores

**FIGURE 7.6** Map of Activities with Parent. Darker shading indicates higher scores

FIGURE 7.7 Map of Television Time. Darker shading indicates more time watching television

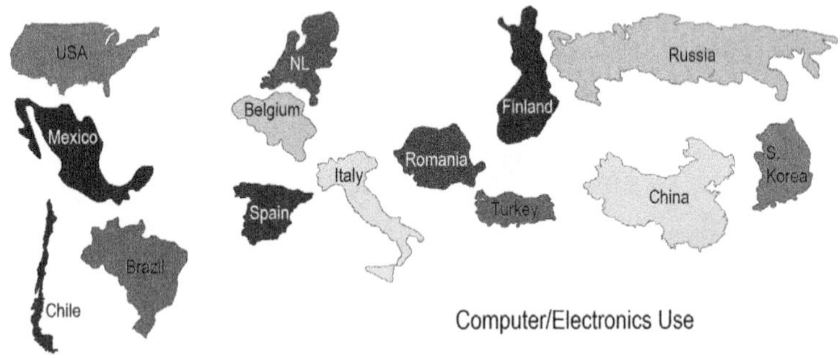


FIGURE 7.8 Map of Computer Time. Darker shading indicates more time on electronic devices

than those from Belgium, the US, Romania, Spain, Finland, and China; with Brazil and Mexico also reporting more TV watching than Italy, South Korea, and the Netherlands. Turkey watched more than the four lowest countries. There was wide variability within all countries in the use of computer and other electronics. Mexico, Chile, and Finland reported significantly higher use than Italy and China.

## *Relations to Cultural Orientation Dimensions*

To explore connections between play variables and established cultural distinctions, Pearson's correlations were calculated between average country scores (marginal means) on play, TV/media, engagement with parent and Hofstede's six cultural orientation dimensions.

With respect to play, both Low-Intensity Toy Play and High-Intensity Toy Play were highest in cultures characterized by Short-Term Orientation, $r_s(12) = -0.58$ and $-0.55$, $p_s < 0.05$. Play with Purpose was marginally associated with high Power Distance scores, $r(12) = 0.47$, $p < 0.10$. In regards to other activities, Short-Term Orientation was also associated with greater Time spent on Computer and engagement with parents, $r_s(12) = -0.69$ and $-0.60$, $p_s < 0.01$ and $0.05$, respectively. Computer time was also correlated with Indulgence, $r(12) = 0.57$, $p < 0.05$. Marginal associations suggested more Television Watching in Collectivist countries, $r(12) = -0.52$, $p < 0.10$ and more Computer Use in more Feminine cultures, $r(12) = -0.46$, $p < 0.10$.

## Discussion

In this chapter, we addressed cross-cultural differences in play and other activities among JETTC sites. A variety of differences emerged, indicating that high- and low-intensity play; and purposeful as well as entertainment-focused play; differed across multiple cultures. Cross-cultural variability was also noted in TV/media exposure, and parental involvement of toddlers in activities (e.g., housework).

Although the US and Spain were ranked the highest for high-intensity play, which was consistent with our hypotheses, they were also rated the highest in low-intensity play. Short-Term Orientation was associated with more frequent high- and low-intensity play, suggesting that cultural emphasis on immediate gratification predicts more frequent play behavior, overall.

Our findings regarding TV/media exposure were also partially consistent with our hypotheses, with more individualistic US parents reporting significantly less TV watching than more collectivistic caregivers from Brazil and Turkey. Collectivism was marginally associated with television watching, with more collectivistic countries reporting more TV exposure than generally individualistic cultures. Use of electronics other than TV was only marginally associated with more a feminine culture and appeared otherwise more variable than TV watching. Our findings regarding the frequency of media exposure were not consistent with those reported by Singer et al. (2009), as only the Netherlands maintained its relative ranking across TV watching and other electronic usage indicators. Singer et al. (2009) included a substantially broader age-range (i.e., 1–12 years of age), noting that exposure to media was positively correlated to age. Thus, future research should include longitudinal designs capable of elucidating changes in parenting practices related to TV/media exposure, and the role of culture in shaping these trajectories.

Cross-cultural differences in the duration of exposure to TV, versus the pattern of results reflecting the use of other electronic media, may be a function of these activities being viewed as serving different purposes. For example, in a comparison of Japanese and US mothers' views of children watching TV, US parents were significantly more cautious about what their children watched, whereas Japanese parents expressed more openness and a positive appraisal of their children's TV watching (Komaya & Bowyer, 2000). Content of TV and electronic media may differ significantly between cultures, which should be examined in future research.

## References

Bornstein, M. H., Haynes, O. M., Pascual, L., Painter, K. M., & Galperín, C. (1999). Play in two societies: Pervasiveness of process, specificity of structure. *Child Development*, *70*(2), 317–331.

Bornstein, M. H., & Tamis-LeMonda, C. S. (1995). Parent-child symbolic pay: Three theories in search of an effect. *Developmental Review*, *15*(4), 382–400.

Chessa, D., Lis, A., Riso, D. D., Delvecchio, E., Mazzeschi, C., Russ, S. W., & Dillon, J. (2012). A cross-cultural comparison of pretend play in U.S. and Italian children. *Journal of Cross-Cultural Psychology*, *44*(4), 640–656.

Feldman, R. (2007). Mother-infant synchrony and the development of moral orientation in childhood and adolescence: Direct and indirect mechanisms of developmental continuity. *American Journal of Orthopsychiatry*, 77(4), 582–597.

Haight, W. L., Wang, X. L., Fung, H. H., Williams, K., & Mintz, J. (1999). Universal, developmental, and variable aspects of young children's play: A cross-cultural comparison of pretending at home. *Child Development*, *70*(6), 1477–1488.

Harkness, S., Zylicz, P. O., Super, C. M., Welles-Nyström, B., Bermúdez, M. R., Bonichini, S., . . . Mavridis, C. J. (2011). Children's activities and their meanings for parents: A mixed-methods study in six Western cultures. *Journal of Family Psychology*, *25*(6), 799–813.

Hofstede, G., Hofstede, G. J., & Minkov, M. (2010). *Cultures and organizations: Software of the mind* (Rev. 3rd ed.). New York, NY: McGraw-Hill.

Komaya, M., & Bowyer, J. (2000). College-educated mothers' ideas about television and their active mediation of viewing by three- and five-year-old children: Japan and the U.S.A. *Journal of Broadcasting and Electronic Media*, *44*(3), 349–363.

Manganello, J. A., & Taylor, C. A. (2009). Television exposure as a risk factor for aggressive behavior among 3-year-old children. *Archives of Pediatrics & Adolescent Medicine, 163*(11), 1037–1045.

Nielsen, M. (2012). Imitation, pretend play, and childhood: Essential elements in the evolution of human culture? *Journal of Comparative Psychology, 126*(2), 170–181.

Nielsen, M., Cucchiaro, J., & Mohamedally, J. (2012). When the transmission of culture is child's play. *PLoS ONE,* 7(3), e34066.

Parmar, P., Harkness, S., & Super, C. M. (2004). Asian and Euro-American parents' ethnotheories of play and learning: Effects on preschool children's home routines and school behaviour. *International Journal of Behavioral Development, 28*(2), 97–104.

Parmar, P., Harkness, S., & Super, C. M. (2008). Teacher or playmate? Asian immigrant and Euro-American parents' participation in their young children's daily activities. *Social Behavior and Personality: An International Journal, 36*(2), 163–176.

Pellegrini, A. D. (1995). A Longitudinal study of boys' rough- and-tumble play and dominance during early adolescence. *Journal of Applied Developmental Psychology, 16*(1), 77–93.

Piaget, J. (1951). *Play, dreams, and imitation in childhood.* London, UK: Routledge and Kegan Paul.

Roopnarine, J. L., & Davidson, K. L. (2015). Parent-child play across cultures: Advancing play research. *American Journal of Play,* 7(2), 228–252.

Singer, D. G., Singer, J. L., Agostino, H. D., & Delong, R. (2009). Children's pastimes and play in sixteen nations is free-play declining? *American Journal of Play, 1*(3), 283–312.

White, L. K., & Brinkerhoff, D. B. (1981). Children's work in the family: Its significance and meaning. *Journal of Marriage and the Family, 43*(4), 789–798.

Zimmerman, F. J., & Bell, J. F. (2010). Associations of television content type and obesity in children. *American Journal of Public Health, 100*(2), 334–340.

# 8

# CROSS-CULTURAL DIFFERENCES IN CHILDREN'S SLEEP

*Blanca Huitron, Guadalupe Domínguez-Sandoval, Amanda Prokasky, Carmen González-Salinas, and Sae-Young Han*

Sleep plays a critical role in the physiological, neuroanatomical, and clinical domains of brain development. Continuous night sleep is necessary to ensure maturation, restoration, and reorganization of arousal, affect, and attentional systems, essential to functioning in multiple areas. Sleep makes particularly significant contributions to behavioral functioning in early childhood (Dahl, 1996; Domínguez-Sandoval, 2017). In this chapter, we explore differences between the JETTC cultures in sleep patterns of children, and the techniques used by parents to promote child sleep (see Figure 8.1).

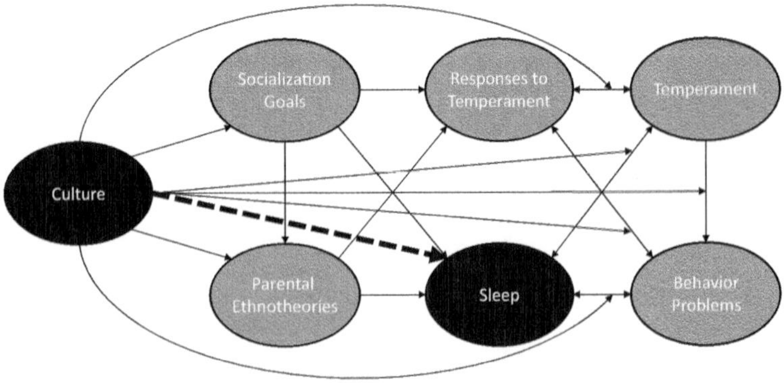


**FIGURE 8.1** Sleep in the JETTC Conceptual Model

Culture interacts with biology to establish developmental norms and expectations regarding children's sleep (Jenni & O'Connor, 2005). Harkness and Super (2002) note that the organization of sleep is a highly structured aspect of cultural practice that is relatively resistant to change. Routines and strategies before bed, bedtimes, wake times, and sleep problems are culturally constructed, and not necessarily rooted in sleep biology (Jenni & O'Connor, 2005), as evidenced by cross-cultural variability in sleep practices. For example, Super et al. (1996) found that Dutch parents encouraged more sleep and a more regular bedtime schedule than did United States (US) parents. Dutch children slept more, and were more regular in their sleep schedule than US children at similar ages (Super et al., 1996). In contrast, Ottaviano, Giannotti, Cortesi, Bruni, and Ottaviano (1996) reported that bedtime for children from southern European countries such as Italy, Spain, and Greece is typically unstructured and flexible.

Parent involvement is a determining factor for sleep-related practices, with child sleeping hours established according to the daily commitments of the caregivers (working hours, housework, and social activities) (Harkness et al., 2011; Morelli, Rogoff, Oppenheim, & Goldsmith, 1992). Describing parenting practices in different cultural communities elucidates the extent to which structure of these sleep-related routines is universal or organized according to culture-specific considerations. New and Richman (1996) reported that Italian children have no clear bedtime schedules or rituals, and go to bed later than American children. Italian parents were also less concerned about their children's sleep habits than were American parents, and believed their children were getting adequate amounts of sleep, despite Italian children going to bed later and waking up earlier than children in other countries (New & Richman, 1996; Ottaviano et al., 1996).

In a large study of sleep patterns in US and Canadian children from birth to 3 years old, Sadeh, Mindell, Luedtke, and Wiegand (2008) found that extended and more consolidated sleep in children was associated with parental behaviors that encouraged independence and self-soothing (e.g., having the child fall asleep independently), while more active interactions, such as nursing or rocking the child to sleep, were associated with shorter and more fragmented sleep. In US samples, parental involvement and lack of self-soothing skills were highly associated with night wakings and difficulties falling asleep in infants (Adair, Bauchner, Philipp, Levenson, & Zuckerman, 1991; Anders, Halpern, & Hua, 1992). Conversely, Mindell et al. (2010) noted that parents from primarily Asian countries were much more likely to be engaged with their children at bedtime and following night wakings compared to parents from primarily Caucasian countries, and this engagement with children at bedtime did not impact children's sleep in primarily Asian countries.

Information concerning parental activities as these relate to children's sleep allows us to enhance our understanding of the extent to which children's sleep patterns are biologically determined versus culturally constructed. In this chapter, we explore strategies that parents in 14 countries use to help their children sleep, including passive strategies such as cuddling or reading stories, active strategies such as walking around or going for a car ride, staying with the child, and letting the child cry it out (no parental intervention). We also examined child sleep characteristics, including bedtime, wake time, amount of nighttime sleep, and length of daytime naps.

## Results

### Cross-Cultural Patterns of Parenting

**TABLE 8.1** Effects of culture, age, and sex on sleep

| *Sleep variable* | *Age* | *Culture* | *Sex* | *Culture × Sex* |
|---|---|---|---|---|
| Parental behaviors | | | | |
| Active Sleep Techniques | 5.29* | 12.69** | 1.42 | 1.23 |
| Gentle Sleep Techniques | 5.78* | 12.11** | 0.44 | 1.16 |
| Stay with Child | 1.43 | 15.01** | 0.46 | 0.79 |
| Cry it Out | 10.10* | 6.78** | 2.65 | 1.73# |
| Child sleeping patterns | | | | |
| Bed time | 0.54 | 85.22** | 0.86 | 1.55# |
| Waking time | 8.39* | 27.13** | 2.12 | 0.80 |
| Nighttime sleep | 4.69* | 32.43** | 0.67 | 0.83 |
| Naps | 30.27** | 5.68** | 4.43* | 0.80 |

Note: ANOVAs, with age as covariate, gender, and country as factors. Waking Time Dfs for age and sex = 1,805; Dfs for culture and culture × sex = 13,805. Bed Time Dfs for age and sex = 1,799; Dfs for culture and culture × sex = 13,799. Nighttime Sleep Dfs for age and sex = 1,796; Dfs for culture and culture × sex = 13,796. For all other variables, Dfs for age and sex = 1,812; Dfs for culture and culture × sex = 13,812. $^{**}p < 0.001$, $^{*}p < 0.05$, $^{\#}p < 0.10$

As shown in Table 8.1, substantial cross-cultural effects for all variables were revealed through sex by culture Analyses of Variance (ANOVAs), with age as a covariate. Age effects indicated less use of Active and Cry it Out techniques, more Gentle Techniques and Waking Child, fewer naps, earlier waking times, and less nighttime sleep for older children. More naps were reported for males. Sex × Culture effects were not significant.

### *Sleep Preparation/Maintenance Strategies*

Figures 8.2 and 8.3 indicate marginal means on parental sleep-promoting behaviors for each country; descriptive statistics available upon request from the volume editors. Overall, use of active techniques was relatively

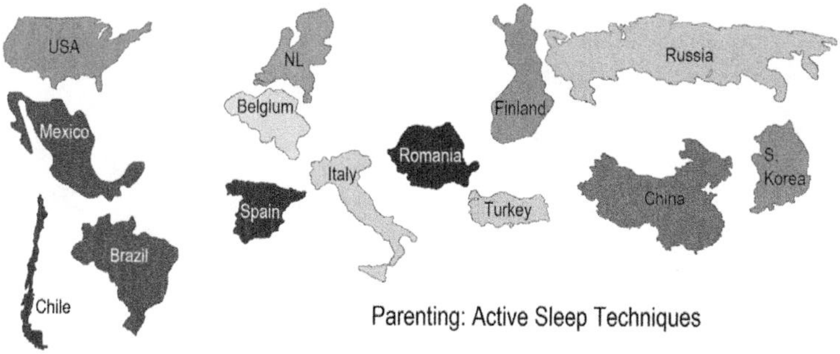


**FIGURE 8.2** Map of parental Active Sleep Techniques marginal means. Darker shading indicates higher scores

**FIGURE 8.3** Map of parental Gentle Sleep Techniques marginal means. Darker shading indicates higher scores

**FIGURE 8.4** Map of parental Stay with Child sleep technique marginal means. Darker shading indicates higher scores

**FIGURE 8.5** Map of parental Cry it Out sleep technique marginal means. Darker shading indicates higher scores

**FIGURE 8.6** Map of child bedtime marginal means. Darker shading indicates later bedtimes

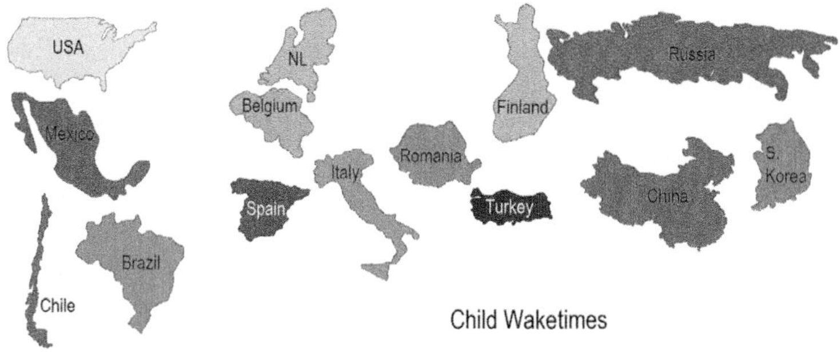


**FIGURE 8.7** Map of child waketime marginal means. Darker shading indicates later waketimes

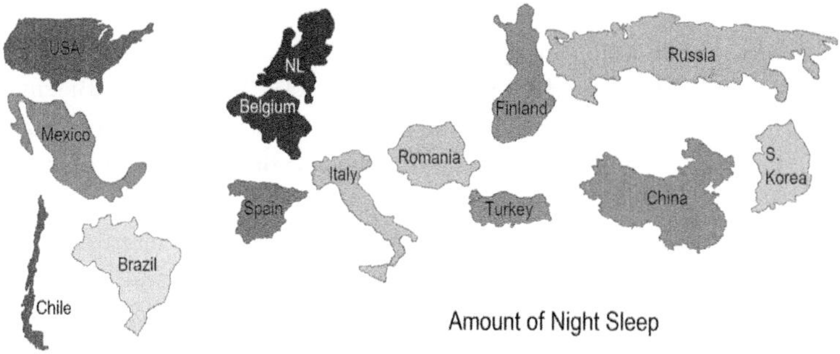


**FIGURE 8.8** Map of night sleep marginal means. Darker shading indicates greater time sleeping

**FIGURE 8.9** Map of naps marginal means. Darker shading indicates higher frequency of naps

low across countries. Main effects comparisons (Bonferroni adjustment) indicated that parents from Romania, Spain, Chile, Mexico, and Brazil used these techniques more than parents from the five lowest-scoring countries: Belgium, Italy, Turkey, Russia, and the Netherlands. In addition, Chile, Spain, and Romania scored higher than the US and Finland, with Spain and Romania also scoring higher than Korea, and Romania higher than China.

Gentle strategies were used more frequently in all 14 countries than Active Strategies. For gentle techniques, main effects comparisons indicated that parents from the US, Finland, Netherlands, Romania, and Spain used these more than parents from the four lowest-scoring countries: China, Turkey, South Korea, and Mexico. Chile, Belgium, and Italy also used these more than mothers from China and Turkey. Mothers from the US used this technique more than mothers from Brazil, Russia, Italy, and Belgium.

Staying with Child was more common in South Korea and Brazil than in Belgium, Netherlands, Turkey, and the US (Figure 8.4). Brazilians also stayed with children more than parents in Finland and Spain. Belgian and Dutch parents reported very infrequent use of this technique, scoring lower than all other countries.

Letting children Cry it Out was a rare practice in all participating countries. Leaving children to cry it out was more common in Mexico, Korea, Netherlands, China, and the US than in Russia and Romania (Figure 8.5). Mexico and the Netherlands were also higher than Finland, with the Netherlands additionally significantly higher than Italy and Belgium. Russia also scored lower than Brazil, Turkey, and Spain.

## *Cross-Cultural Patterns of Child Sleep*

Figures 8.6 and 8.7 reflect marginal means for each country on children's sleeping patterns. Regarding bed times, main effects comparisons (Bonferroni adjustment) indicated that children from the Netherlands, Belgium, the US, Finland, and Chile went to bed at earlier times than children from China, Spain, Mexico, Romania, South Korea, Brazil, Russia, and Turkey. Bedtimes in Finland were also earlier than those in Italy; and bedtimes in the US, Belgium, and Netherlands were earlier than those in Finland and Chile. Turkish bedtimes were significantly later than those in all other countries.

Patterns were somewhat similar regarding waking times, as children from the US, Finland, the Netherlands, and Belgium woke earliest, and significantly earlier than those from Turkey, Spain, Mexico, Russia, Chile, and China. Children from the US rose earlier than children from all countries other than Finland, the Netherlands, and Belgium. Wake times in Mexico were also later than those in Italy; those in Spain were later than those in Korea, Romania, Brazil, and Italy; and wake times in Turkey were later than in all other countries.

Regarding amount of nighttime sleep (Figure 8.8), children from the Netherlands slept more than those from all other countries, and those from Belgium slept more than all but the Dutch children. Children from these countries slept nearly 2 hours more, on average relative to those in the countries reporting the least sleep. In addition, children from Spain, US, and Chile slept more at night than those from Korea, Romania, Italy, and Russia; US and Chilean children also slept more than those from China and Finland; and US children more than Mexican and Turkish counterparts. Naps were more commonly reported in South Korea, Romania, and China than Spain, Russia, and the US (Figure 8.9). These were additionally more common in Romania and South Korea than Chile and the Netherlands, with Korea also reporting significantly more naps than the Netherlands.

### *Connections between Parental Behaviors and Child Sleep*

Pearson's correlations were calculated between average country scores on parental sleep-promoting techniques and child sleep parameters. Countries in which parents used gentle soothing techniques had children who went to bed earlier, got up earlier, and were less likely to nap, $r_s(14) = -0.67$, $-0.67$, and $-0.59$, $p_s < 0.01$, 0.01, and 0.05, respectively. Countries in which parents stayed with their child had children who went to bed later and slept less during the night, $r_s(14) = -0.75$ and $-0.90$, $p_s < 0.01$.

### *Relations to Cultural Orientation Dimensions*

To explore connections between sleep variables and established cultural distinctions (Hofstede et al., 2010), Pearson's correlations were calculated between average country scores (marginal means) on sleep variables and Hofstede's six cultural orientation dimensions.

With respect to parenting, the use of gentle sleep techniques was most common in Individualist and cultures low in Power Distance,

$r_s(14) = 0.72$ and $-0.54$, $p_s < 0.01$ and 0.05, respectively. Staying with the child was more common in Collectivist cultures, $r(14) = 0.66$, $p = 0.01$. Marginal associations suggested more Active Sleeping Techniques in Collectivist countries, $r(14) = -0.51$, $p < 0.10$, and more leaving the child to cry in more Indulgent cultures, $r(14) = -0.47$, $p < 0.10$.

Later bed times, later waking times, and more napping were associated with Collectivism, $r_s(14) = -0.74$, $-0.66$, and $-0.55$, $p_s < 0.01$, 0.05, and 0.05, respectively. Later bed times and waking times were also linked to high Power Distance, $r_s(14) = 0.61$ and 0.53, $p_s < 0.05$. In addition, total sleep time was marginally associated with Individualism and Indulgence, $r_s(14) = 0.53$ and 0.50, $p_s < 0.10$.

## Discussion

In all countries participating in this research, parents reported using passive strategies more frequently than active ones to help their children prepare for sleep. It was common to endorse comforting children with hugs, swaying or patting, playing music or singing songs, speaking with soft voice, or reading children stories. It was infrequent for caregivers to leave the child crying to calm down themselves. Reliance on passive rather than active strategies suggests that caregivers preferred to use a lower level of intervention with their child in helping to induce sleep across our sample of countries. Passive strategies may also be most effective in supporting child self-regulation in the transition from wakefulness to sleep, important because self-regulation around sleep helps to ensure quality and stability of sleep across the lifespan, supporting performance on tasks in an alert state (Sheldon, 2014). Parents from countries with a more individualistic orientation, short Power Distance, and an emphasis on Indulgence, tended to use more gentle techniques, allowing the child to cry it out more frequently. It may be that parents from more indulgent and individualistic cultures, and those with a small power distance, are more likely to facilitate child self-regulation in situations such as onset/maintenance of sleep. The use of gentle techniques and letting children "cry it out" may seem inconsistent, yet both can support the development of self-regulation, with the emphasis on giving the child an opportunity to learn to self-soothe.

Staying near the child's bed was also a common practice in all countries (except Belgium and the Netherlands), especially those characterized by a more collectivist orientation. Parents in collectivist societies also used more active strategies in regulation and preparation for sleep, expressing a preference for picking children up, walking them around, or playing games in anticipation of sleep. Using these strategies accentuates the differentiation between sleep and wake activities and may facilitate children sleeping through the night by making this distinction salient.

Most children of participating countries started sleeping between 8 and 10 pm, and only in the Netherlands, Belgium, and US was sleep for the average child initiated before 8 pm. Children's waking hours in most countries began around 7–8 am, and only US children got up, on average, before 7 am. Despite differences in bedtime and waking hours across cultures, most children slept approximately 11–12 hours per night. Differing cultural norms dictate typical parental work schedules, meal times, and other factors that can indirectly influence bedtimes and wake times. By comparison, daytime sleep schedule varied widely among the different countries. In particular, Spanish children rarely took naps longer than 2 hours, whereas in Romania and Korea longer naps were frequent. Touchette et al. (2013) demonstrated that variations in the duration of daytime sleep were regulated more by environmental aspects, unlike the duration and continuity of night sleep, modulated primarily by biological factors.

## References

Adair, R., Bauchner, H., Philipp, B., Levenson, S., & Zuckerman, B. (1991). Night waking during infancy: Role of parental presence at bedtime. *Pediatrics, 87*, 500–504.

Anders, T. F., Halpern, L. F., & Hua, J. (1992). Sleeping through the night: A developmental perspective. *Pediatrics, 90*, 554–560.

Dahl, R. E. (1996). The regulation of sleep and arousal: Development and psychopathology. *Development and Psychopathology, 8*, 3–27.

Domínguez-Sandoval, G. (2017). *Efectos de la teofilina y el dormer solos y acompañados en la estructura de sueño y variables respiratorias de neonatos* (Tesis para obtener grado). Doctor en psicología, Neurociencias de la conducta, Universidad Nacional Autonoma de México, México City.

Harkness, S., & Super, C. M. (2002). Culture and parenting. In M. H. Bornstein (Ed.), *Handbook of parenting: Biology and ecology of parenting* (pp. 253–280). Mahwah, NH: Lawrence Erlbaum Associates Publishers.

Harkness, S., Super, C. M., & Mavridis, C. J. (2011). Parental ethnotheories about children's socioemotional development. In X. Chen & K. H. Rubin (Eds.), *Socioemotional development in cultural context* (pp. 73–98). New York: Guilford.

Hofstede, G., Hofstede, G. J. & Minkov, M. (2010). *Cultures and Organizations: Software of the Mind* (Rev. 3rd ed.). New York: McGraw-Hill.

Jenni, O. G., & O'Connor, B. B. (2005). Children's sleep: An interplay between culture and biology. *Pediatrics, 115*(Suppl. 1), 204–216.

Mindell, J. A., Sadeh, A., Kohyama, J., & Ti Hwei, H. (2010). Parental behaviors and sleep outcomes in infants and toddlers: A cross-cultural comparison. *Sleep Medicine, 11*, 393–399.

Morelli, G., Rogoff, B., Oppenheim, D., & Goldsmith, D. (1992). Cultural variation in infants' sleeping arrangements: Questions of independence. *Developmental Psychology, 28*, 604–613.

New, R. S., & Richman, A. L. (1996). Maternal beliefs and infant care practices in Italy and the United States. In S. Harkness & C. M. Super (Eds.), *Parents' cultural belief systems: Their origins, expressions, and consequences* (pp. 385–404). New York, NY: Guilford.

Ottaviano, S., Giannotti, F., Cortesi, F., Bruni, O., & Ottaviano, C. (1996). Sleep characteristics in healthy children from birth to 6 years of age in the urban area of Rome. *Sleep, 19*, 1–3.

Sadeh, A. V. I., Mindell, J. A., Luedtke, K., & Wiegand, B. (2009). Sleep and sleep ecology in the first 3 years: A web-based study. *Journal of Sleep Research, 18*, 60–73.

Sheldon, S. (2014). Diagnostic methods in pediatric sleep medicine. *Sleep Medicine Clinics, 2*, 343–351.

Super, C. M., Harkness, S., van Tijen, N., van der Vlugt, E., Fintelman, M., & Dijkstra, J. (1996). The three R's of Dutch childrearing and the socialization of infant arousal. In S. Harkness & C. M. Super (Eds.), *Parents' cultural belief systems: Their origins, expressions, and consequences* (pp. 447–466). New York, NY: Guilford.

Touchette, E., Dionne, G., Forget-Dubois, N., Peit, D., Pérusse, D., Falissard, B., . . . Montplaisir, J. Y. (2013). Genetic and environmental influences on daytime and nighttime sleep duration in early childhood. *Pediatrics, 131*, 2012–2284.

# 9

# CROSS-CULTURAL DIFFERENCES IN DISCIPLINE

*Samuel P. Putnam, Oana Benga, Rosario Montirosso, Mirjana Majdandžić, and Sara Casalin*

A universal task inherent to parenting involves the correction of undesirable behaviors. Cultures not only differ in the conduct they deem to be inappropriate, they also differ in terms of the parental behaviors that are most frequently used in response to child misbehavior. The second and third years of life are often viewed as a challenge for parents, as they balance their offspring's increasing desire and capability for autonomy with socializing their young children to conform to societal expectations (Edwards & Liu, 1995). Because cultures differ dramatically with respect to the ages at which they expect children to gain various competencies

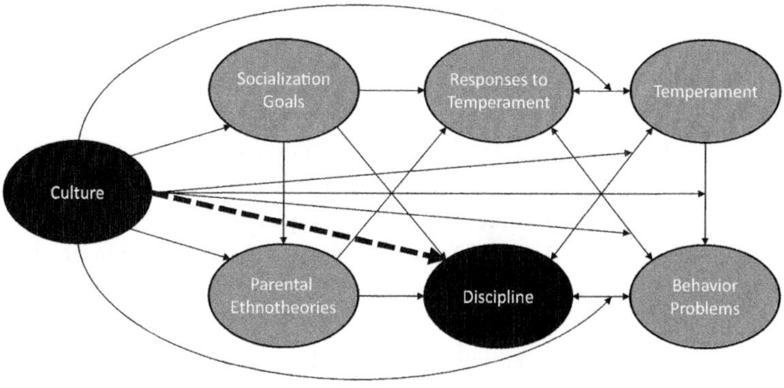


**FIGURE 9.1** Discipline in the JETTC Conceptual Model

(Goodnow, 1995; Super & Harkness, 1986), as well as the nature of the characteristics they wish to promote (Keller et al., 2006), cultural differences in the use of discipline may be particularly pronounced during the toddler period. In this chapter, we explore differences between the JETTC cultures in discipline techniques reported by parents (see Figure 9.1).

Discipline strategies vary in terms of the mechanisms that are presumed to result in changes to children's behavior (e.g., Hoffman, 1975). Power assertive techniques, such as hitting, yelling, removing privileges, or separating the child from others (i.e., "time out"), rely on the parent's relatively greater physical size and their control of important resources. In contrast, inductive discipline communicates the rationale for parental expectations and provides guidance regarding how to address a previous wrongdoing. These types of discipline are not mutually exclusive and a cultures' characteristic use of one strategy does not preclude frequent use of another.

Corporal punishment has been most thoroughly studied, both in traditional developmental psychology and the cross-cultural literatures. A number of studies indicate frequent use of corporal punishment in East Asian cultures (see Giles-Sims & Lockhart, 2005; Lau, 2010). However, recent research suggests diminishing use of physical punishment in China (Chang, Lansford, Schwartz, & Farver, 2004), with Lansford et al. (2005) reporting lower rates of physical discipline in China than in five other countries, including Italy, which scored highest. Also relevant are studies of immigrant families from Central America and East Asia, who have endorsed corporal punishment more frequently than other cultural groups in their host nations of the United States (US), Canada, and Australia (Gorman, 1998; Hong & Hong, 1991; Kulig, 1998; Papps, Walker, Trimboli, & Trimboli, 1995). A study of six countries (including four Joint Effort Toddler Temperament Consortium (JETTC) cultures) by duRivage et al. (2015) relating corporal punishment to laws regarding its use reported infrequent levels in the Netherlands and Germany, with relatively higher use in Romania and Turkey. In sum, the results of previous comparative studies lead us to anticipate higher levels of corporal punishment in East Asia and Latin America, and lower levels in northern than in southern and eastern Europe.

As noted by Gershoff et al. (2010), there is almost no research on global variation in parenting techniques beyond corporal punishment. This may be surprising in light of the relative infrequency of physical discipline. In a sample of 24 developing countries (of which none are included in the JETTC), Lansford and Deater-Deckard (2012) reported that nearly 80 percent of caregivers reported that their child had received an explanation for why a behavior was wrong in the past month, whereas around 40 percent had spanked their child. In a study of 11 discipline techniques used by parents in Kenya, Philippines, Thailand, India, China, and Italy, Gershoff et al. (2010) found teaching, requiring an apology, and yelling were more commonly used than techniques such as time outs or corporal punishment. Comparisons of the two JETTC countries included in the Gershoff et al. (2010) study suggests considerably higher use of time outs and yelling or scolding by Italian parents, and higher withdrawal of love by Chinese parents, but few substantial differences in other techniques including teaching, asking the child to apologize, or taking away privileges.

Anthropological perspectives (e.g., Ember & Ember, 2005) have suggested that reliance on agriculture, social stratification, increased economic complexity, and autocratic political decision making are associated with greater use of corporal punishment. Ember and Ember (2005) argue that these factors result in power inequalities, and that corporal punishment may be used by parents to promote strict obedience and to prepare children "to accept that some people are more powerful than others" (p. 612). The Power Distance dimension of Hofstede's model reflects this cultural difference, as democratic political systems to be representative of low Power Distance (Hofstede, Hofstede, & Minkov, 2010). Thus, we anticipated an association between high Power Distance and spanking or hitting in our data. Collectivism also places value on conformity and obedience (Park & Lau, 2016; Rudy & Grusec, 2006), leading to expectations of a similar relationship between high use of corporal punishment and Collectivism. Our predictions regarding corporal punishment extended to other forms of power assertion, and we hypothesized that removal of privileges and yelling or swearing may also be high in high Power Distance and collectivist cultures. Expectations regarding associations between other cultural dimensions and inductive discipline practices are elusive, and analyses of these relations were considered exploratory.

## Results

As shown in Table 9.1, substantial cross-cultural effects for all variables were revealed through 2 (Sex) by 14 (Culture) Analyses of Variance (ANOVAs), with age as a covariate. Age effects indicated increased use of all techniques except hitting at older child ages. No sex effects were significant, although the Sex × Culture interaction was significant for withdrawing privileges. Tests of simple effects of sex by country for this technique indicated higher scores for parents of males than females in the Netherlands and (marginally) Belgium, but marginally higher scores for females in Turkey.

Examining the marginal means (available from volume editors), suggested that talking the issue over and asking the child to repair the damage were frequently used responses to misbehavior in all countries, with average scores in all countries suggesting that parents used these techniques sometimes or often (i.e., scores of 2 or 3 on the Daily Activities Questionnaire). In contrast, across the JETTC samples, shouting and hitting were infrequent, with many indicating these were used never or rarely (i.e., scores of 0 or 1).

**TABLE 9.1** Effects of culture, age, and sex on discipline

| *Variable* | *Age* | *Culture* | *Sex* | *Culture × Sex* |
|---|---|---|---|---|
| Talk the problem over | 23.61** | 7.20** | 0.70 | 0.46 |
| Ask child to repair the damage | 29.99** | 3.03** | 0.82 | 0.58 |
| Tell child to think about misbehavior | 52.07** | 6.77** | 0.03 | 0.92 |
| Shout or swear | 7.97** | 11.51** | 1.38 | 1.41 |
| Hit or spank | 1.80 | 13.56** | 0.14 | 1.37 |
| Separate child from others | 40.09** | 10.56** | 0.23 | 0.92 |
| Withdraw privileges | 25.86** | 3.54** | 0.36 | 1.77* |

Note: ANOVAs, with age as covariate, gender and country as factors. Dfs for age and sex =1,812; Dfs for country and country × sex = 13,812. $^{**}p < 0.001$, $^{*}p < 0.05$, $^{\#}p < 0.10$

**FIGURE 9.2** Map of shouting discipline marginal means. Darker shading indicates higher scores

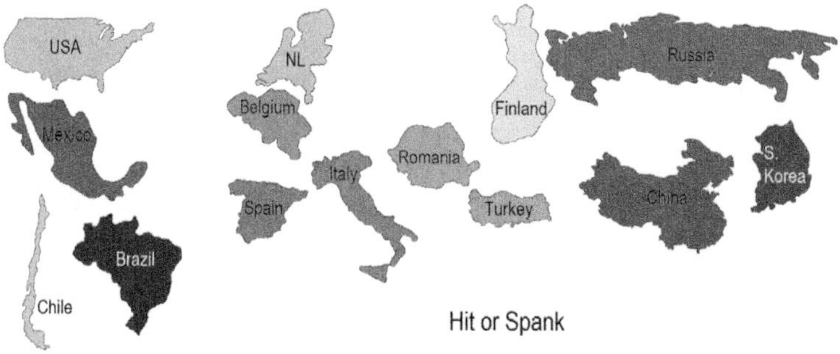


**FIGURE 9.3** Map of hitting discipline marginal means. Darker shading indicates higher scores

**FIGURE 9.4** Map of take privilege away discipline marginal means. Darker shading indicates higher scores

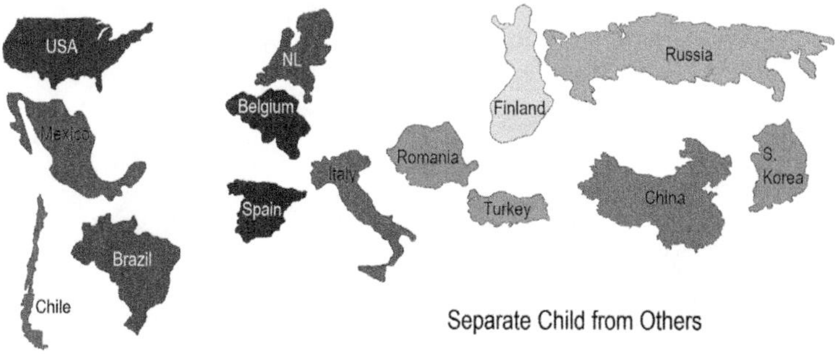


**FIGURE 9.5** Map of separate child discipline marginal means. Darker shading indicates higher scores

**FIGURE 9.6** Map of talk about it discipline marginal means. Darker shading indicates higher scores

**FIGURE 9.7** Map of repair damage discipline marginal means. Darker shading indicates higher scores

**FIGURE 9.8** Map of think about it discipline marginal means. Darker shading indicates higher scores

### *Power Assertive Strategies*

China, Russia, and Brazil reported high use of shouting or swearing, scoring higher than parents from Chile, the US, Turkey, the Netherlands, Romania, Mexico, and Spain (Figure 9.2). China and Russia additionally outscored South Korea. Italian and Finnish parents reported more use than Chile, US, Turkey, and the Netherlands. Belgium also reported more use than the US and Chile, and South Korea more than Chile.

Regarding hitting or spanking the child, main effects comparisons (Bonferroni adjustment) indicated that Brazilian, Korean, Chinese, Mexican, and Russian parents reported significantly more frequent use than Finnish, Chilean, Dutch, and American parents (Figure 9.3). China, South Korea, and Brazil additionally scored higher than Romania and Turkey, with Korea and Brazil also reporting higher levels of corporal punishment than Belgians, and Brazilians more than Italians, Spanish, and Russians. Finland and Netherlands also reported less use than Spain, with Finland also lower than Italy.

Taking privileges away from the child was more frequently used by parents in Spain than those in Russia, Italy, and the Netherlands (Figure 9.4). Brazil and China also reported more use of this technique than Russia.

Separating the child from others (i.e., "time out") was more common among parents from Spain, Belgium, and the US than those from Finland, Russia, Turkey, South Korea, and Romania (Figure 9.5). Belgians and Russians also used this approach more than Chinese parents. Brazil and the Netherlands scored higher than Finland and Russia, with the Netherlands also scoring higher than Turkey. Finland relied less on separation than Chile, Italy, and Mexico.

### *Inductive Strategies*

Regarding talking the issue over (Figure 9.6), parents from Brazil, Romania, Finland, Italy, Spain, and Mexico used this strategy more than those from Russia and China. Parents in the four highest-scoring countries also used this technique more than those from Belgium; and Romanians and Brazilians more than Chileans and Dutch parents.

Asking the child to repair the damage was more frequently used by parents in Spain and Mexico than those in Turkey (Figure 9.7).

Telling the child to think about their misbehavior was more commonly used in Brazil, China, Mexico, Romania, Italy, Russia, and

Turkey than in the US. Brazilian and Chinese also used this technique more than Dutch parents, with Brazilians reporting greater use than Finns (Figure 9.8).

### *Relations to Cultural Orientation Dimensions*

To explore connections between discipline techniques and established cultural distinctions, Pearson's correlations were calculated between average country scores (marginal means) on the discipline variables and Hofstede's six cultural orientation dimensions.

Requiring the child to think about their misbehavior was most common in high Power Distance and collectivist cultures, *rs*(14) = 0.62 and –0.53, *ps* < 0.05. High Power Distance and Collectivism were also marginally predictive of a high use of hitting/spanking, *rs*(14) = 0.50 and –0.49, *ps* < 0.10. Asking the child to repair damage was most common in countries characterized by Short-term Orientation and Indulgence, *rs*(14) = –0.63 and 0.58, *ps* < 0.05. Conversely, shouting was more common in countries associated with Long-term Orientation and (marginally) low Indulgence, *rs*(14) = 0.56 and –0.50, $p < 0.05$ and $p <$ 0.10, respectively. Talking the issue over was also marginally linked to Short-term Orientation, $r(14) = -0.48$, $p < 0.10$.

## Discussion

Our analyses reveal substantial cultural differences in the relative use of different forms of discipline. Before focusing on these differences, however, it is worth noting a degree of similarity. Across the different nations, inductive techniques such as talking over the issue and asking the child to repair damage were more frequently used than physically and psychologically aggressive techniques, with mild power assertion (i.e., taking away privileges and giving a "time out") used at moderate levels.

Findings regarding corporal punishment were largely consistent with our predictions. As in previous studies, the four cultures reporting greatest reliance on hitting or spanking were in East Asia and Latin America, and parents in northern Europe tended to report lower use of corporal punishment than those in southern Europe. The cultural dimensions of Power Distance and Collectivism were marginally predictive of high levels of physical discipline, consistent with a connection between societal values emphasizing conformity and the use of parental power to control children's behavior (Ellis & Petersen, 1992; Ember & Ember, 2005).

Surprisingly, requiring the child to think about their misbehavior—conceived of as an inductive discipline technique, demonstrated a similar pattern in relation to Power Distance and Collectivism. One explanation of this finding concerns the integration among different techniques. Parents typically use these approaches synergistically, with a power-assertive technique such as hitting being used to direct children's focus to think about the induction message (Hoffman, 1975). In cultures emphasizing obedience, concerted efforts to ensure that the child remember his/her misdeed by combining spanking with pressure to reflect, may be viewed as important for preventing repetition of the forbidden act.

Cultures with philosophies allowing for indulgence and a focus on short-term rewards tended to ask children to repair damage they had caused, whereas caregivers in cultures emphasizing constraint and long-term goals were more likely to shout or swear at their children in response to misbehavior. A focus on immediate solutions and reciprocal relationships in short-term societies appears to be consistent with expectations that toddlers apologize or otherwise address most salient effects of the current situation. In contrast, long-term societies place value in shame and recognition of social status (Hofstede et al., 2010), and shouting or swearing at a child may instill and reinforce emotions and cognitions associated with these values.

Separating the child from others (i.e., "time out") was not clearly linked to cultural orientation, but did exhibit a geographical pattern, such that it was more frequently used in western than eastern cultures. Although concerns have been voiced regarding the use of time out, it is included as a component in multiple evidence-based programs aimed at parental management of preschooler's conduct problems (Morawska & Sanders, 2010), and reportedly used by over 80 percent of US parents. Our results suggest that this practice is far less common in Asian cultures. Cultural values not included in Hofstede's model could also be relevant. Whereas separation may be perceived as a firm but benign consequence for misbehavior in western cultures, it is viewed as cruel in countries placing more value on physical proximity.

This potential for differing perceptions by parents has been previously characterized as the distinction between form and function (Bornstein, 1995; Bornstein & Lansford, 2010). Appreciation of cultural context involves the recognition that different behaviors may serve the same function in different cultures, and similar behaviors may be used for differing purposes. Given the common challenge of addressing unwanted toddler behaviors, parents in the JETTC sites chose to respond in ways that reflect and maintain their cultural values. The meaning of a given discipline technique is also likely to vary according to the context in which it is displayed. These differing meanings, in turn, may result in inconsistencies between cultures in the ways that parent discipline techniques and child behaviors are related, an issue we address in Chapter 15.

It is important to recognize that parenting patterns, including those which are culturally-influenced, are not static. For instance, corporal punishment becomes less acceptable with increasing child age (Ellonen, Lucas, Tindberg, & Janson, 2017), and it has long been acknowledged that parent and child behavior are reciprocal (e.g., Bell, 1968; Pastorelli et al., 2016). Finally, the use and acceptability of discipline techniques in a culture can shift in accordance to legislation, as demonstrated by decreases in corporal punishment in the years after it was banned in multiple countries (duRivage et al., 2015; Zolotor & Puzia, 2010), including the JETTC countries of Finland, the Netherlands, Spain, and Romania, which showed low rates of spanking in our data.

## References


Bell, R. Q. (1968). A reinterpretation of the direction of effects in studies of socialization. *Psychological Review, 75*, 81–95.

Bornstein, M. H. (1995). Form and function: Implications for studies of culture and human development. *Culture & Psychology, 1*, 123–137.

Bornstein, M. H., & Lansford, J. E. (2010). Parenting. In M. H. Bornstein (Ed.), *Handbook of cultural developmental science* (pp. 259–277). New York, NY: Psychology Press.

Chang, L., Lansford, J. E., Schwartz, D., & Farver, J. M. (2004). Marital quality, maternal depressed affect, harsh parenting, and child externalizing in Hong Kong Chinese families. *International Journal of Behavioral Development, 28*, 311–318.

duRivage, N., Keyes, K., Leray, E., Pez, O., Bitfoi, A., Koç, C., et al. (2015). Parental use of corporal punishment in Europe: intersection between public health and policy. *PLoS ONE, 10*, e0118059.

Edwards, C. P., & Liu, W.-L. (1995). Parenting toddlers. In M. Bornstein (Ed.), *Handbook of parenting* (2nd ed., Vol. 1, pp. 45–71). Mahwah, NJ: Lawrence Erlbaum Associates.

Ellis, G., & Petersen, L. R. (1992). Socialization values and parental control techniques: A cross-cultural analysis of child-rearing. *Journal of Comparative Family Studies, 23*, 39–54.

Ellonen, N., Lucas, S., Tindberg, Y., & Janson, S. (2017). Parents' self-reported use of corporal punishment and other humiliating upbringing practices in Finland and Sweden – A comparative study. *Child Abuse Review, 26*, 289–304.

Ember, C. R., & Ember, M. (2005). Explaining corporal punishment of children: A cross-cultural study. *American Anthropologist, 107*, 609–619.

Gershoff, E. T., Grogan-Kaylor, A., Lansford, J. R., Chang, L., Zelli, A., Deater-Deckard, K., & Dodge, K. A. (2010). Parent discipline practices in an international sample: Associations with child behaviors and moderation by perceived normativeness. *Child Development, 81*, 487–502.

Giles-Sims, J., & Lockhart, C. (2005). Culturally shaped patterns of disciplining children. *Journal of Family Issues, 26*, 196–218.

Goodnow, J. J. (1995). Parents' knowledge and expectations. In M. H. Bornstein (Ed.), *Handbook of parenting* (2nd ed., Vol. 3, pp. 305–332). Hillsdale, NJ: Lawrence Erlbaum Associates.

Gorman, J. C. (1998). Parenting attitudes and practices of immigrant Chinese mothers of adolescents. *Family Relations, 47*, 73–80.

Hoffman, M. (1975). Moral internalization, parental power, and the nature of parent-child interaction. *Developmental Psychology, 11*, 228–239.

Hofstede, G., Hofstede, G. J., & Minkov, M. (2010). *Cultures and organizations: Software of the mind* (Rev. 3rd ed.). New York, NY: McGraw-Hill.

Hong, G. K., & Hong, L. K. (1991). Comparative perspectives on child abuse and neglect: Chinese versus Hispanics and Whites. *Child Welfare, 70*, 463–475.

Keller, H., Lamm, B., Abels, M., Yovsi, R., Borke, J., Jensen, H., . . . Chaudhary, N. (2006). Cultural models, socialization goals, and parenting ethnotheories: A multicultural analysis. *Journal of Cross-Cultural Psychology, 37*, 155–172.

Kulig, J. C. (1998). Family life among El Salvadorans, Guatemalans and Nicaraguans: A comparative study. *Journal of Comparative Family Studies, 29*, 469–479.

Lansford, J. E., & Deater-Deckard, K. (2012). Childrearing discipline and violence in developing countries. *Child Development, 83*, 62–75.

Lansford, J. E., Chang, L., Dodge, K. A., Malone, P. S., Oburu, P., Palmerus, K., Quinn, N. (2005). Cultural normativeness as a moderator of the link between physical discipline and children's adjustment: A comparison of China, India, Italy, Kenya, Philippines, and Thailand. *Child Development, 76*, 1234–1246.

Lau, A. S. (2010). Physical discipline in Chinese American immigrant families: An adaptive culture perspective. *Cultural Diversity and Ethnic Minority Psychology, 16*, 313–322.

Morawska, A., & Sanders, M. (2010). Parental use of time out revisited: A useful or harmful parenting strategy? *Journal of Child and Family Studies, 20*, 1–8.

Papps, F., Walker, M., Trimboli, A., & Trimboli, C. (1995). Parental discipline in Anglo, Greek, Lebanese, and Vietnamese cultures. *Journal of Cross-Cultural Psychology, 26*, 49–64.

Park, H., & Lau, A. S. (2016). Socioeconomic status and parenting priorities: Child independence and obedience around the world. *Journal of Marriage & Family, 78*, 43–59.

Pastorelli, C., Lansford, J., Luengo Kanacri, B. P., Malone, P. S., DiGiunta, L., Bacchini, D., Sorbring, E. (2016). Positive parenting and children's prosocial behavior in eight countries. *Journal of Child Psychology & Psychiatry, 57*, 824–834.

Rudy, D., & Grusec, J. E. (2006). Authoritarian parenting in individualist and collectivist groups: Associations with maternal emotion and cognition and children's self-esteem. *Journal of Family Psychology*, *20*, 68–78.

Super, C., & Harkness, S. (1986). The developmental niche: A conceptualization at the interface of child and culture. *International Journal of Behavioral Development*, *9*, 545–569.

Zolotor, A. J., & Puzia, M. E. (2010). Bans against corporal punishment: A systematic review of the laws, changes in attitudes and behaviors. *Child Abuse Review*, *19*, 229–247.

# 10

# CROSS-CULTURAL DIFFERENCES IN PARENTS' RESPONSES TO CHILD TEMPERAMENT

*Sae-Young Han, Seong-Yeon Park, Eun Gyoung Lee, Maria Beatriz Martins Linhares, and Helena Slobodskaya*

Although individual differences in reactivity and self-regulation are constitutionally based and remain relatively stable over time, they are also shaped by contextual factors such as parent-child interactions. Parents respond to children's negative emotions, either demonstrating tolerance or rejection, and when children express positive emotions, varying in the degree to which these are attended/encouraged. Through multiple exchanges with caregivers, children learn the extent to which different

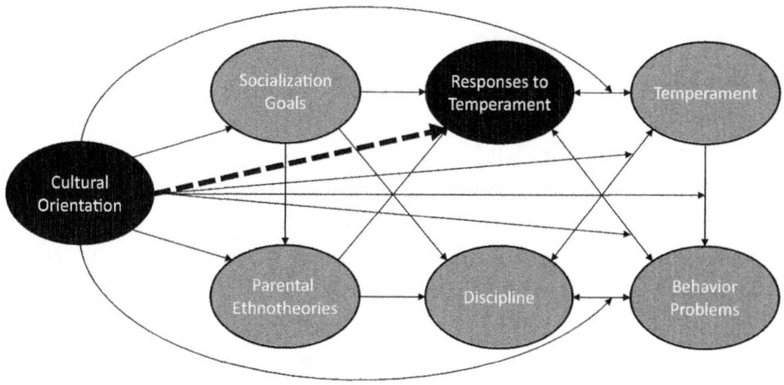


**FIGURE 10.1** Parent's responses in the JETTC Conceptual Model

emotional expressions are socially acceptable, and which require modulation. Caregiver responses are shaped by perceptions of their children's characteristics, in turn greatly influenced by the cultural meaning associated with particular domains of emotional/behavioral development or regulation (Cole & Tan, 2015; Super et al., 2008). In this chapter, we explore differences between the JETTC cultures in the ways parents respond to child behaviors associated with Surgency (SUR), Negative Affectivity (NEG) and Effortful Control (EFF; see Figure 10.1).

Parental reactions to children's displays of negative emotions have been shown to vary across cultures. Chinese mothers showed more authoritarian (i.e., emphasizing control/discipline over warmth/affection) attitudes than United States (US) mothers toward child NEG (Porter et al., 2005), expecting control over these expressions. Indian immigrant mothers were more likely than White American mothers to report unsupportive reactions to their preschool children's negative emotions (McCord & Raval, 2016). In a similar vein, Fäsche et al. (2011) found that Indian and Nepalese mothers, in comparison to German and US mothers, were more likely to express distress to children's display of negative emotions.

In a study examining parental reactions to positive emotion expression in 6-year-old children, Park, Trommsdorff, and Lee (2012) found that Korean mothers showed slightly more supportive than unsupportive reactions. This finding is in line with Korean mothers' beliefs that Surgency (SUR) is a desirable temperament trait in toddlers (Yun & Park, 2013). Chinese mothers of toddlers reported higher punishment and lower acceptance of positive emotion expressions, relative to Canadian mothers, implying that Chinese parents may consider positive affect as less important, possibly due to their collectivistic values (Chen et al., 1998). Finnish mothers also showed low affection and high control to their 7–8-year-old children's displays of high activity level (Katainen, Raikkonen, & Keltikangas-Jarvinen, 1997; Laukkanen, Ojansuu, Tolvanen, Alatupa, & Aunola, 2014).

With respect to EFF, compared to Canadian parents, Chinese parents expected their children to maintain a high level of control over emotions and behaviors (Chen et al., 2003). Similarly, Korean mothers perceived high EFF as a desirable temperamental trait (Yun & Park, 2013), reflecting a high societal value placed on self-control. For East Asian parents, use of authoritarian parenting was associated with children's low EFF and high dispositional anger/frustration (Zhou, Eisenberg, Wang, & Reiser, 2004).

In societies with dominant individualistic values, emphasizing autonomy and self-assertiveness, parents are more likely to encourage children to express their emotions (Rothbaum, Nagaoka, & Ponte, 2006). On the other hand, in societies embracing collectivistic values, interdependence and group harmony are emphasized, as parents discourage children's display of emotions, emphasizing behavioral control (Cole, Tamang, & Shrestha, 2006). When caregivers in collectivist countries approach children with emotional warmth, it is generally to enhance acceptance of the group norms and values, for example when mothers respond to infants in an anticipatory manner that blurs the self-other distinction. Caregivers in individualistic cultures, on the other hand, encourage expression of positive emotions and support flexible self-regulation (Greenfield, Keller, Fuligni, & Maynard, 2003).

Beyond Individualism/Collectivism, the Long-Term versus Short-Term Orientation dimension appears especially relevant to EFF (Krassner et al., 2016). Putnam and Gartstein (2017) showed that higher SUR was related to low Long-Term Orientation, indicating that children growing up in short-term oriented cultures get more opportunities to seek immediate gratification of needs, whereas children in long-term oriented cultures are likely discouraged from expressing their immediate pleasure-seeking tendencies.

For the current study, the primary goal was to compare 14 JETTC cultures on the four facets of Parental Responses to Temperament Displays (PRTD): Encouraging NEG, Encouraging SUR, Punishing Low EFF, and Rewarding High EFF, with cross-cultural differences anticipated. Although few a priori hypotheses could be formulated regarding specific countries in terms of PRTD differences, there were several specific expectations for links with Hofstede's cultural orientation dimensions. Mothers from highly collectivist cultures and those high in Long-Term Oriention were expected to show less encouragement with respect to toddlers' expression of both negative and positive emotions. We also expected these caregivers to score higher on Punishing Low EFF and Rewarding High EFF, stressing the importance of children's self-control.

## Results

As shown in Table 10.1, substantial cross-cultural effects for all four scales were revealed through 2 (Sex) by 14 (Culture) ANOVAs, with age as a covariate. Age effects indicated higher likelihood of punishing low EFF in older children. Sex and Sex × Culture effects were non-significant for all scales.

**TABLE 10.1** Effects of culture, age, and sex on parental responses to temperament displays

| *PRTD scale* | *Age* | *Culture* | *Sex* | *Culture × Sex* |
|---|---|---|---|---|
| Encouraging Negative Affectivity | 1.58 | 18.10** | 1.58 | 0.82 |
| Encouraging Surgency | 0.61 | 5.29** | 0.22 | 0.76 |
| Punishing Low Effortful Control | 5.20* | 7.40** | 0.02 | 0.57 |
| Rewarding High Effortful Control | 0.98 | 9.54** | 0.53 | 0.64 |

** $p < 0.1$, * $p < 0.05$

Note: ANOVAs, with age as covariate, sex and country as factors. Dfs for age and sex = 1,805. Dfs for culture and culture × sex = 13,805

**FIGURE 10.2** Map of Encouraging Negative Affectivity marginal means. Darker shading indicates higher scores

**FIGURE 10.3** Map of Encouraging Surgency marginal means. Darker shading indicates higher scores

Main effects comparisons (Bonferroni adjustment) for Encouragement of NEG indicated that Spanish mothers scored higher than those from all countries but South Korea and Finland. Korean and Finnish mothers scored higher than those from multiple countries, and lower than none (Figure 10.2). Mothers from the US and China also scored higher than multiple countries. Mothers from Turkey, Belgium, Italy, Mexico, and Chile, Russian, and Netherlands scored lower than several countries, but higher than Brazil. Brazilian mothers scored lower than those from all other countries but Romania, with Romanians also scoring lower than five groups.

Regarding encouragement of SUR (Figure 10.3), Finnish mothers scored highest, with pairwise comparisons indicating significantly higher

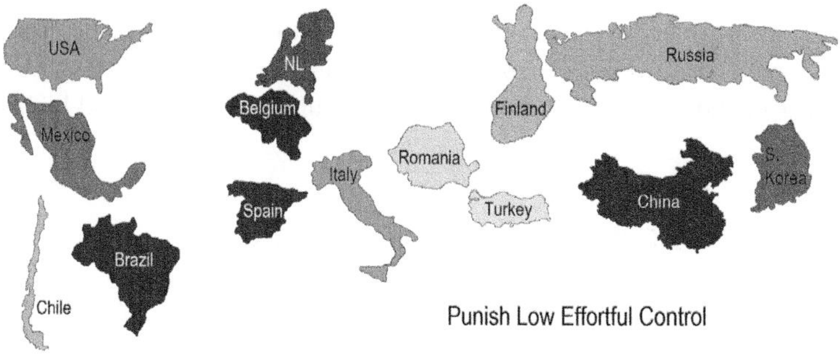


**FIGURE 10.4** Map of Punish Low Effortful Control. Darker shading indicates higher scores

**FIGURE 10.5** Map of Reward High Effortful Control. Darker shading indicates higher scores

scores than those from Italy, Brazil, and China. Chileans also scored higher than Italians and Brazilians; and Spanish, Mexican, Russian, and American parents were higher in SUR Encouragement than those from Italy.

Across all countries, mothers reported relatively low levels of Punish-Ment Low EFF. Chinese mothers scored significantly higher than seven other groups (Figure 10.4). Spanish, Brazilian, Belgian, and Dutch mothers also scored higher than mothers from at least one other nation, and lower than none. Italy, US, Russia, Chile, and Finland scored lower than at least one other country, and higher than none; and Romania and Turkey scored lower than the highest five countries on this dimension.

Rewarding of High EFF (Figure 10.5) was highest among Belgian and Dutch mothers, who scored significantly higher than mothers from five and seven countries, respectively. Mothers from Russia, China, Turkey, Brazil, and Spain were also higher than two or three countries, and lower than none, on this dimension. Rewarding high EFF was lowest in Chile, Mexico, and Italy, who scored lower than multiple countries, and higher than none.

## Relations to Cultural Orientation Dimensions

Pearson's correlations were calculated between average country scores on the four parenting variables and Hofstede's six cultural orientation dimensions (Hofstede et al., 2010). High tendencies to Reward High EFF were associated with Long-Term Orientation, $r(14) = 0.57$, $p < 0.05$.

## Discussion

The purpose of this study was to explore cross-cultural differences in mothers' responses to their children's temperament displays across 14 JETTC cultures, and results revealed such differences abound. The observed pattern of results was also consistent with hypotheses concerning links between Hofstede's Long-Term versus Short-Term Orientation dimension and parental responses to child emotional/behavioral expressions.

Observed differences were not entirely consistent with expectations. US mothers scored relatively high on encouragement of both NEG and SUR, presumably reflecting the individualistic value of encouraging child emotional expressions (Rothbaum et al., 2006). However, mothers from some collectivistic (Chile and Spain) and mixed-values cultures

(Russia and Korea) were also likely to encourage the expressions of both negative and positive emotions. In China, a collectivistic culture presumably emphasizing the importance of controlling emotional expressions, mothers reported high encouragement of NEG similar to the US. Chinese mothers, however, scored low on Encouragement of SUR, likely reflecting a lack of emphasis on positive affect (Chen et al., 1998). Consistent with previous research suggesting strong promotion of self-control by Chinese parents (Chen et al., 2003), Chinese mothers scored highest on punishment of low EFF and among the highest in rewarding of successful restraint.

Consistent with expectations, mothers from long-term oriented countries received the highest scores for rewarding high EFF, whereas mothers from short-term oriented societies showed relatively lower levels. Short-term cultural orientation may translate into acceptance of immediate need fulfillment in the offspring, rather than prioritizing regulation. Additionally, JETTC results may be explained by the finding that Chilean mothers tend to perceive their infants as high in EFF (Farkas & Vallotton, 2016), potentially affording the ability to forgo instillment of further advancement of regulation.

Mothers from all 14 countries reported relatively low levels of punishment for low EFF, coupled with relatively high levels of endorsement of rewarding high EFF. Mothers were more likely to punish low EFF in older toddlers across JETTC sites, likely a function of the fact that Effortful Control undergoes rapid development throughout this period (Posner, Rothbart, Sheese, & Voelker, 2012). Accordingly, modulation of behaviors and emotions is likely to gain in importance as toddlers approach the end of their third year of life. Although not considered in this study, children with higher EFF may elicit more supportive caregiving (Li, Pawan, & Stansbury, 2014), and this possibility should be examined in future research.

## References

Chen, X., Hastings, P. D., Rubin, K. H., Chen, H., Cen, G., & Stewart, S. L. (1998). Child-rearing attitudes and behavioral inhibition in Chinese and Canadian toddlers: A cross-cultural study. *Developmental Psychology, 34*(4), 677–686.

Chen, X., Rubin, K. H., Liu, M., Chen, H., Wang, L., Li, D., Li, B. (2003). Compliance in Chinese and Canadian toddlers: A cross-cultural study. *International Journal of Behavioral Development, 27*(5), 428–436.

Cole, P. M., Tamang, B. L., & Shrestha, S. (2006). Cultural variations in the socialization of young children's anger and shame. *Child Development*, 77(5), 1237–1251.

Cole, P. M., & Tan, P. Z. (2015). Emotion socialization from a cultural perspective. In. J. E. Grusec & P. D. Hastings (Ed.), *Handbook of socialization: Theory and research* (pp. 516–542). New York, NY: Guilford.

Farkas, C., & Vallotton, C. (2016). Differences in infant temperament between Chile and the US. *Infant Behavior and Development*, *44*, 208–218.

Fäsche, A., Trommsdorff, G., Heikamp, T., Cole, P. M., Mishra, R. C., Niraula, S., & Park, S.-Y. (2011). Cultural differences in mothers' beliefs about sensitivity and maternal reactions to children's distress. In E. M. Leerkes & J. A. Nelson (Chairs), *Racial and cultural differences in parents' emotion socialization beliefs*. Symposium conducted at the SRCD Biennial Meeting, Montreal, Canada, April.

Greenfield, P. M., Keller, H., Fuligni, A., & Maynard, A. (2003). Cultural pathways through universal development. *Annual Review of Psychology*, *54*(1), 461–490.

Hofstede, G., Hofstede, G. J. & Minkov, M. (2010). *Cultures and organizations: Software of the mind* (Rev. 3rd ed.). New York: McGraw-Hill.

Katainen, S., Raikkonen, K., & Keltikangas-Jarvinen, L. (1997). Childhood temperament and mother's child-rearing attitudes: Stability and interaction in a three-year follow-up study. *European Journal of Personality*, *11*(4), 249–265.

Krassner, A. M., Gartstein, M. A., Park, C., Dragan, W. L., Lecannelier, F., & Putnam, S. P. (2016). East-west, collectivist-individualist: A cross-cultural examination of temperament in toddlers from Chile, Poland, South Korea, and the U.S. *European Journal of Developmental Psychology*, *14*(4), 449–464.

Laukkanen, J., Ojansuu, U., Tolvanen, A., Alatupa, S., & Aunola, K. (2014). Child's difficult temperament and mothers' parenting styles. *Journal of Child and Family Studies*, *23*(2), 312–323.

Li, I., Pawan, C., & Stansbury, K. (2014). Emerging effortful control in infancy to toddlerhood and maternal support: A child driven or parent driven model? *Infant Behavior and Development*, *37*(2), 216–224.

McCord, B. L., & Raval, V. V. (2016). Asian Indian immigrant and white American maternal emotion socialization and child socio-emotional functioning. *Journal of Child and Family Studies*, *25*(2), 464–474.

Park, S. Y., Trommsdorff, G., & Lee, E. G. (2012). Korean mothers' intuitive theories regarding emotion socialization of their children. *International Journal of Human Ecology*, *13*(1), 39–56.

Porter, C. L., Hart, C. H., Yang, C., Robinson, C. C., Olsen, S. F., Zeng, Q., Jin, S. (2005). A comparative study of child temperament and parenting in Beijing, China, and the western United States. *International Journal of Behavioral Development*, *29*(6), 541–551.

Posner, M. I., Rothbart, M. K., Sheese, B. E., & Voelker, P. (2012). Control networks and neuromodulators of early development. *Developmental Psychology*, *48*(3), 827.

Putnam, S. P., & Gartstein, M. A. (2017). Aggregate temperament scores from multiple countries: Associations with aggregate personality traits, cultural dimensions, and allelic frequency. *Journal of Research in Personality, 67*, 157–170.

Rothbaum, F., Nagaoka, R., & Ponte, I. C. (2006). Caregiver sensitivity in cultural context: Japanese and US teachers' beliefs about anticipating and responding to children's needs. *Journal of Research in Childhood Education, 21*(1), 23–40.

Super, C. M., Axia, G., Harkness, S., Welles-Nystrom, B., Zylicz, P.O., Parmar, P., McGurk, H. (2008). Culture, temperament, and the "difficult child": A study in seven Western cultures. *European Journal of Developmental Science, 2*(1–2), 136–157.

Yun, K. B., & Park, S. Y. (2013). Korean mothers' beliefs regarding toddlers' temperament, and their reactions to what they view as desirable and undesirable behavior. *Korean Journal of Child Studies, 34*(1), 103–121.

Zhou, Q., Eisenberg, N., Wang, Y., & Reiser, M. (2004). Chinese children's effortful control and dispositional anger/frustration: Relations to parenting styles and children's social functioning. *Developmental Psychology, 40*(3), 352–366.

# 11

# INTEGRATING THE DEVELOPMENTAL NICHE

## Relations among Socialization Goals, Parental Ethnotheories, Daily Activities, and Parental Responses to Temperament

*Mirjana Majdandžić, Marlis Cornelia Kirchhoff, Katri Räikkönen, Oana Benga, and Emine Ahmetoglu*

In this chapter, we integrate findings regarding the developmental niche by exploring relations of parental socialization goals (SG) and ethnotheories (PE) with daily activities involving the child, and parental reactions to child temperament displays (see Figure 11.1). SG (parents' beliefs regarding desired outcomes for children) and PE (desired parental behaviors to

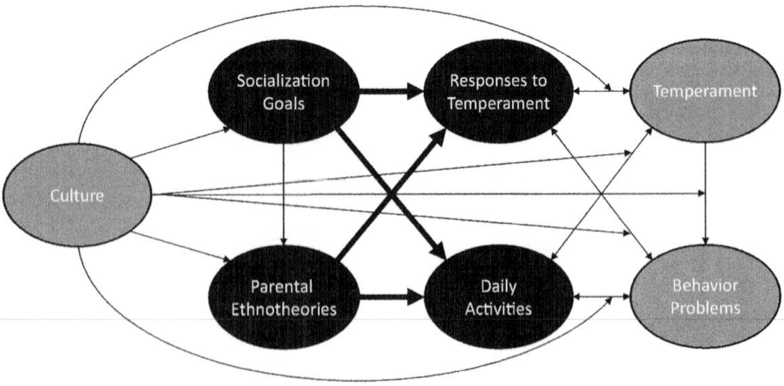


**FIGURE 11.1** Niche element associations in the JETTC Conceptual Model

achieve these outcomes) are expected to influence a wide array of daily routines, including play, preparation for sleep/soothing, and discipline strategies; as well as how parents appraise and respond to their child's behavior. Specifically, temperament displays that are consistent with desired child outcomes are expected to be encouraged and displays considered undesirable are likely to be discouraged. Cultural norms pertaining to "proper parenting" are also likely to affect the way caregivers respond to expressions of Negative Affectivity (NEG) and Surgency (SUR), and displays of Effortful Control (EFF).

Cultures favoring relational SG and PE emphasize helping others, obedience, controlling emotions, and prompt responses to child distress. Cultures that value acceptance of norms and hierarchies as contributors to the harmonic functioning of the social unit are characterized by a proximal parenting style: seeking synchrony in mother–child exchanges (Carra, Lavelli, Keller, & Kärtner, 2013), more frequent references to the social context, moral correctness (Kärtner et al., 2006), a focus on obedience and responsibility for the group (Harkness & Super, 1992), and encouragement of proper demeanor (Leyendecker, Lamb, Harwood, & Schölmerich, 2002). Play in such cultures is more often connected to a purpose such as academic enrichment (Parmar, Harkness, & Super, 2008). Less parental encouragement of independence and bedtime routines such as rocking or nursing are also more likely in this relational cultural context and have been linked to shorter and more fragmented child sleep (Sadeh, Mindell, Luedtke, & Wiegand, 2009). Regarding discipline, corporal punishment is more often used in cultures that emphasize power hierarchy (Ember & Ember, 2005).

Cultures favoring autonomous SG and PE emphasize self-confidence, competitiveness, and autonomy. Such cultures are characterized by a distal parenting style, preferring face-to-face interactions, play with objects, and high responsivity to positive affect (Carra et al., 2013; Keller et al., 2006). Rough-and-tumble play is more prevalent in individualistic cultures (Roopnarine & Davidson, 2015), where play is primarily used for entertainment (Parmar et al., 2008). Encouraging independence in falling asleep and reliance on greater self-soothing is consistent with autonomous values and predicts longer and more consolidated sleep (Sadeh et al., 2009). Findings on discipline suggest corporal punishment is seldom applied in cultures low in power hierarchy (Ember & Ember, 2005).

According to the literature relevant to parental responses to temperament displays, discussed in Chapter 10, positive and negative emotional expressions tend to be discouraged in countries high in relatedness (Chen et al., 1998; Porter et al., 2005), whereas EFF is valued (Cole, Tamang, & Shrestha, 2006; Yun & Park, 2013). Delay of gratification, an expression of EFF, was described as higher, and emotional expressiveness as lower, in interdependent cultures (Lamm et al., 2018). In contrast, emotional expression, and particularly SUR, is often encouraged in countries valuing autonomy (Rothbaum, Nagaoka, & Ponte, 2006), with expressions of EFF valued less.

Countries high on Relational SG emphasize obedience, caring for others and emotional control, and were expected to score high on Play with a Purpose and low on Play for Entertainment (Parmar et al., 2008). The finding that children in collectivist countries watch more television (Singer, Singer, Agostino, & Delong, 2009), suggest that children in countries high on relational goals will engage more in this activity. The emphasis on obedience in relational goals is expected to translate into positive links with the use of power-assertive discipline techniques, consistent with theories relating values emphasizing conformity with the use of corporal punishment (Ember & Ember, 2005). Relational SG may also predict parents' discouragement of negative and positive emotional expressions (Chen et al., 1998; Porter et al., 2005). Parental promotion of EFF in countries valuing relatedness was expected, given the emphasis on obedience and emotional control (Cole et al., 2006; Lamm et al., 2018).

Autonomous socialization goals, valuing self-confidence and independence, are conceptually linked to individualism. Chapter 8 revealed positive links between Individualism and gentle sleep-aiding techniques, and between Indulgence and leaving the child alone to cry, suggesting that countries high on autonomous goals score higher on these sleep routines. Chapter 9 results indicating that corporal punishment is lower in individualistic countries suggests that countries high in autonomous goals use less hitting/spanking and other power-assertive discipline strategies. The positive correlation between Indulgence and asking the child to repair the damage (Chapter 9) suggests greater use of this disciplining technique in countries endorsing autonomous goals. Because emphasis on independence has been linked with more expressed emotions (Rothbaum et al., 2006), countries high in autonomous goals are predicted to encourage NEG and SUR in their toddlers. Because of an emphasis on comforting the child, countries high on Relational PE are expected to use more sleep-aiding techniques, to stay with their child during bedtime, and not leave the child alone to cry. Autonomous PE reflect ideals of training children to sleep and play alone and show positive links

**TABLE 11.1** Between-country correlations between countries' marginal means of socialization goals/parental ethnotheories and family context variables

| | *Socialization goals* | | *Parental ethnotheories* | |
|---|---|---|---|---|
| | *Relational* | *Autonomous* | *Relational* | *Autonomous* |
| Daily activities | | | | |
| Low-Intensity Toy Play | 0.18 | 0.18 | 0.31 | –0.10 |
| High-Intensity Toy Play | 0.49[#] | 0.26 | –0.03 | 0.33 |
| Play with Purpose | 0.03 | 0.14 | –0.26 | 0.13 |
| Play for Entertainment | –0.64* | –0.31 | 0.08 | –0.26 |
| Activities with Parent | 0.08 | 0.44 | 0.36 | 0.05 |
| Watching Television | 0.65* | 0.27 | –0.41 | 0.32 |
| Computer/Electronics | 0.27 | 0.55* | 0.24 | 0.14 |
| Parenting regarding child sleep | | | | |
| Active Techniques | 0.31 | 0.14 | 0.27 | –0.09 |
| Gentle Techniques | –0.19 | 0.20 | 0.49[#] | –0.16 |
| Stay with Child | 0.17 | –0.39 | 0.02 | –0.40 |
| Cry it Out | 0.43 | 0.29 | –0.52[#] | 0.39 |
| Children's sleep patterns | | | | |
| Bed time | 0.07 | –0.34 | –0.20 | –0.09 |
| Waking time | 0.25 | 0.04 | –0.26 | 0.38 |
| Nighttime sleep | 0.12 | 0.54* | 0.08 | 0.46[#] |
| Naps | –0.26 | –0.12 | –0.20 | –0.30 |
| Discipline | | | | |
| Talk about issue | –0.31 | 0.00 | 0.04 | –0.24 |
| Repair damage | 0.22 | 0.15 | 0.21 | 0.05 |
| Think about misbehavior | 0.23 | –0.38 | –0.16 | 0.05 |
| Shout or swear | –0.10 | –0.80** | 0.09 | –0.33 |
| Hit or spank | 0.43 | –0.42 | –0.43 | –0.19 |
| Remove child from others | 0.38 | 0.24 | –0.25 | 0.29 |
| Take away privileges | 0.29 | –0.02 | –0.01 | 0.14 |
| Responses to temperament | | | | |
| Encouraging NEG | 0.00 | –0.22 | 0.14 | –0.13 |
| Encouraging SUR | 0.28 | 0.39 | 0.37 | 0.10 |
| Punish low EFF | 0.41 | –0.27 | –0.15 | 0.06 |
| Reward high EFF | 0.07 | –0.15 | –0.10 | 0.12 |

Note: $N = 14$, $^{**}p < 0.01$, $^{*}p < 0.05$, $^{\#}p < 0.10$

to Indulgence (Chapter 6). Therefore, predictions resemble those for Autonomous SG. The ideal of training the child to sleep alone predicts higher use of "cry it out", lower frequency of staying with child, less use of sleep-aiding techniques, and longer child nighttime sleep (Sadeh et al., 2009).

## Results

Relational SG were associated with more time watching television and low endorsement of play for entertainment; and marginally associated with more high-intensity toy play. Autonomous goals were linked to frequent use of computers and other electronics, more nighttime sleep, and less reliance on shouting/swearing as a discipline technique.

No correlations between PE and parenting behavior were significant, but countries with higher Relational PE were marginally more likely to use gentle bedtime techniques and not have their children cry it out at bedtime; and countries high on Autonomous PE reported marginally more sleep. There were no significant correlations between mothers' SG/PE and their responses to their child's temperament displays.

## Discussion

The aim of this chapter was to integrate the developmental niche by exploring how parental SG and PE translate into child-related daily routines and responses to temperament displays. Few significant associations between parental psychology and family context variables emerged. Relational SG were expected to translate into more play with a purpose, yet mothers in countries high in these goals engaged children less in play for entertainment. Thus, cultures holding relational values regard play less as a purely entertaining activity, consistent with an emphasis on obedience and following rules. Children in countries endorsing relational goals spent more time watching television, in line with previous findings (Singer et al., 2009), and with the marginal positive association between Collectivism and television exposure (Chapter 7). Watching television is often a group activity, and the idea of shared time together is consistent with relational values.

Children in countries that value autonomous goals spent more time on computers and other electronic devices. Playing with devices such as tablets and computers entails a solo activity, which is consistent with prioritizing autonomy and independence. Autonomously oriented cultures may regard playing with electronic devices as an appropriate means for children to spend leisure time. Children in these countries slept more during the night, in line with previous links between encouragement of independence and extended sleep in children (Sadeh et al., 2009). A substantial correlation was found between higher endorsement of autonomous goals and less shouting and swearing as a discipline technique. Shouting/swearing likely conveys a negative message about the child and may lower self-confidence—an outcome antithetical to the autonomous socialization agenda.

The developmental niche has been conceptualized as a framework that confers cultural influences onto the next generation. Research has demonstrated coherent culture-specific pathways adaptive in different environmental contexts (Keller, 2015). Yet, such coherence between systems was largely absent in the present investigation. Yet, several strong correlations between elements of the developmental niche indicate important influences of cultural values on child rearing relevant to temperament development.

## References

Carra, C., Lavelli, M., Keller, H., & Kärtner, J. (2013). Parenting infants: Socialization goals and behaviors of Italian mothers and immigrant mothers from West Africa. *Journal of Cross-Cultural Psychology, 20*(10), 1–17.

Chen, X., Hastings, P. D., Rubin, K. H., Chen, H., Cen, G., & Stewart, S. L. (1998). Child-rearing attitudes and behavioral inhibition in Chinese and Canadian toddlers: A cross-cultural study. *Developmental Psychology, 34*, 677–686.

Cole, P. M., Tamang, B. L., & Shrestha, S. (2006). Cultural variations in the socialization of young children's anger and shame. *Child Development, 77*, 1237–1251.

Ember, C. R., & Ember, M. (2005). Explaining corporal punishment of children: A cross-cultural study. *American Anthropologist, 107*(4), 609–619.

Harkness, S., & Super, C. (1992). Parental ethnotheories in action. In S. Harkness & C. M. Super (Eds.), *Parental belief systems: The psychological consequences for children* (2nd ed.). Hillsdale, NJ: Lawrence Erlbaum Associates.

Kärtner, J., Keller, H., Lamm, B., Abels, M., Yovsi, R., & Chaudhary, N. (2007). Manifestations of autonomy and relatedness in mothers' account of their ethnotheories regarding child care across five cultural communities. *Journal of Cross-Cultural Psychology, 38*, 613–628.

Keller, H. (2015). Psychological autonomy and hierarchical relatedness as organizers of developmental pathways. *Philosophical Transactions of the Royal Society B, 371*, 20150070.

Keller, H., Lamm, B., Abels, M., Yovis, R., Borke, J., Jensen, H., . . . Chaudhary, N. (2006). Cultural models, socialization goals, and parenting ethnotheories: A multicultural analysis. *Journal of Cross-Cultural Psychology, 37*, 155–172.

Lamm, B., Keller, H., Teiser, J., Yovsi, R., Poloczek, S., Suhrke, J., . . . Lohaus, A. (2018). Waiting for the second treat: Developing culture-specific modes of self-regulation. *Child Development, 89*(3), e261–e277.

Leyendecker, B., Lamb, E., Harwood, R. L., & Schölmerich, B. (2002). Mother's socialization goals and evaluations of desirable and undesirable everyday situations in two diverse cultural groups. *International Journal or Behavioral Development, 26*, 248–258.

Parmar, P., Harkness, S., & Super, C. M. (2008). Teacher or playmate? Asian immigrant and Euro-American parents' participation in their young children's daily acitvities. *Social Behavior and Personality: An International Journal, 36*(2), 163–176.

Porter, C. L., Hart, C. H., Yang, C., Robinson, C. C., Olsen, S. F., Zeng, Q., Jin, S. (2005). A comparative study of child temperament and parenting in Beijing, China, and the western United States. *International Journal of Behavioral Development, 29*, 541–551.

Roopnarine, J. L., & Davidson, K. L. (2015). Parent-child play across cultures: Advancing play research. *American Journal of Play*, 7(2), 228–252.

Rothbaum, F., Nagaoka, R., & Ponte, I. C. (2006). Caregiver sensitivity in cultural context: Japanese and US teachers' beliefs about anticipating and responding to children's needs. *Journal of Research in Childhood Education, 21*, 23–40.

Sadeh, A. V. I., Mindell, J. A., Luedtke, K., & Wiegand, B. (2009). Sleep and sleep ecology in the first 3 years: A web-based study. *Journal of Sleep Research, 18*(1), 60–73.

Singer, D. G., Singer, J. L., Agostino, H. D., & Delong, R. (2009). Children's pastimes and play in sixteen nations: Is free-play declining? *American Journal of Play, 1*(3), 283–312.

Yun, K. B., & Park, S. Y. (2013). Korean mothers' beliefs regarding toddlers' temperament, and their reactions to what they view as desirable and undesirable behavior. *Korean Journal of Child Studies, 34*, 103–121.

# PART 3

# The Niche and the Child

## Links between Parental Psychology, Developmental Context, and Child Outcomes

# 12

# SOCIALIZATION GOALS, PARENTAL ETHNOTHEORIES, TODDLER TEMPERAMENT, AND BEHAVIOR PROBLEMS

*Rosario Montirosso, Lorenzo Giusti, Niccolò Butti, Zhengyan Wang, and Mirjana Majdandžić*

Parental ethnotheories (PE) and socialization goals (SG) constitute key components of the developmental niche, as experienced by the developing child (Döge & Keller, 2014; Harkness & Super, 1996), and represent culture-related dimensions of parents' expectations concerning child-rearing practices. Most previous research into SG and PE has addressed their associations with parental practices (Harkness & Super, 2002). However, these factors also have a substantial impact upon children's

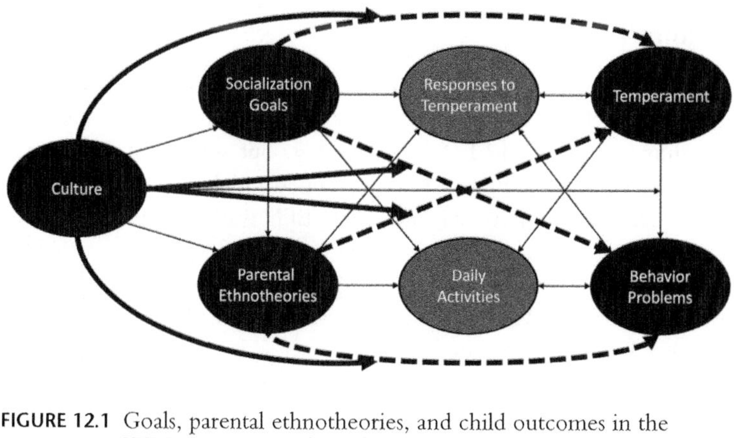


**FIGURE 12.1** Goals, parental ethnotheories, and child outcomes in the JETTC Conceptual Model

social-emotional development. Indeed, cross-cultural studies indicate that child-rearing goals and beliefs likely mediate cultural influences on child development (e.g., Super & Harkness, 1986). For instance, Chen, Rubin, and Li (1995) and Chen et al. (1998) suggested that cultural beliefs regarding the appropriateness of assertive and attention-seeking behaviors resulted in differences in the prevalence of behavioral inhibition between Chinese and Canadian children. To date, culturally driven parental goals and ethnotheories have been insufficiently studied in association with temperament and behavioral-emotional problems. Although the literature addressing parental attitudes/beliefs is extensive, it has focused on discrete, relatively stable cultural contexts (Georgas, Berry, Van de Vijver, Kagitçibasi, & Poortinga, 2006; Harkness & Super, 1996; Levine & New, 2008). Although Relational/Autonomous SG and PE have not been directly associated with temperament and behavior problems, we expected such relations to emerge for Negative Affectivity (NEG), Surgency (SUR), Effortful Control (EFF), as well as internalizing (INT) and externalizing (EXT) problems, in the JETTC dataset (see Figure 12.1).

Thus, an exploratory approach was adopted with the following aims: to (1) investigate associations between Relational/Autonomous SG and PE, children's temperament and behavior problems for the JETTC multicultural sample as a whole; (2) determine how differences between cultures with respect to PE and SG are associated with cultural variability in child characteristics; and (3) examine within-country associations to ascertain the degree to which relations between parent and child variables are common or unique across countries.

## Results

Initial correlations calculated using the entire sample of individual families, which conflate within-country and between-country differences, are shown in Table 12.1. Several modest, but significant, correlations were apparent. With respect to temperament, high NEG was associated with low Autonomous SG, and high EFF was associated with high Relational and Autonomous SG. With respect to behavior problems, high INT and total problems were associated with low levels of Autonomous SG, Relational, and Autonomous PE. High EXT was also associated with low Relational PE.

The results of between-country correlations, shown in Table 12.2 and Figure 12.2 suggest that countries with high SUR also indicated high levels of Relational PE.

**TABLE 12.1** Correlations between temperament/behavior problems and socialization goals/parental ethnotheories for the entire sample

| | *Socialization goals* | | *Parental ethnotheories* | |
|---|---|---|---|---|
| | *Relational* | *Autonomous* | *Relational* | *Autonomous* |
| Negative Affectivity | 0.05 | $-0.07^{*}$ | –0.04 | –0.01 |
| Surgency | 0.00 | $0.07^{\#}$ | 0.03 | $0.07^{\#}$ |
| Effortful Control | $0.09^{*}$ | $0.15^{**}$ | 0.04 | 0.03 |
| Internalizing | $0.07^{\#}$ | $-0.08^{*}$ | $-0.14^{**}$ | $-0.08^{*}$ |
| Externalizing | 0.03 | –0.06 | $-0.10^{**}$ | –0.06 |
| Total problems | 0.04 | $-0.09^{*}$ | $-0.12^{**}$ | $-0.09^{*}$ |

Note: ns range from 830 to 837. $^{**}p < 0.01$, $^{*}p < 0.05$, $^{\#}p < 0.10$

**TABLE 12.2** Between-country correlations between countries' marginal means of temperament/behavior problems and socialization goals/parental ethnotheories

| | *Socialization goals* | | *Parental ethnotheories* | |
|---|---|---|---|---|
| | *Relational* | *Autonomous* | *Relational* | *Autonomous* |
| Negative Affectivity | 0.19 | –0.30 | –0.02 | 0.05 |
| Surgency | –0.19 | –0.09 | $0.86^{**}$ | –0.17 |
| Effortful Control | 0.26 | 0.22 | –0.14 | $-0.49^{\#}$ |
| Internalizing | 0.21 | –0.18 | –0.14 | 0.33 |
| Externalizing | 0.25 | 0.02 | 0.44 | 0.27 |
| Total problems | 0.28 | –0.15 | 0.19 | 0.32 |

Note: $N = 14$, $^{**}p < 0.01$, $^{\#}p < 0.10$

**TABLE 12.3** Average within-country correlations between temperament/behavior problems and socialization goals/parental ethnotheories

| | *Socialization goals* | | *Parental ethnotheories* | |
|---|---|---|---|---|
| | *Relational* | *Autonomous* | *Relational* | *Autonomous* |
| Negative Affectivity | $0.02^{1}$ | $-0.04^{1}$ | $-0.05^{0}$ | $-0.01^{1}$ |
| Surgency | $0.02^{1}$ | $0.08^{0}$ | $-0.05^{1}$ | $0.08^{1}$ |
| Effortful Control | $0.08^{1}$ | $0.15^{4}$ | $0.05^{1}$ | $0.06^{0}$ |
| Internalizing | $0.01^{1}$ | $-0.04^{0}$ | $-0.12^{4}$ | $-0.01^{1}$ |
| Externalizing | $0.00^{4}$ | $-0.05^{1}$ | $-0.15^{3}$ | $0.04^{1}$ |
| Total problems | $-0.01^{2}$ | $-0.06^{2}$ | $-0.14^{3}$ | $-0.01^{2}$ |

Note: Superscripts indicate the number of countries (out of 14) for which the correlation was significant to $p < 0.05$

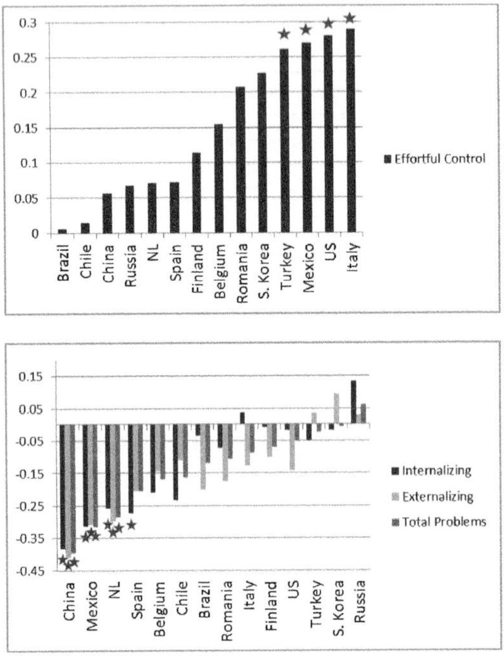


Autonomous Socialization Goals predicting Effortful Control

Relational Parental Ethnotheories predicting Behavior Problems

**FIGURE 12.2** Goals/parental ethnotheories–child outcome correlations for JETTC countries

⋆ indicates significant correlation

The average within-culture correlations are shown in Table 12.3 and demonstrate limited support for links between child outcomes and parenting psychology. In the interest of brevity, we only describe relations that were significant in three or more countries. The relation between Autonomous SG and EFF was significant and positive in Italy, the US, Mexico, and Turkey (see Figure 12.2). Regarding behavior problems, Relational PE was negatively correlated with INT, EXT, and total problems in Mexico, the Netherlands, and China; and also with INT in Spain.

## Discussion

Our results suggest some links between parental SG, PE, and children's temperament/behavior problems. These associations were obtained across the entire sample, and within multiple JETTC cultures. These findings provide a glimpse of the complex pattern of interactions between cultural dimensions, parental psychology, and children development.

First, our analyses with the entire sample suggested multiple associations between parental goals and beliefs concerning child-rearing practices and both children temperament and behavior problems. Although correlations were generally low, these suggested that expectations for autonomy in children, both in terms of SG and PE, were linked with diminished levels of internalizing behavior. Curiously, relational PE were also associated with low levels of behavior problems. It was similarly notable that both Relational and Autonomous SG were associated with children's ability to regulate themselves. Given the seemingly paradoxical nature of these findings, further consideration of analyses from a within-country perspective is warranted.

Regarding the second aim of the study, a single significant association between SG/PE and child outcomes was obtained at the between-country level. Countries in which parents ascribe to more relational PE also have children higher in SUR. This finding could be a function of practices associated with relational PE, such as motor stimulation, body contact, and prompt soothing. Tactile experiences such as these, consistently offered by multiple adults in a child's life, may allow for comfort in active and risky activities associated with SUR.

The third aim regarded associations of SG/PE with temperament and behavior problems at the within-country level in order to ascertain the degree to which relations between parent and child variables were generalizable across JETTC countries. As noted above, the consistent but low correlations between parenting psychology and child outcomes across the full sample begs the question of why these associations are found in some countries, but not others. Two different patterns could be discerned. The first association, between promotion of autonomy and EFF found in Italy, US, Mexico, and Turkey, suggests that in these cultures, mothers fostering self-confidence, competition, and self-control had better-regulated children. The fact that this association was significant in these countries—and not in the others—may be interpreted in the light of Masculinity/Femininity dimension (i.e., the extent to which a society is driven by competition, achievement, and success, rather than cooperation, modesty, nurturance, and a focus on consensus; Hofstede, Hofstede, & Minkov, 2010). Italy, Mexico, and the US are three of the four most masculine of the JETTC nations, and parents in these countries may facilitate high levels of EFF in their toddlers to meet the challenges. The second association concerns the link between relational PE and lower behavior problems in Mexico, the Netherlands, China (INT and EXT), and Spain (INT). Parents who emphasized quick comforting and a proximal approach tended to have children with fewer behavioral difficulties, but only in China, Netherlands, and Mexico, all at the lower end of Uncertainty Avoidance. It may be that adults from these countries, who are not excessively threatened by ambiguous or unknown situations, translate this cultural orientation into child rearing, a possibility to be explored in future research.

Alternative interpretations of these findings concern how parental values may influence the representation of child characteristics. This level of interpretation must be taken into consideration, since the parental and child dimensions were both evaluated by the mother. For instance, the link between autonomy promotion and EFF in masculine countries may reflect high social desirability of these two constructs in cultures valuing competition and confidence. Disentangling parent perception from objective differences in child behavior is a consistent challenge in all research of this nature, deserving more extensive investigation in cross-cultural context.

## References

Chen, X., Hastings, P. D., Rubin, K. H., Chen, H., Cen, G., & Stewart, S. L. (1998). Child-rearing attitudes and behavioral inhibition in Chinese and Canadian toddlers: A cross-cultural study. *Developmental Psychology*, *34*(4), 677.

Chen, X., Rubin, K. H., & Li, B. (1995). Social and school adjustment of shy and aggressive children in China. *Development and Psychopathology*, 7(2), 337–349.

Döge, P., & Keller, H. (2014). Similarity of mothers' and preschool teachers' evaluations of socialization goals in a cross-cultural perspective. *Journal of Research in Childhood Education*, *28*(3), 377–393.

Georgas, J., Berry, J. W., Van de Vijver, F. J., Kagitçibasi, Ç., & Poortinga, Y. H. (Eds.). (2006). *Families across cultures: A 30-nation psychological study*. Cambridge, UK: Cambridge University Press.

Harkness, S., & Super, C. M. (Eds.). (1996). *Parents' cultural belief systems: Their origins, expressions, and consequences*. New York, NY: Guilford.

Harkness, S., & Super, C. M. (2002). Culture and parenting. *Handbook of Parenting*, *2*, 253–280.

Hofstede, G., Hofstede, G. J., & Minkov, M. (2010). *Cultures and organizations: Software of the mind* (Rev. 3rd ed.). New York, NY: McGraw-Hill.

Levine, R. A., & New, R. S. (Eds.). (2008). *Anthropology and child development: A cross-cultural reader*. Oxford, UK: Blackwell Publishing.

Super, C. M., & Harkness, S. (1986). The developmental niche: A conceptualization at the interface of child and culture. *International Journal of Behavioral Development*, *9*(4), 545–569.

# 13

# PLAY/ACTIVITIES, TEMPERAMENT, AND BEHAVIOR PROBLEMS

*Oana Benga, Georgiana Susa-Erdogan, Roseriet Beijers, Mirjana Majdandžić, and Sara Casalin*

As a critical component of the developmental niche, daily activities reflect the cultural organization of children's lives (Harkness, Mavridis, Liu, & Super, 2015) and are therefore expected to affect child development. The Daily Activities Questionnaire (DAQ) allows for a multifaceted assessment of parental practices with toddlers, of which the domains of play (including intensity and purpose), engagement with parent and media exposure will be considered, along with temperament and emotional/behavior problems, across the 14 JETTC countries (see Figure 13.1).

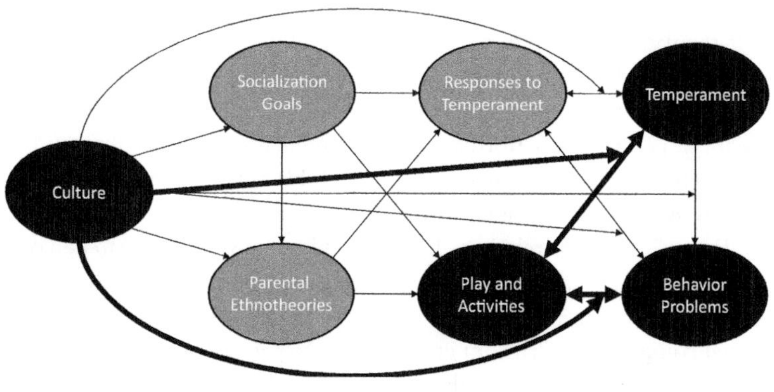


**FIGURE 13.1** Activities and child outcomes in the JETTC Conceptual Model

Play is generally considered central for optimal child development in western families, while South American/Asian caregivers prioritize academic training. Additionally, parents from western societies are active play partners, whereas those from other societies often perceive this role as "outside their job description" (Bornstein, 2007). Thus, existing literature, along with evidence from Chapters 7 and 11, suggest that in interdependent cultures, play is not a goal in itself, but an instrument for early instilment of values and responsibilities, including academic success. On the other hand, in independent countries, play—in particular highly stimulating, exploratory play—is encouraged, and the parent is significantly involved. We expect such cultural variations to influence temperament and adjustment.

Relationships of play with temperament were explored in a few studies, mostly from the perspective of child propensities to engage in certain types of play (e.g., with peers, Spinrad et al., 2004). In this book, and elsewhere in the literature, an opposite direction of effects is considered, asking questions regarding play contributing to temperament development. For example, Sharp et al. (2017) showed a negative correlation (for boys only) of outdoor play with Negative Affectivity (NEG) and a positive correlation with Surgency (SUR). Relations between play and Effortful Control (EFF) are less clear, yet there is some evidence that (pretend) play may foster child self-regulation (Lillard, 2017). Findings concerning early parent-child play appear consistent with this pattern of results, with caregiver support of interest in play exerting a longterm positive influence on cognitive and social independence, supported by self-regulation (Landry, Smith, Swank, & Miller-Loncar, 2000). Comparative longitudinal studies show an earlier emergence of self-regulation in toddlers, and superior abilities at age 4, for interdependent rather than independent families, with the former characterized by a more directive, controlling mother–infant interaction style (Lamm et al., 2017). Better performance on self-regulatory tasks by Korean (Oh & Lewis, 2008) and Chinese preschool children (Sabbagh, Xu, Carlson, Moses, & Lee, 2006) aligns with the latter data.

Regarding the relation between play and emotional/behavior adjustment, an extensive review on high-intensity outdoor play (including rough-and-tumble play) highlighted its positive effects on social competence (Brussoni et al., 2015). Negative correlations between father-child rough-and-tumble play and child externalizing problems (EXT) were also reported (Anderson, Qiu, & Wheeler, 2017; St George, Fletcher, & Palazzi, 2017). Ahnert et al. (2017) showed that quality of father-child physical and pretend play negatively correlated with internalizing problems (INT) of young children.

Media exposure (via TV or other electronic devices) is another important aspect of daily activities, yet links between media and temperament have been largely unexplored. Longitudinal positive correlations between TV watching and NEG and SUR were recently reported throughout the first 18 months (Thompson, Adair, & Bentley, 2017). Poor self-regulation and executive functioning were correlated with media use, and more detrimental effects were noted for infancy exposure (Kostyrka-Allchorne, Cooper, & Simpson, 2017). Similarly, relations between TV and emotional/behavior adjustment suggest withdrawn behavior, inattention, and EXT are consequences of increased TV exposure, particularly in early childhood (Özmert, Toyran, & Yurdakök, 2002; Tremblay et al., 2011; Verlinden et al., 2012). On the other hand, limited research concerning other media (e.g., computer) exposure suggests positive relations with self-regulation (Huber, Yeates, Meyer, Fleckhammer, & Kaufman, 2018).

We hypothesized relations between play and temperament: play with high-intensity toys and play for entertainment to be related with higher SUR; play with purpose (that reduces child's degrees of freedom) to be associated with NEG, at least in individualist countries; low-intensity toy play (via books, role-playing, learning and cuddly toys) to be related to high EFF. We also anticipated all types of play would be associated with low INT and EXT. Second, negative associations were anticipated for TV exposure and EFF, along with positive relations for NEG, SUR, INT, and EXT. The relations were expected to be stronger in more collectivist cultures, given evidence from Chapter 7. All other analyses should be considered exploratory.

## Results

Initial correlations calculated using the entire sample of individual families, which conflate within-country and between-country differences, are shown in Table 13.1. Play with low-intensity toys was linked to high EFF and low behavior problems of all types. Play with high-intensity toys was associated with high SUR, high EFF, and low INT. Play with Purpose was linked to high NEG, high EFF, and low EXT. Play for entertainment only was associated with high NEG and SUR. Engagement with Parent was associated with high SUR and EFF; and low NEG, INT and total problems. More time watching TV was associated with high

**TABLE 13.1** Correlations between temperament/behavior problems and daily activities for the entire sample

| | *Low-Int. Toy Play* | *High-Int. Toy Play* | *Play with Purp.* | *Play for Ent.* | *Activities with Parent* | *TV* | *Elec.* |
|---|---|---|---|---|---|---|---|
| Negative Affectivity | −0.04 | −0.05 | 0.09** | 0.10** | −0.12** | 0.16** | 0.06 |
| Surgency | 0.04 | 0.14** | 0.04 | 0.08* | 0.24** | 0.05 | 0.07# |
| Effortful Control | 0.25** | 0.09** | 0.20** | 0.01 | 0.22** | −0.06# | 0.01 |
| Internalizing | −0.10** | −0.11** | 0.01 | −0.03 | −0.14** | 0.20** | 0.04 |
| Externalizing | −0.14** | −0.04 | −0.09** | −0.03 | −0.04 | 0.16** | 0.09* |
| Total problems | −0.13** | −0.07# | −0.05 | −0.02 | −0.11** | 0.20** | 0.07# |

Note: Low-Int. Toy Play = play with Low-Intensity toys; High-Int. Toy Play = Play with High-Intensity toys; Play with Purp. = Play with Purpose; Play for Ent. = Play solely for Entertainment; Activities with Parent = Activities with Parent; TV = time watching television; Elec. = time with computer or other electronics. $n_s$ = 841 for temperament, 836 for behavior problems. $^{**}p < 0.01$, $^{*}p < 0.05$, $^{\#}p < 0.10$

**TABLE 13.2** Between-country correlations between countries' marginal means of temperament/behavior problems and daily activities

| | *Low-Int. Toy Play* | *High-Int. Toy Play* | *Play with Purp.* | *Play for Ent.* | *Activities with Parent* | *TV* | *Elec.* |
|---|---|---|---|---|---|---|---|
| Negative Affectivity | −0.39 | −0.11 | 0.27 | 0.24 | −0.45 | 0.17 | −0.11 |
| Surgency | 0.40 | 0.07 | −0.38 | −0.12 | 0.49# | −0.23 | 0.31 |
| Effortful Control | 0.48# | 0.32 | 0.07 | −0.13 | 0.33 | 0.02 | 0.49# |

|  |  |  |  |  |  |  |  |
|---|---|---|---|---|---|---|---|
| Internalizing | –0.36 | 0.05 | 0.57* | 0.03 | –0.15 | 0.49# | –0.13 |
| Externalizing | 0.04 | 0.14 | 0.01 | –0.29 | 0.32 | 0.43 | 0.23 |
| Total problems | –0.19 | 0.10 | 0.35 | –0.12 | 0.04 | 0.55* | 0.07 |

Note: Low-Int. Toy Play = Play with Low-Intensity toys; High-Int. Toy Play = Play with High-Intensity toys; Play with Purp. = Play with Purpose; Play for Ent. = Play solely for Entertainment; Activities with Parent = Activities with Parent; TV = time watching television; Elec. = time with computer or other electronics. $N = 14$, $^{*}p < 0.05$, $^{\#}p < 0.10$

**TABLE 13.3** Average within-country correlations between temperament/behavior problems and daily activities

|  | *Low-Int. Toy Play* | *High-Int. Toy Play* | *Play with Purp.* | *Play for Ent.* | *Activities with Parent* | *TV* | *Elec.* |
|---|---|---|---|---|---|---|---|
| Negative Affectivity | $0.00^{1}$ | $-0.03^{1}$ | $0.05^{0}$ | $0.06^{0}$ | $-0.05^{1}$ | $0.14^{2}$ | $0.09^{2}$ |
| Surgency | $0.00^{0}$ | $0.15^{4}$ | $0.08^{2}$ | $0.12^{1}$ | $0.19^{3}$ | $0.07^{2}$ | $0.06^{2}$ |
| Effortful Control | $0.22^{7}$ | $0.09^{1}$ | $0.21^{6}$ | $0.04^{4}$ | $0.21^{6}$ | $-0.06^{0}$ | $-0.03^{3}$ |
| Internalizing | $-0.06^{1}$ | $-0.08^{3}$ | $-0.08^{1}$ | $-0.03^{1}$ | $-0.11^{1}$ | $0.16^{5}$ | $0.09^{2}$ |
| Externalizing | $-0.14^{3}$ | $-0.04^{0}$ | $-0.11^{3}$ | $-0.01^{1}$ | $-0.08^{2}$ | $0.13^{2}$ | $0.10^{2}$ |
| Total problems | $-0.11^{1}$ | $-0.05^{1}$ | $-0.12^{3}$ | $-0.01^{1}$ | $-0.10^{3}$ | $0.17^{3}$ | $0.09^{2}$ |

Note: Low-Int. Toy Play = Play with Low-Intensity toys; High-Int. Toy Play = Play with High-Intensity toys; Play with Purp. = Play with Purpose; Play for Ent. = Play solely for Entertainment; Activities with Parent = Activities with Parent; TV = time watching television; Elec. = time with computer or other electronics. Superscripts indicate the number of countries (out of 14) for which the correlation was significant to $p < 0.05$

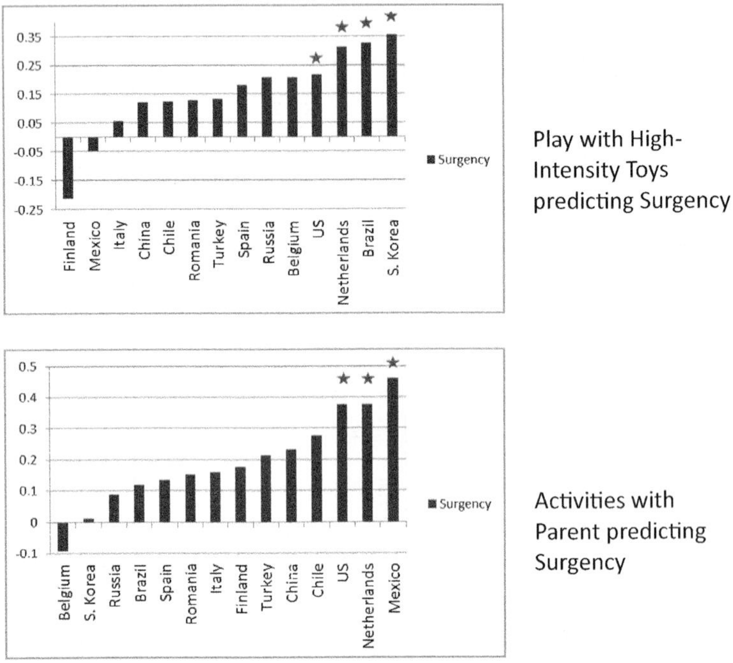


**FIGURE 13.2** Activities-Surgency correlations for JETTC countries

* indicates significant correlation

NEG and all behavior problems variables. Time on computers and other electronics was associated with high EXT.

No significant relations between daily activities and child temperament were noted in between-country analyses (Table 13.2). Marginal associations emerged, such that countries in which children scored higher on SUR had mothers who engaged their child in activities more, and countries in which children scored higher on EFF reported more low-intensity toy play and time on electronic devices. Countries reporting that their children's play was intended to be purposeful had higher toddler INT, and children showed higher total problems in cultures with more extensive TV exposure.

The average within-culture correlations are shown in Table 13.3. In the interest of brevity, we only describe relations that were significant in three or more countries. Regarding temperament, high SUR was associated with high levels of High-Intensity Toy Play and Engagement with Parent in multiple countries (Figure 13.2). EFF was consistently associated with more Low-Intensity Toy Play, Play with Purpose, and Engagement with Parent (Figure 13.3). Inconsistent findings were reported with respect to play being solely for entertainment, which was negatively correlated with EFF in Russia and Chile ($r_s$ = –0.35 and –0.31), and positively correlated with EFF in Brazil and Turkey ($r_s$ = 0.34 and 0.30). Findings for computer use were also inconsistent, demonstrating

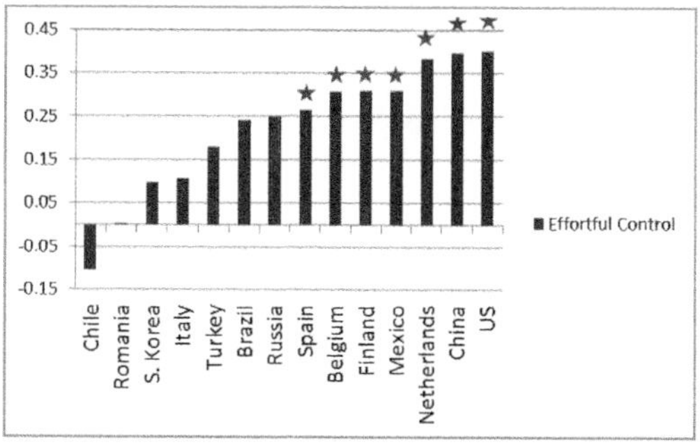


Play with Low-Intensity Toys predicting Effortful Control

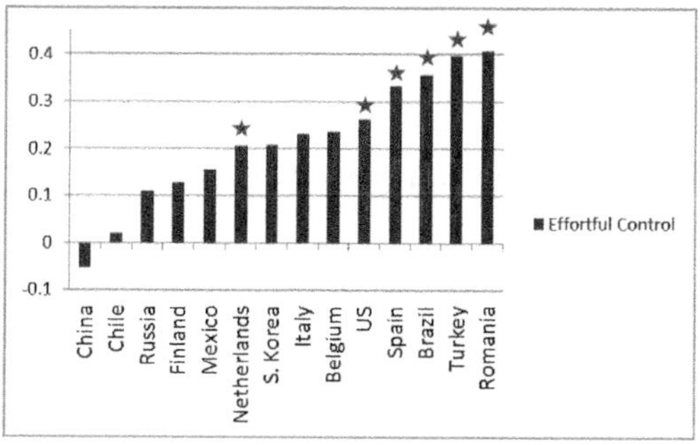


Play with Purpose predicting Effortful Control

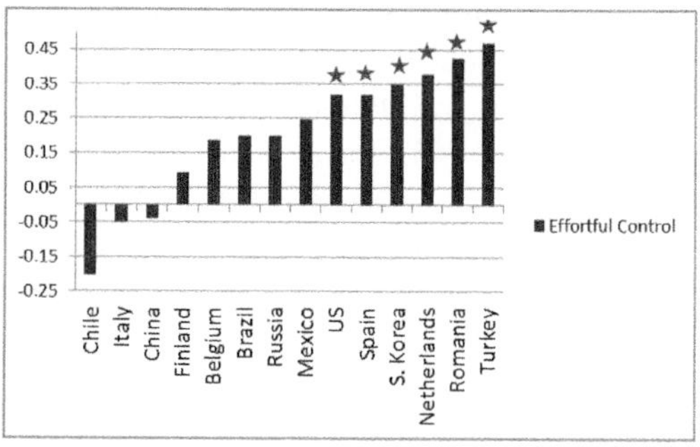


Engagement with Parent predicting Effortful Control

**FIGURE 13.3** Activities-Effortful Control correlations for JETTC countries

⋆ indicates significant correlation

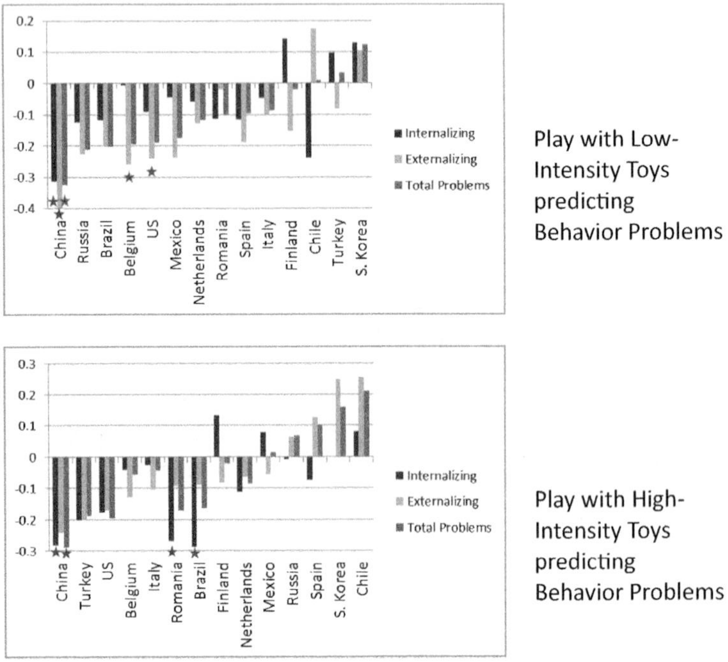


**FIGURE 13.4** Intensity play-behavior problem correlations for JETTC countries

* indicates significant correlation

a positive correlation with EFF in Mexico ($r$ = 0.27), and negative correlations in Chile and Finland ($r_s$ = –0.34 and –0.27).

Regarding behavior problems, findings that were consistent across several countries included Low-Intensity Toy Play predicting low EXT; High-Intensity Toy Play predicting low INT; TV use predicting INT and total behavior problems; and Play with Purpose predicting low total behavior problems (Figures 13.4 and 13.5). Inconsistency was observed for Activities with Parent, which was associated with high behavior problems in Chile ($r$ = 0.30), but with low behavior problems in Turkey and the Netherlands ($r_s$ = –0.31 and –0.23).

## Discussion

Analyses conducted for the entire sample revealed that correlations of play with temperamental reactivity were in line with our predictions, as High-Intensity Toy Play and Play for Entertainment were associated with higher SUR, whereas Play with Purpose was linked with higher levels of NEG. In addition, Play for Entertainment was also associated with higher levels of NEG, whereas child's Activities with Parent was related to higher SUR and lower NEG. Regarding self-regulation, all types of play (except Play for Entertainment) and Activities with Parent were related to higher EFF. This pattern of results suggests that parents across the JETTC cultures make use of play and other parent–child joint daily activities to support the development of self-regulation in their toddlers.

Between and within-country analyses were informative in their own right. Between-country correlational analyses revealed that countries reporting more frequent child Play with Purpose had children with higher INT. In addition, cultures with greater average duration of TV watching exhibited higher total child behavior problems. The within-country analyses revealed a consistent association between higher levels of Low-Intensity Toy Play with higher levels of EFF (US, China,

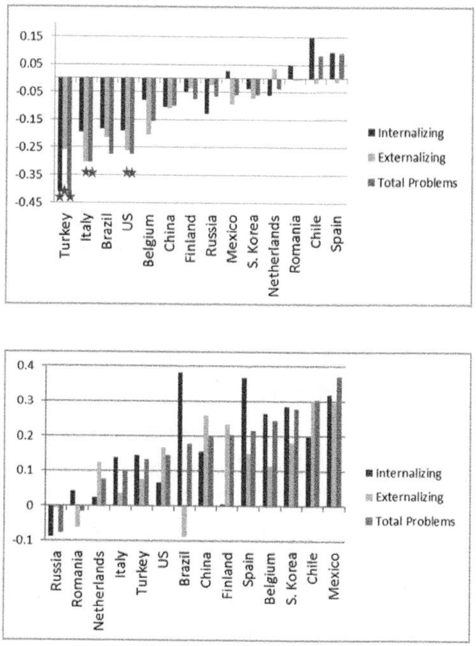


Play with Purpose predicting Behavior Problems

Television use predicting Behavior Problems

**FIGURE 13.5** Activities-behavior problem correlations for JETTC countries

* indicates significant correlation

the Netherlands, Mexico, Finland, Belgium, Spain, and Russia), indicating that the beneficial impact of low-intensity toy play was largely invariant across JETTC cultures. In addition, children high in EFF may enjoy quiet activities of low-intensity toy play that provide a good fit for their advanced attentional abilities.

Inconsistent findings were reported with respect to Play for Entertainment, which was negatively correlated with EFF in Russia and Chile and positively correlated with EFF in Brazil and Turkey. The nature of parent–child interactions during play for entertainment can be different in these countries, due to variability in corresponding socialization values and goals. For example, in more collectivistic cultures such as Chile (in our JETTC Chile scored highest on Collectivism, after China), caregivers tend to be more interested in social harmony and respect for rules, and less likely to encourage strong positive emotions, such as excitement, that typically emerge during play for entertainment elsewhere (Haight, Wang, Fung, Williams, & Mintz, 1999; O'Reilly & Bornstein, 1993). On the other hand, it might be that parents from more collectivistic cultures who perceive their children as lower in EFF, prefer to engage more in play for entertainment, in order to soothe these children, who may be perceived as lower in self-regulation. Positive associations observed between play for entertainment and EFF in Turkey and Brazil require additional research for a conclusive interpretation. In may be, for example, that parents who engage in more entertainment in play with their toddlers in Turkey are more autonomy-oriented, and possibly more actively involved in encouraging child self-expression (Haight, Parke, & Black, 1997).

High levels of Low-Intensity Toy Play, High-Intensity Toy Play, and Play with Purpose were associated with lower INT and EXT, confirming our hypotheses, as was engagement with parent. This pattern of results suggests that, for toddlers around the world, participation in age-appropriate play, along with parental engagement in joint activities, are protective factors for early emotional/behavioral problems. The centrality of play for healthy development has been frequently emphasized, along with its privileged status as an ideal context for parents' full engagement with their children (Ginsburg, 2007). Results for Activities with Parent were more variable, showing an association with high behavior problems in Chile. An increase in child adjustment problems might be explained by the collectivistic orientation of Chilean parents, who likely hold more authoritarian attitudes, emphasizing child obedience, in contrast to prevalent attitudes of Turkish and Dutch parents, likely fostering agency and autonomy in their children (Schaefer & Edgerton, 1985). More engagement might thus provide Chilean children with more instances of problematic (e.g., intrusive) interactions. This interpretation can be further supported by our data regarding Activities with Parent and EFF, as greater engagement with parent was associated with higher EFF for Turkish and Dutch children, but lower EFF for Chilean children, in contrast to Lamm et al. (2017), indicating the need for further studies.

Relations between TV viewing, INT and EXT, were consistent across between- and within-country analyses, and in line with our predictions. In particular, countries with greater TV exposure showed higher total problems (Brazil, China, Russia, Chile, Mexico, and Turkey), and individual children who watched TV more had higher INT, EXT, and total behavior problems, in Mexico, Chile, South Korea, Belgium, Spain, and Brazil. These results are consistent with previous findings (e.g., Tremblay et al., 2011; Verlinden et al., 2012); however, we did not assess media content (e.g., violent programs, non-educational programs), which should be examined in the future.

Exploratory analyses regarding the use of computer and other electronics produced inconsistent results. In considering EFF, associations were positive for Mexico, and negative in Chile and Finland. Research regarding the impact of screen media has lagged considerably behind its rate of adoption; however, Radesky, Schumacher and Zuckerman (2015) noted the use of screen media as a common behavior regulation tool: what the industry terms a "shut-up toy." Unfortunately, we did not obtain data on parental intentions regarding screen media use with toddlers, and these should be collected going forward.

## References


Ahnert, L., Teufl, L., Ruiz, N., Piskernik, B., Supper, B., Remiorz, S., . . . Nowacki, K. (2017). Father-child play during the preschool years and child internalizing behaviors: Between robustness and vulnerability. *Infant Mental Health Journal, 38*(6), 743–756.

Anderson, S., Qiu, W., & Wheeler, S. (2017). The quality of father rough-and-tumble play and toddlers' aggressive behavior in China. *Infant Mental Health Journal, 38*(6), 726–742.

Bornstein, M. H. (2007). On the significance of social relationships in the development of children's earliest symbolic play: An ecological perspective. In A. Gönçü & S. Gaskins (Eds.), *Play and development* (pp. 101–129). Mahwah, NJ: Lawrence Erlbaum Associates.

Brussoni, M., Gibbons, R., Gray, C., Ishikawa, T., Sandseter, H., Bienenstock, A., Tremblay, M. S. (2015). What is the relationship between risky outdoor play and health in children? A systematic review. *International Journal of Environmental Research and Public Health*, *12*(6), 6423–6454.

Ginsburg, K. (2007). The Importance of play in promoting healthy child development and maintaining strong parent–child bonds. *Pediatrics*, *119*(1), 182–191.

Haight, W. L., Parke, R. D., & Black, J. E. (1997). Mothers' and fathers' beliefs about and spontaneous participation in their toddlers' pretend play. *Merrill-Palmer Quarterly*, *43*(2), 271–290.

Haight, W. L., Wang, X., Fung, H. H., Williams, K., & Mintz, J. (1999). Universal, developmental, and variable aspects of young children's play: A cross-cultural comparison of pretending at home. *Child Development*, *70*(6), 1477–1488.

Harkness, S., Mavridis, C. J., Liu, J. J., & Super, C. M. (2015). Parental ethnotheories and the development of family relationships in early and middle childhood. In A. L. Jensen (Ed.), *The oxford handbook of human development and culture: An interdisciplinary perspective*. New York, NY: Oxford University Press.

Huber, B., Yeates, M., Meyer, D., Fleckhamme, L., & Kaufman, J. (2018). The effects of screen media content on young children's executive functioning. *Journal of Experimental Child Psychology*, *170*, 72–85.

Kostyrka-Allchorne, K., Cooper, N. R., & Simpson, A. (2017). The relationship between television exposure and children's cognition and behaviour: A systematic review. *Developmental Review*, *44*, 19–58.

Lamm, B., Keller, H., Teiser, J., Gudi, H., Yovsi, R. D., Freitag, C., . . . Lohaus, A. (2017). Waiting for the second treat: Developing culture-specific modes of self-regulation. *Child Development*, *89*(3), e261–e277.

Landry, S. H., Smith, K. E., Swank, P. R., & Miller-Loncar, C. L. (2000). Early maternal and child influences on children's later independent cognitive and social functioning. *Child Development*, *71*(2), 358–375.

Lillard, A. S. (2017). Why do the children (pretend) play? *Trends in Cognitive Sciences*, *21*, 826–834.

O'Reilly, A. W., & Bornstein, M. H. (1993). Caregiver-child interaction in play. In M. H. Bornstein & A. O'Reilly (Eds.), *New directions for child development: The role of play in the development of thought* (pp. 55–66). San Francisco, CA: Jossey-Bass.

Oh, S., & Lewis, C. (2008). Korean preschoolers' advanced inhibitory control and its relation to other executive skills and mental state understanding. *Child Development*, *79*(1), 80–99.

Özmert, E., Toyran, M., & Yurdakök, K. (2002). Behavioral correlates of television viewing in primary school children evaluated by the child behavior checklist. *Archives of Pediatrics & Adolescent Medicine*, *156*(9), 910–914.

Radesky, J. S., Schumacher, J., & Zuckerman, B. (2015). Mobile and interactive media use by young children: The good, the bad, and the unknown. *Pediatrics*, *135*(1), 1–3.

Sabbagh, M. A., Xu, F., Carlson, S. M., Moses, L. J., & Lee, K. (2006).The development of executive functioning and theory of mind. *Psychological Science, 17*(1), 74–81.

Schaefer, E. S., & Edgerton, M. (1985). Parent and child correlates of parental modernity. In I. E. Sigel (Ed.), *Parental belief systems: The psychological consequences for children* (pp. 287–318). New York, NY: Psychology Press.

Sharp, J. R., Maguire, J. L., Carsley, S., Abdullah, K., Chen, Y., Perrin, E. M., . . . On Behalf of TARGet Kids! Collaboration. (2018). Temperament is associated with outdoor free play in young children: A TARGet Kids! Study. *Academic Pediatrics, 18*(4), 445–451.

Spinrad, T. L., Eisenberg, N., Harris, E., Hanish, L., Fabes, R. A., Kupanoff, K., . . . Holmes, J. (2004). The relation of children's everyday nonsocial peer play behavior to their emotionality, regulation, and social functioning. *Developmental Psychology, 40*(1), 67–80.

St George, J., Fletcher, R., & Palazzi, K. (2017). Comparing fathers' physical and toy play and links to child behaviour: An exploratory study. *Infant and Child Development, 26,* e1958.

Thompson, A. L., Adair, L. S., & Bentley, M. E. (2013). Maternal characteristics and perception of temperament associated with infant TV exposure. *Pediatrics, 131*(2), e390–e397.

Tremblay, M. S., LeBlanc, A. G., Kho, M. E., Saunders, T. J., Larouche, R., & Colley, R. C. (2011). Systematic review of sedentary behaviour and health indicators in school-aged children and youth. *The International Journal of Behavioral Nutrition and Physical Activity, 8,* 98.

Verlinden, M., Tiemeier, H., Hudziak, J. J., Jaddoe, V. W. V., Raat, H., Guxens, M., . . . Jansen, P. W. (2012). Television viewing and externalizing problems in preschool children: The Generation R Study. *Archives of Pediatrics and Adolescent Medicine, 166*(10), 919–925.

# 14

# SLEEP, TEMPERAMENT, AND BEHAVIOR PROBLEMS

*Amanda Prokasky, Felipe Lecannelier, Noelia Sánchez-Pérez, and Maria A. Gartstein*

Relationships between sleep, temperament, and behavior problems have been established. For example, in a study of Canadian toddlers, Reid, Hong, and Wade (2009) found links between sleep problems, difficult temperament, characterized by high negative affectivity and low adaptability, and behavior problems. Similarly, Bates, Viken, Alexander, Beyers, and Stockton (2002) reported that preschool children experiencing more sleep disruptions also had more teacher-reported behavior and

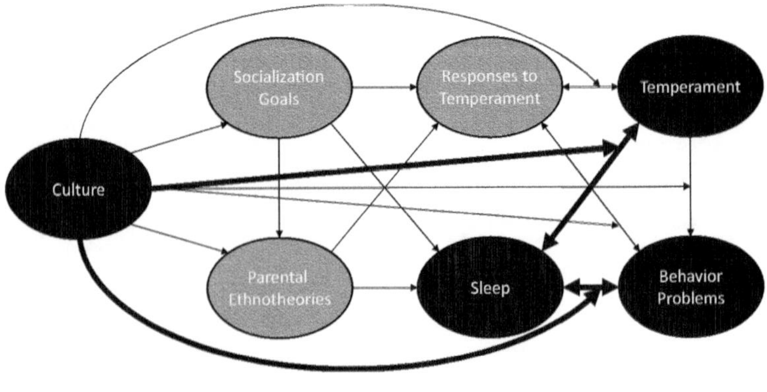


**FIGURE 14.1** Sleep and child outcomes in the JETTC Conceptual Model

adjustment problems. Molfese et al. (2015) found that United States (US) children higher in activity level and lower in soothability had less actigraph-recorded nighttime sleep, whereas toddlers higher in fear had more variable sleep onset times. Much of this work was completed in western cultures, particularly the US, and has primarily focused on sleep problems such as night wakings or bedtime resistance. Fewer studies examined how temperament relates to basic sleep indicators, such as bedtime, wake time, amount of nighttime sleep, or naps; and even fewer still examined these relations from a cross-cultural perspective. The current chapter addresses this shortcoming in the developmental literature, exploring cultural patterns surrounding child sleep as they are related to temperament and behaviour problems (see Figure 14.1).

Parents use a variety of strategies to help their children fall asleep at night, but research addressing whether these strategies relate to children's temperament or behavior problems has been limited. In one study of US preschoolers, Wilson et al. (2015) found that consistent bedtime routines and avoiding arousing activities at bedtime were associated with less bedtime resistance in preschool children with more difficult temperament, and unrelated to bedtime resistance in children who were less difficult. However, Johnson and McMahon (2008) found no relations between temperament, parental interactions at bedtime, or children's sleep in a sample of Australian preschoolers.

The developmental niche framework conceptualized organization of child sleep as highly structured by culture and relatively resistant to change (Harkness & Super, 2002). For instance, in their cross-cultural study of the daily lives of US and Dutch children, US parents viewed sleep as almost entirely determined by age and individual child characteristics, including temperament, whereas Dutch parents viewed children's sleep as the result of instituting a regular sleep schedule (Harkness & Super, 2006). These differing parental ethnotheories concerning children's sleep suggest that links with temperament and behavior problems may be moderate or strong in some cultures, but not others. Likewise, cross-cultural variability in temperament, behavior problems, and parental activities around bedtime (see Chapters 3, 4, and 9; this volume), suggest that links between these variables likely differ cross-culturally. Therefore, this chapter aims to elucidate whether between-country differences in child temperament and behavior problems are related to cultural differences in sleep and sleep-related parenting behaviors; and whether links between child behavior and sleep measures are consistent across the 14 JETTC countries.

## Results

Initial correlations calculated using the entire sample of individual families, which conflate within-country and between-country differences, are shown in Tables 14.1 and 14.2. For parental sleep-promoting behaviors, Active Techniques (e.g., walking, car ride, and special activity) were linked to high levels of all temperament traits and behavior problems scores; Gentle Techniques (e.g., talking, cuddling) were associated with high Surgency (SUR) and Effortful Control (EFF), and low Negative Affectivity (NEG), Internalizing (INT), and total problems. Staying with

**TABLE 14.1** Correlations between temperament/behavior problems and parental behaviors regarding child sleep for the entire sample

| | *Parenting behaviors regarding child sleep* | | | |
|---|---|---|---|---|
| | *Active Techniques* | *Gentle Techniques* | *Stay with Child* | *Cry it Out* |
| Negative Affectivity | 0.18** | –0.08* | 0.19** | 0.08* |
| Surgency | 0.08* | 0.12** | 0.02 | –0.05 |
| Effortful Control | 0.07* | 0.20** | 0.10** | –0.03 |
| Internalizing | 0.11** | –0.12** | 0.12** | 0.12** |
| Externalizing | 0.08* | –0.04 | 0.05 | 0.09** |
| Total problems | 0.11** | –0.09** | 0.13** | 0.11** |

Note: $n_s$ = 841 for temperament, 836 for behavior problems. $^{**}p < 0.10$, $^{*}p < 0.05$

**TABLE 14.2** Correlations between temperament/behavior problems and children's sleeping patterns for the entire sample

| | *Children's sleeping patterns* | | | |
|---|---|---|---|---|
| | *Bed Time* | *Waking Time* | *Nighttime Sleep* | *Naps* |
| Negative Affectivity | 0.28** | 0.20** | –0.13** | 0.07 |
| Surgency | –0.03 | –0.02 | 0.03 | –0.01 |
| Effortful Control | –0.01 | –0.03 | –0.02 | –0.06 |
| Internalizing | 0.26** | 0.23** | –0.12** | –0.00 |
| Externalizing | 0.11** | 0.11** | –0.03 | –0.03 |
| Total problems | 0.24** | 0.21** | –0.10** | –0.02 |

Note: $n_s$ range from 820 to 841. $^{**}p < 0.10$

Child was linked to high NEG, EFF, INT, and total problems; letting the child Cry it Out was linked to high NEG and all behavior problems scores; and waking the child in the morning was associated with high NEG. With respect to child sleep measures, later bedtimes, later waking times, and less nighttime sleep were all associated with greater NEG, higher INT, and total problems. Late bed and waking times were also associated with high Externalizing problems (EXT).

Between-country correlations indicate that countries in which parents report using high levels of Gentle Techniques also have children rated high in SUR, low in NEG, and low INT (see Table 14.3). With respect

**TABLE 14.3** Between-country correlations between countries' marginal means of temperament/behavior problems and parental behaviors regarding child sleep

| | *Parenting behaviors regarding child sleep* | | | |
|---|---|---|---|---|
| | *Active Techniques* | *Gentle Techniques* | *Stay with Child* | *Cry it Out* |
| Negative Affectivity | 0.28 | –0.73** | 0.42 | 0.34 |
| Surgency | 0.15 | 0.63* | –0.18 | –0.47# |
| Effortful Control | 0.48# | 0.23 | 0.31 | 0.24 |
| Internalizing | 0.26 | –0.68** | 0.45 | 0.00 |
| Externalizing | 0.26 | –0.01 | 0.09 | –0.32 |
| Total problems | 0.34 | –0.44 | 0.40 | –0.16 |

Note: $N = 14$, $^{**}p < 0.10$, $^{*}p < 0.05$, $^{\#}p < 0.10$

**TABLE 14.4** Between-country correlations between countries' marginal means of temperament/behavior problems and children's sleeping patterns

| | *Children's sleeping patterns* | | | |
|---|---|---|---|---|
| | *Bed Time* | *Waking Time* | *Nighttime Sleep* | *Naps* |
| Negative Affectivity | 0.55* | 0.54* | –0.34 | 0.55* |
| Surgency | –0.36 | –0.40 | 0.30 | –0.46 |
| Effortful Control | –0.21 | –0.02 | –0.15 | 0.12 |
| Internalizing | 0.67** | 0.72** | –0.49# | 0.37 |
| Externalizing | 0.18 | 0.10 | 0.02 | –0.23 |
| Total problems | 0.53# | 0.54* | –0.34 | 0.09 |

Note: $n_s$ range from 820 to 841. $^{**}p < 0.10$, $^{*}p < 0.05$, $^{\#}p < 0.10$

to children's sleep measures, countries with later bedtimes and waking times also have children with higher NEG, INT, and for waking times, higher total problems (see Table 14.4). In addition, frequent napping was linked to NEG.

In the interest of brevity, we only describe relations that were significant in three or more countries for average within-culture correlations (Tables 14.5 and 14.6). With respect to temperament and parenting behaviors, patterns that were consistent across several countries (Figure 14.2) included significant positive correlations between Active Soothing and NEG;

**TABLE 14.5** Average within-country correlations between temperament/behavior problems and parental behaviors regarding child sleep

| | *Parenting behaviors regarding child sleep* | | | |
|---|---|---|---|---|
| | *Active Techniques* | *Gentle Techniques* | *Stay with Child* | *Cry it Out* |
| Negative Affectivity | $0.16^{6}$ | $0.07^{3}$ | $0.10^{4}$ | $0.07^{1}$ |
| Surgency | $0.05^{1}$ | $0.06^{1}$ | $0.04^{0}$ | $-0.02^{0}$ |
| Effortful Control | $0.03^{2}$ | $0.21^{6}$ | $0.07^{3}$ | $-0.05^{2}$ |
| Internalizing | $0.07^{2}$ | $-0.03^{2}$ | $0.06^{1}$ | $0.12^{3}$ |
| Externalizing | $0.04^{2}$ | $-0.04^{1}$ | $0.03^{0}$ | $0.12^{3}$ |
| Total problems | $0.06^{1}$ | $-0.04^{0}$ | $0.08^{1}$ | $0.13^{3}$ |

Note: Superscripts indicate the number of countries (out of 14) for which the correlation was significant to $p < 0.05$

**TABLE 14.6** Average within-country correlations between temperament/behavior problems and children's sleeping patterns

| | *Children's sleeping patterns* | | | |
|---|---|---|---|---|
| | *Bed time* | *Waking Time* | *Nighttime Sleep* | *Naps* |
| Negative Affectivity | $0.09^{1}$ | $0.08^{1}$ | $-0.02^{2}$ | $0.00^{1}$ |
| Surgency | $0.05^{0}$ | $0.01^{1}$ | $-0.04^{1}$ | $0.02^{0}$ |
| Effortful Control | $-0.01^{0}$ | $-0.01^{2}$ | $0.01^{1}$ | $-0.05^{2}$ |
| Internalizing | $0.13^{3}$ | $0.11^{1}$ | $-0.02^{0}$ | $-0.02^{2}$ |
| Externalizing | $0.11^{3}$ | $0.08^{1}$ | $-0.05^{1}$ | $-0.03^{1}$ |
| Total problems | $0.15^{4}$ | $0.11^{2}$ | $-0.05^{0}$ | $-0.03^{2}$ |

Note: Superscripts indicate the number of countries (out of 14) for which the correlation was significant to $p < 0.05$

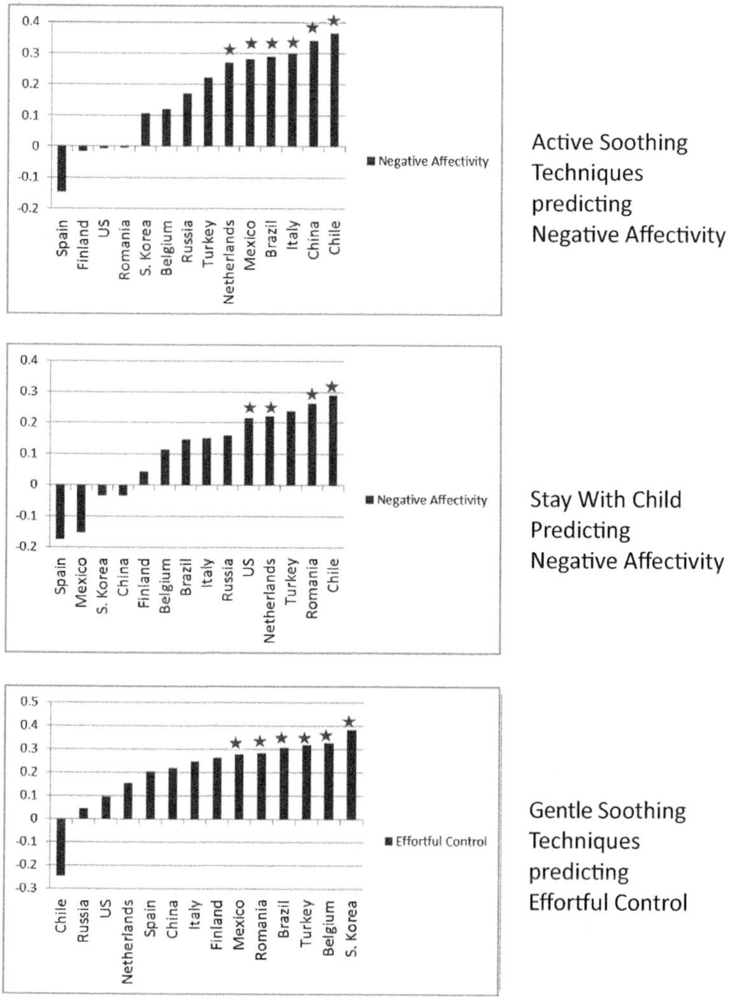


**FIGURE 14.2** Sleep strategies–temperament correlations for JETTC countries

⋆ indicates significant correlation

Staying with Child and NEG; and Gentle Techniques and EFF. Contradictory patterns were apparent for the association between Gentle Techniques and NEG, which were positive in Mexico and Chile ($r_s$ = 0.34 and 0.38), but negative in Spain ($r$ = –0.45); and for Staying with Child and EFF, for which correlations were positive in Belgium and Finland ($r_s$ = 0.28 and 0.28), but negative in Turkey ($r$ = –0.36).

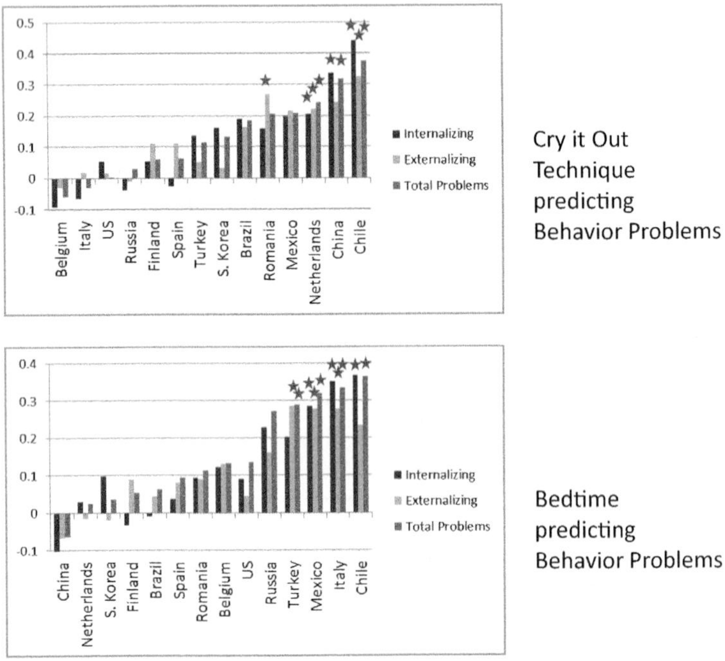


**FIGURE 14.3** Sleep strategies–behavior problem correlations for JETTC countries

* indicates significant correlation

No consistent patterns were observed between children's sleeping patterns and temperament.

Regarding behavior problems and parental sleep-promotion, the most consistent pattern was for the use of Crying it Out to be associated with INT, EXT and/or total problems (Figure 14.3). Later bedtimes were associated with INT, EXT, and/or total problems in several countries.

## Discussion

At the between-country level, countries in which parents frequently use passive soothing techniques, such as talking or cuddling with their child at bedtime, reported higher levels of SUR, and lower levels of NEG and INT in their children. Parental behaviors around bedtime serve to establish a sleep-promoting routine, with caregivers also determining an appropriate bedtime, consistent with their own daily/nighttime schedule. However, culture largely defines parental practices regarding sleep, how parents view and interpret connections between sleep, and children's behavior (Owens, 2004), and relations between these constructs may not apply universally in all cultures. For example, US parents are generally concerned with their child's sleep, expanding time and effort in attempts to establish consistent sleeping patterns for their infants (Harkness & Super, 1994). In contrast, Italian parents have less concern for their children's sleep and more for their children's eating habits, instead focusing attention on child nutrition (New, 1988). Not surprisingly, US parents are more likely to view children with inconsistent sleeping habits as temperamentally difficult, while Italian parents are not (Harkness & Super, 1994; New, 1988). Cultures that identify sleep as a correlate of children's health, behavior, and development are more likely to invest parental time and resources (i.e., parental practices at bedtime) into ensuring their adequate and consistent sleep.

Sleep patterns, such as bedtime and wake time, are also influenced by culture (Owens, 2004), and in the present study, the between-country correlations illustrate that in countries with later bedtimes and wake times, children were rated higher in NEG and INT, and in the case of later wake times, higher total problems. In addition, in countries with more napping, children were rated as higher in NEG. These relations between sleep patterns and temperament/behavior problems likely reflect how cultures differ in their expectations and interpretation of sleep behaviors in children (Jenni & O'Connor, 2005). For example, southern European countries such as Italy, Spain, and Greece typically have flexible and unstructured bedtimes (Jenni & O'Connor, 2005) and are therefore less likely to view later bedtimes as problematic or related to maladaptive temperament traits such has higher NEG or increased behavior problems.

At the within-country level, relations between NEG and parental behaviors at bedtime were consistent with previous research noting relations between "difficult" temperament (typically characterized by high levels of NEG and lower EFF) and sleep problems, including resistance to bedtime (e.g., Goodnight et al., 2007). In addition, the relations between gentle techniques and EFF suggest that these activities may help children learn to self-soothe, thus enhancing the development of EFF. Alternatively, it could be that children higher in EFF, which includes dimensions like attention, cuddliness, and low-intensity pleasure, prefer gentle techniques to more active ones. However, relations between temperament and parental sleep-promoting behaviors were not found in every country, implying culture-specific mechanisms (Harkness & Super, 2006; Jenni & O'Connor, 2005). Concerning behavior problems, the "cry it out" technique was related to INT, EXT, and total behavior problems in three countries. The lack of more universal associations within countries could be due to a lack of variability, as this technique was a rare practice across all countries (see Chapter 8; this volume).

Discernable patterns between sleep measures and temperament did not emerge at the within-country level. However, behavior problems were related to later bedtimes in several countries. The more consistent relations between behavior problems and sleep measures may be due to the fact that inadequate sleep exacerbates existing behavior problems, making these more salient to parents than temperamental characteristics (Dahl, 1996; Gregory & O'Connor, 2002). Together these results are largely consistent with research linking child temperament, behavior problems, as well as parental behaviors at bedtime to sleep (e.g., Goodnight et al., 2007; Sadeh, Lavie, & Scher, 1994).

## References


Bates, J. E., Viken, R., Alexander, D., Beyers, J., & Stockton, L. (2002). Sleep and adjustment in preschool children: Sleep diary reports by mothers relate to behavior reports by teachers. *Child Development*, 7, 62–74.

Dahl, R. E. (1996). The regulation of sleep and arousal: Development and psychopathology. *Development and Psychopathology*, *8*(3), 3–27.

Goodnight, J. A., Bates, J. E., Staples, A. D., Pettit, G. S., & Dodge, K. A. (2007). Temperamental resistance to control increases the association between sleep problems and externalizing behavior development. *Journal of Family Psychology*, *21*(1), 39.

Gregory, A. M., & O'Connor, T. G. (2002). Sleep problems in childhood: A longitudinal study of developmental change and association with behavioral problems. *Journal of the American Academy of Child & Adolescent Psychiatry*, *41*, 964–971.

Harkness, S., & Super, C. M. (2002). Culture and parenting. *Handbook of Parenting*, *2*, 253–280.

Harkness, S., & Super, C. M. (2006). Themes and variations: Parental ethnotheories in Western cultures. In K. H. Rubin & O. B. Chung (Eds.), *Parenting beliefs, behaviors, and parent-child relations: A cross-cultural perspective* (pp. 61–80). New York, NY: Psychology Press.

Jenni, O. G., & O'Connor, B. B. (2005). Children's sleep: An interplay between culture and biology. *Pediatrics*, *115*(Suppl. 1), 204–216.

Johnson, N., & McMahon, C. (2008). Preschoolers' sleep behaviour: Associations with parental hardiness, sleep-related cognitions and bedtime interactions. *Journal of Child Psychology and Psychiatry*, *49*(7), 765–773.

Molfese, V. J., Rudasill, K. M., Prokasky, A., Champagne, C., Holmes, M., Molfese, D., & Bates, J. E. (2015). Relations between toddler sleep characteristics, sleep problems, and temperament. *Developmental Neuropsychology, 40*(3), 138–154.

New, R. S. (1988). Parental goals and Italian infant care. *New Directions in Child Development, 40*, 51–63.

Owens, J. A. (2004). Sleep in children: Cross-cultural perspectives. *Sleep and Biological Rhythms, 2*, 165–173.

Reid, G. J., Hong, R. Y., & Wade, T. J. (2009). The relation between common sleep problems and emotional and behavioral problems among 2- and 3-year-olds in the context of known risk factors for psychopathology. *Journal of Sleep Research, 18*(1), 49–59.

Sadeh, A., Lavie, P., & Scher, A. (1994). Sleep and temperament: Maternal perceptions of temperament of sleep-disturbed toddlers. *Early Education and Development, 5*(4), 311–322.

Wilson, K. E., Lumeng, J. C., Kaciroti, N., Chen, S. Y. P., LeBourgeois, M. K., Chervin, R. D., & Miller, A. L. (2015). Sleep hygiene practices and bedtime resistance in low-income preschoolers: Does temperament matter? *Behavioral Sleep Medicine, 13*(5), 412–423.

# 15

# DISCIPLINE, TEMPERAMENT, AND BEHAVIOR PROBLEMS

*Oana Benga, Georgiana Susa-Erdogan, Blanca Huitron, Elena Kozlova, and Emine Ahmetoglu*

Toddlerhood represents a challenging time for parent-child relationships, requiring a recalibration of parenting strategies to the child's growing need for independence, and also to significant parental role changes (e.g., prevention of injuries, teaching of social values, and culturally-acceptable behaviors). Consequently, parenting strategies are reshaped, with an increasing reliance on discipline (Klimes-Dougan & Kopp, 1999; Laible & Thompson, 2002). To properly meet the new demands of autonomy

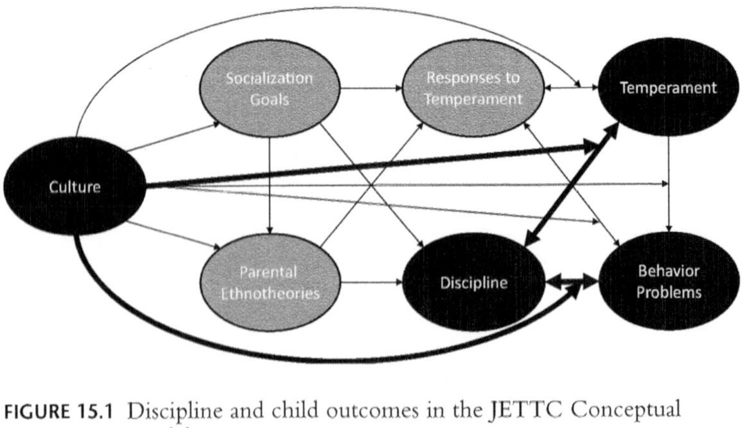


**FIGURE 15.1** Discipline and child outcomes in the JETTC Conceptual Model

seeking, as well as those of building self-regulation, parents of toddlers need to provide support, structure, and guidance (Pope-Edwards & Liu, 2002; Rinaldi & Howe, 2012), and this parental task is generally thought to be universal. The present chapter explores the limits of this assumption from a cross-cultural perspective (see Figure 15.1), given that parenting beliefs and strategies are acknowledged to be significantly influenced by culture (Bornstein, 2012).

Parental disciplinary strategies such as higher control and power-assertive disciplinary strategies have been linked to temperament (Braungart-Rieker, Garwood, & Stifter, 1997; Coplan & Weeks, 2009), child Negative Affectivity (NEG) in particular. These findings from western samples were replicated in Chinese dyads, as child NEG was associated with maternal (but not paternal) psychological and physical aggression (Xing, Zhang, Shao, & Wang, 2017). Power assertive strategies, in particular harsh or negative punishments, were also associated with increases in parameters related to Surgency (SUR; e.g., impulsivity), in children from the United States (US) and China (Rubin, Burgess, Dwyer, & Hastings, 2003; Xu, Zhang, & Farver, 2009). In contrast, clear, consistent discipline (Lengua, Wolchik, Sandler, & West, 2000) and high behavioral control (Bates, Pettit, Dodge, & Ridge, 1998; Xu et al., 2009) were associated with reduced impulsivity. Power-assertive discipline techniques, as well as low sensitivity, were associated with low levels of Effortful Control (EFF; Gartstein & Fagot, 2003; Kochanska, Murray, & Harlan, 2000; Piotrowski, Lapierre, & Linebarger, 2013), whereas inductive discipline techniques, like positive redirection and reasoning, were associated with higher EFF (Cipriano & Stifter, 2010; Karreman, van Tuijl, van Aken, & Deković, 2008).

Discipline strategies have been associated with child emotional and behavior adjustment across development and cultures. Child internalizing (INT) and externalizing behaviors (EXT) were predicted by reliance on corporal punishment and psychological control, low levels of warmth and high parental rejection (Lansford et al., 2005; McLeod et al., 2007; Mulvaney & Mebert, 2007). Gershoff et al. (2010) found maternal use of corporal punishment and expressing disappointment to be associated with both increased child aggression and anxiety; yelling or scolding linked to aggression; and time out and shaming specifically related to anxiety, in an international sample from six countries (including two JETTC countries—China and Italy). Wang and Liu (2018) also demonstrated that parental harsh discipline predicted child EXT, with parent-driven effects becoming stronger over time in China. Psychological control was related to INT and EXT in the US, and EXT in Russia, but unrelated to behavior problems in China (Olsen et al., 2002).

Based on the existing literature, we hypothesized that power-assertive discipline would be related to higher NEG, poorer EFF, and higher behavior problems across JETTC cultures; however, we expected these associations to be stronger for toddlers from cultures in East Asia, Latin America, and eastern Europe, that are high in Collectivism, Power Distance, Long-Term Orientation and Restraint, and where power-assertive strategies are more frequently used. In contrast, we expected inductive discipline strategies to be related to greater EFF, lower levels of reactivity and reduced behavior problems. We anticipated these associations to be more prominent for toddlers from more individualist cultures (North America and western Europe), where parents use such strategies more frequently to provide rules and reasoning that can be further internalized and used to support self-control.

## Results

Initial correlations calculated using the entire sample of individual families, which conflate within-country and between-country differences, are shown in Table 15.1. Regarding inductive strategies, talking the problem over with the child was associated with high EFF, low EXT, and total problems. Asking the child to repair the damage was associated with high SUR, high EFF, and high EXT, and asking the child to think about their misbehavior was associated with high NEG, EFF, INT, EXT, and total problems. Regarding power assertion, all strategies were associated with high NEG, EXT, and total problems. Shouting and swearing, giving the child a time out, were linked to high SUR; shouting and swearing, and hitting, to low EFF; and shouting, hitting, and taking away privileges to INT.

Between-country correlations (Table 15.2) indicated that countries in which parents report using high levels of hitting have children rated as high in NEG. Countries in which parents ask the child to think about their misbehavior report high levels of INT and total problems in their children.

Only average within-culture correlations significant in three or more countries are presented (Table 15.3). The most consistent and extensive findings were for shouting and swearing at children, which was associated with high NEG, high SUR, low EFF, and high levels of all behavior problems in multiple countries (Figures 15.2 and 15.3). Regarding other power-assertive strategies, in several countries, hitting children was

**TABLE 15.1** Correlations between temperament/behavior problems and discipline techniques for the entire sample

| | *Inductive strategies* | | *Power assertive strategies* | | | | |
|---|---|---|---|---|---|---|---|
| | *Talk* | *Repair* | *Think* | *Shout* | *Hit* | *Time Out* | *Take Away* |
| Negative Affectivity | –0.06 | 0.00 | 0.16** | 0.25** | 0.24** | 0.08* | 0.20** |
| Surgency | 0.06# | 0.15** | 0.05 | 0.14** | 0.07# | 0.10** | 0.07# |
| Effortful Control | 0.29** | 0.18** | 0.14** | –0.22** | –0.16** | –0.01 | –0.01 |
| Internalizing | –0.06# | 0.04 | 0.12** | 0.28** | 0.23** | 0.03 | 0.11** |
| Externalizing | –0.12** | 0.08* | 0.07* | 0.34** | 0.25** | 0.13** | 0.15** |
| Total problems | –0.10** | 0.07# | 0.09* | 0.36** | 0.27** | 0.08* | 0.14** |

Note: Talk = talk the problem over, Repair = ask child to repair the damage, Think = tell child to think about misbehavior, Shout = shout or swear, Hit = hit or spank, Time Out = separate child from others, Take Away = withdraw privileges. $n_s$ = 841 for temperament, 836 for behavior problems. $^{**}p < 0.01$, $^{*}p < 0.05$, $^{\#}p < 0.10$

**TABLE 15.2** Between-country correlations between countries' marginal means of temperament/behavior problems and discipline techniques

| | *Inductive strategies* | | *Power assertive strategies* | | | | |
|---|---|---|---|---|---|---|---|
| | *Talk* | *Repair* | *Think* | *Shout* | *Hit* | *Time Out* | *Take Away* |
| Negative Affectivity | –0.19 | –0.28 | $0.47^{\#}$ | 0.21 | $0.54^{*}$ | –0.15 | 0.35 |
| Surgency | 0.14 | $0.48^{\#}$ | –0.17 | 0.00 | –0.44 | 0.05 | –0.01 |
| Effortful Control | 0.45 | 0.40 | –0.04 | –0.34 | 0.18 | 0.22 | 0.27 |
| Internalizing | –0.10 | –0.16 | $0.72^{**}$ | 0.38 | $0.49^{\#}$ | 0.31 | 0.38 |
| Externalizing | –0.04 | 0.44 | 0.37 | 0.26 | 0.06 | –0.04 | 0.20 |
| Total problems | –0.09 | 0.13 | $0.65^{*}$ | 0.39 | 0.35 | –0.25 | 0.24 |

Note: $N = 14$, $^{**}p < 0.10$, $^{*}p < 0.05$, $^{\#}p < 0.10$

**TABLE 15.3** Average within-country correlations between temperament/behavior problems and discipline techniques

| | *Inductive strategies* | | *Power assertive strategies* | | | | |
|---|---|---|---|---|---|---|---|
| | *Talk* | *Repair* | *Think* | *Shout* | *Hit* | *Time Out* | *Take Away* |
| Negative Affectivity | $-0.05^{1}$ | $0.01^{0}$ | $0.08^{2}$ | $0.22^{5}$ | $0.15^{1}$ | $0.13^{3}$ | $0.18^{3}$ |
| Surgency | $0.05^{0}$ | $0.11^{1}$ | $0.07^{2}$ | $0.15^{3}$ | $0.12^{1}$ | $0.11^{1}$ | $0.06^{2}$ |
| Effortful Control | $0.26^{6}$ | $0.15^{3}$ | $0.15^{3}$ | $-0.22^{4}$ | $-0.20^{4}$ | $-0.04^{2}$ | $-0.02^{3}$ |
| Internalizing | $-0.06^{2}$ | $0.05^{1}$ | $0.05^{4}$ | $0.24^{8}$ | $0.14^{4}$ | $0.09^{1}$ | $0.08^{2}$ |
| Externalizing | $-0.11^{3}$ | $0.05^{1}$ | $0.04^{4}$ | $0.35^{11}$ | $0.27^{7}$ | $0.18^{5}$ | $0.13^{2}$ |
| Total problems | $-0.10^{3}$ | $0.05^{1}$ | $0.03^{3}$ | $0.34^{10}$ | $0.23^{7}$ | $0.14^{3}$ | $0.12^{2}$ |

Note: Superscripts indicate the number of countries (out of 14) for which the correlation was significant to $p < 0.05$

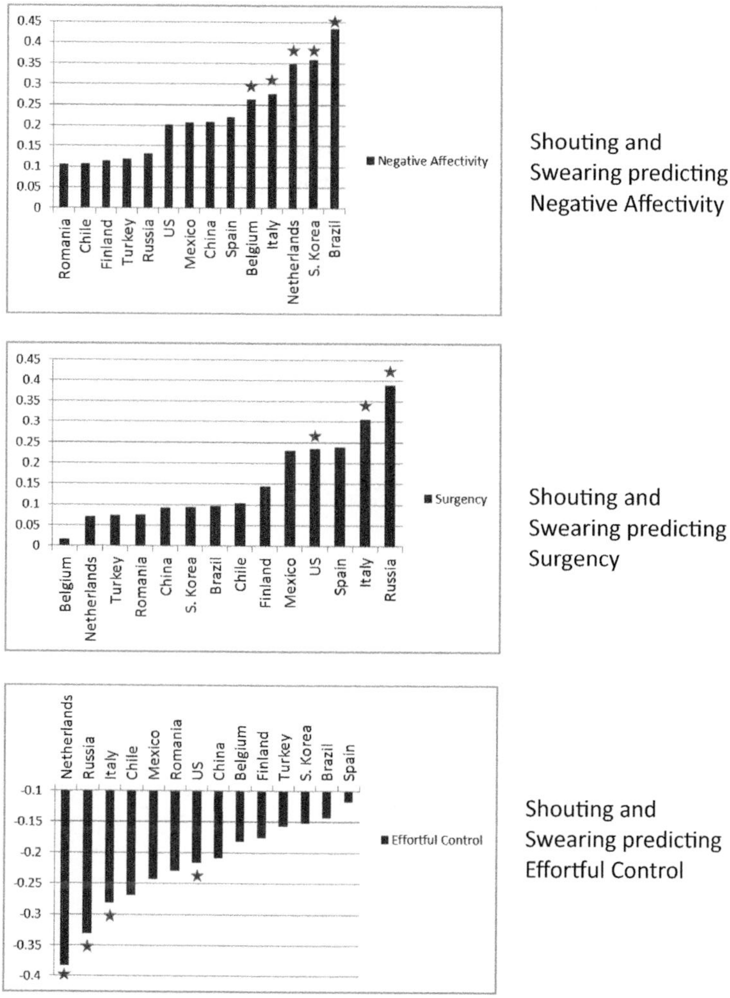


**FIGURE 15.2** Shouting–temperament correlations for JETTC countries

★ indicates significant correlation

associated with low EFF and all behavior problems; time outs were linked to high NEG, EXT, and total problems; and taking privileges was associated with NEG (Figures 15.3 and 15.4). Inconsistent relations were obtained for taking away privileges, which was significantly associated with high EFF in Finland ($r$ = 0.28), but low EFF in the Netherlands and China ($r_s$ = –0.33 and –0.32).

With respect to inductive strategies, all parental variables were tied to high EFF in several countries (Figure 15.5). Talking about the issue was associated with low EXT and/or total behavior problems in several countries (Figure 15.6). Inconsistent findings were obtained for asking the child to think about the misbehavior, which was associated with high levels of behavior problems in several countries, but low problems in one other.

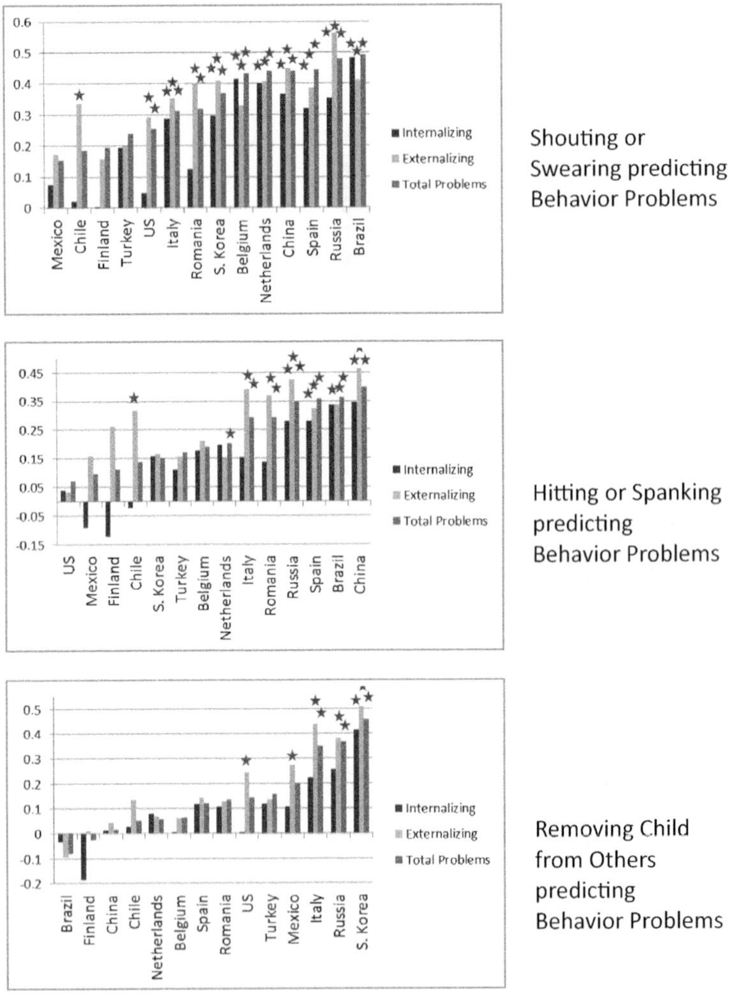


**FIGURE 15.3** Power assertion–behavior problem correlations for JETTC countries

★ indicates significant correlation

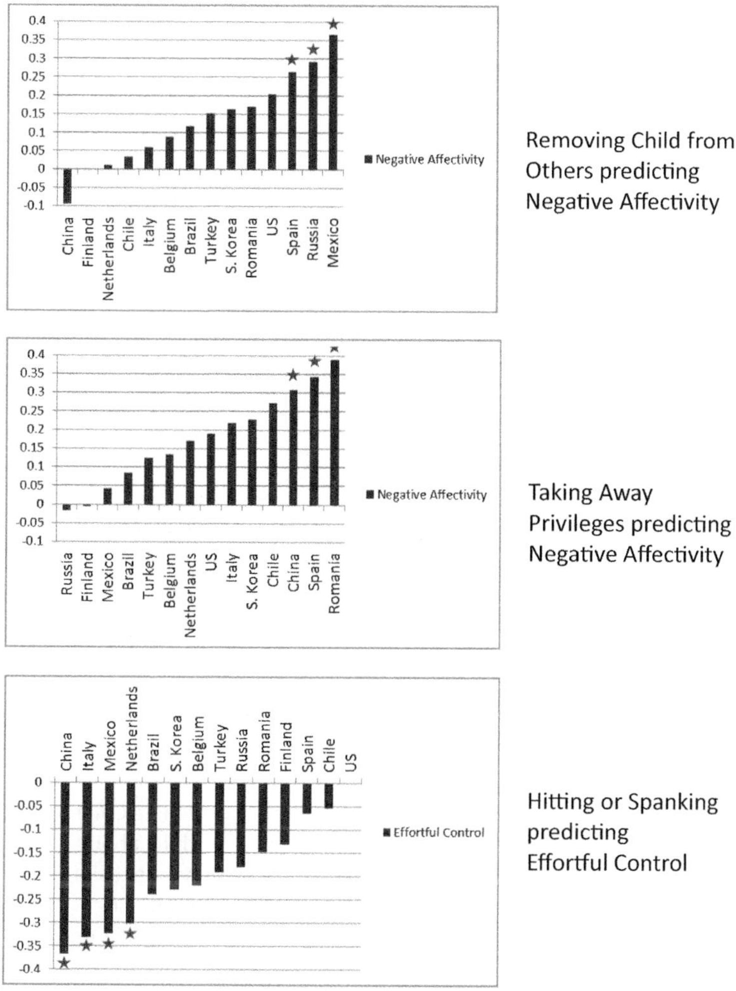


**FIGURE 15.4** Non-shouting power assertion–temperament correlations for JETTC countries

⋆ indicates significant correlation

## Discussion

Analyses at the level of the entire sample partly confirmed our general predictions: power-assertive discipline strategies were all related to high NEG, EXT, and total problems; highly aggressive strategies (shouting/swearing and hitting) were also associated with low EFF and INT;

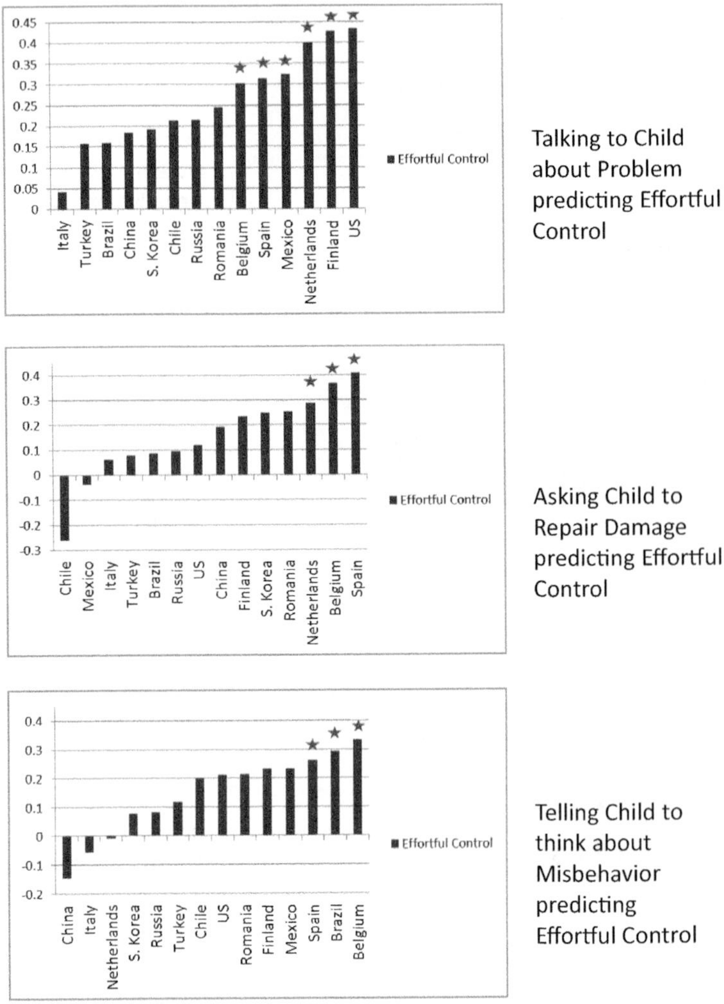


**FIGURE 15.5** Inductive parenting–Effortful Control correlations for JETTC countries

⋆ indicates significant correlation

whereas verbal aggression and time out were linked to SUR. Inductive strategies were all related to high EFF; however, reduced reactivity and behavior problems were evident only for talking the problem over. On the contrary, telling the child to think about misbehavior was associated with high NEG, INT, and total behavior problems.

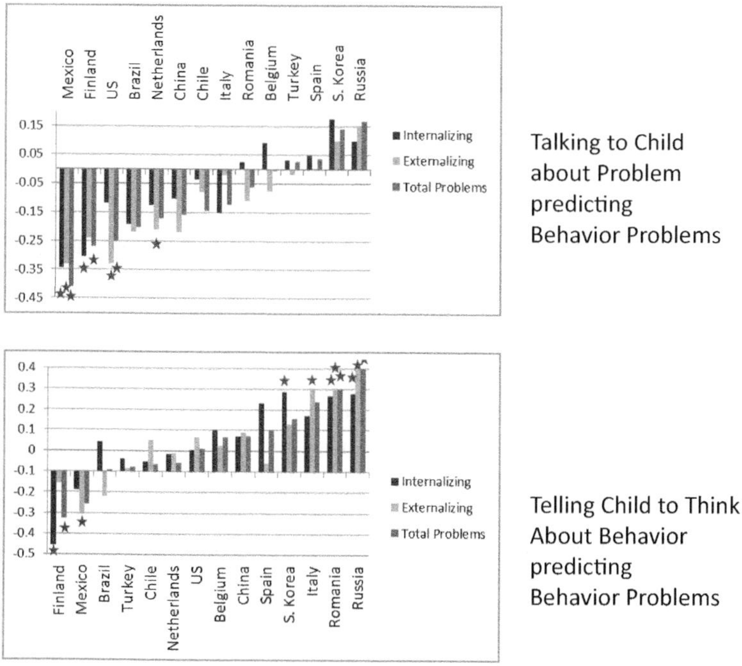


**FIGURE 15.6** Inductive parenting–behavior problem correlations for JETTC countries

* indicates significant correlation

Analyses produced evidence of cultural specificity, as certain relations between parental disciplinary strategies and child outcomes were consistent across different cultures, but not others. Between-country correlations indicated that high levels of hitting were reported in countries where children were perceived as high in NEG (China, South Korea, Brazil), yet within-country analyses did not confirm this relationship. Instead, children who were spanked were perceived as lower in EFF (China, Italy, Mexico, Netherlands) and as displaying higher levels of problems. Hitting or spanking predicted INT (China, Brazil, Spain, Russia), EXT (same countries plus Romania, Italy, Chile), and total problems (all mentioned previously plus Netherlands, not Chile). As a general comment, one should not forget that in our (middle-class, educated) sample, hitting or spanking was not frequently reported by parents.

Across the different cultures, shouting/swearing was significantly associated with higher levels of behavior problems for most countries, and also linked to higher NEG and SUR for children in multiple nations. This verbally aggressive/psychologically controlling strategy thus appears an important path from the developmental niche to child temperament and adjustment.

Greater use of time out was associated with higher NEG and behavior problems in several sites, while taking away privileges was related to higher NEG, and inconsistently associated with EFF (lower EFF in China and Netherlands, higher EFF in Finland). Both of these power-assertive, behaviorally controlling strategies are more popular in the west, the US in particular, compared to eastern countries (e.g., Cheah & Rubin, 2004; Raval, Raval, Salvina, Wilson, & Writer, 2013), possibly due to more tolerance for firm disciplinary practices that increase interpersonal distance to teach child self-control. Most correlations reported here correspond to countries outside of the US and northern Europe, where such strategies are counter-prescribed, which likely contributed to the direction of effects largely conducive to reactivity/dysregulation and behavior problems. Inconsistent relations for taking away privileges were noted and require further study.

Our hypotheses regarding links between inductive discipline strategies, child temperament, and behavior problems were partially confirmed. All inductive strategies were linked to higher EFF in several countries. Thus, our study further supports the importance of parental inductive discipline for promoting EFF (Cipriano & Stifter, 2010). Inductive discipline techniques that involve reasoning and autonomy promotion facilitate the skills involved in effortful self-regulation, and parents of toddlers from countries high in Individualism are more prone to use such techniques.

Telling the child to think about misbehavior was inconsistent in its linkage, associated with greater behavior problems in Russia, Romania, Italy, and South Korea; but lower levels in Finland and Mexico, suggesting that similar behaviors may be used for differing purposes in different cultural contexts. Russia and Romania scored highest on Power Distance and South Korea scored high on Collectivism, suggesting this strategy is associated with more troubling behavior problems in countries distinguished by such cultural orientations. As shown in Chapter 9, this strategy was most common in high Power Distance and Collectivist cultures. By contrast, Finland scored the lowest in Power Distance. Thus, it might be the case that, in high Power Distance and Collectivist cultures, parents are inclined to emphasize their power over the child, in order to get obedience, and can induce, as a result, feelings of guilt and shame. The high level of maladjustment linked to this strategy suggests it is not as benign as expected from a relational induction strategy and might have been used for shaming rather than teaching by parents in our sample. Although we focused exclusively on parent-to-child effects, bidirectional effects between parenting and child temperament should be considered in the future.

## References


Bates, J. E., Pettit, G. S., Dodge, K. A., & Ridge, B. (1998). Interaction of temperamental resistance to control and restrictive parenting in the development of externalizing behavior. *Developmental Psychology, 34*(5), 982–995.

Bornstein, M. H. (2012). Cultural approaches to parenting. *Parenting, Science and Practice, 12*(2–3), 212–221.

Braungart-Rieker, J., Garwood, M. M., & Stifter, C. A. (1997). Compliance and noncompliance: The roles of maternal control and child temperament. *Journal of Applied Developmental Psychology, 18*(3), 411–428.

Cheah, C. S. L., & Rubin, K. H. (2004). Comparison of European American and Mainland Chinese Mothers' responses to aggression and social withdrawal in preschoolers. *International Journal of Behavioral Development, 28*(1), 83–94.

Cipriano, E. A., & Stifter, C. A. (2010). Predicting preschool effortful control from toddler temperament and parenting behavior. *Journal of Applied Developmental Psychology, 31*(3), 221–230.

Coplan, R. J., & Weeks, M. (2009). Shy and soft-spoken: Shyness, pragmatic language, and socio-emotional adjustment in early childhood. *Infant and Child Development, 18*(3), 238–254.

Gartstein, M. A., & Fagot, B. I. (2003). Parental depression, parenting and family adjustment, and child effortful control: Explaining externalizing behaviors for preschool children. *Journal of Applied Developmental Psychology, 24*(2), 143–177.

Gershoff, E. T., Grogan-Kaylor, A., Lansford, J. E., Chang, L., Zelli, A., Deater-Deckard, K., & Dodge, K. A. (2010). Parent discipline practices in an international sample: Associations with child behaviors and moderation by perceived normativeness. *Child Development, 81*(2), 487–502.

Karreman, A., van Tuijl, C., van Aken, M. A. G., & Deković, M. (2008). Parenting, coparenting, and effortful control in preschoolers. *Journal of Family Psychology, 22*(1), 30–40.

Klimes-Dougan, B., & Kopp, C. B. (1999). Children's conflict tactics with mothers: A longitudinal investigation of the toddler and preschool years. *Merrill-Palmer Quarterly, 45*(2), 226–241.

Kochanska, G., Murray, K. T., & Harlan, E. T. (2000). Effortful control in early childhood: Continuity and change, antecedents, and implications for social development. *Developmental Psychology, 36*(2), 220–232.

Laible, D. J., & Thompson, R. A. (2002). Mother–child conflict in the toddler years: Lessons in emotion, morality, and relationships. *Child Development, 73*(4), 1187–1203.

Lansford, J. E., Chang, L., Dodge, K. A., Malone, P. S., Oburu, P., Palmérus, K., . . . Quinn, N. (2005). Physical discipline and children's adjustment: Cultural normativeness as a moderator. *Child Development, 76*(6), 1234–1246.

Lengua, L. J., Wolchik, S. A., Sandler, I. N., & West, S. G. (2000). The additive and interactive effects of parenting and temperament in predicting adjustment problems of children of divorce. *Journal of Clinical Child and Adolescent Psychology, 29*(2), 232–244.

McLeod, B. D., Weisz, J. R., & Wood, J. J. (2007). Examining the association between parenting and childhood depression: A meta-analysis. *Clinical Psychology Review, 27*(8), 986–1003.

Mulvaney, M. K., & Mebert, C. J. (2007). Parental corporal punishment predicts behavior problems in early childhood. *Journal of Family Psychology, 21*(3), 389–397.

Olsen, S. F., Yang, C., Hart, C. H., Robinson, C. C., Wu, P., Nelson, D. A., . . . Wo, J. (2002). Maternal psychological control and preschool children's behavioral outcomes in China, Russia, and the United States. In B. K. Barber (Ed.), *Intrusive parenting: How psychological control affects children and adolescents* (pp. 235–262). Washington, DC: American Psychological Association.

Piotrowski, J. T., Lapierre, M. A., & Linebarger, D. L. (2013). Investigating correlates of self-regulation in early childhood with a representative sample of English-Speaking American families. *Journal of Child and Family Studies, 22*(3), 423–436.

Pope-Edwards, C. P., & Liu, W. (2002). Parenting toddlers. In M. L. Bornstein (Ed.), *Handbook of parenting: Children and parenting* (2nd ed., Vol. 1, pp. 45–72). Hillsdale, NJ: Lawrence Erlbaum Associates.

Raval, V. V., Raval, P. H., Salvina, J. M., Wilson, S. L., & Writer, S. (2013). Mothers' socialization of children's emotion in India and the USA: A cross- and within-culture comparison. *Social Development, 22*, 467–484.

Rinaldi, C. M., & Howe, N. (2012). Mothers' and fathers' parenting styles and associations with toddlers' externalizing, internalizing, and adaptive behaviors. *Early Childhood Research Quarterly, 27*(2), 266–273.

Rubin, K. H., Burgess, K. B., Dwyer, K. M., & Hastings, P. D. (2003). Predicting preschoolers' externalizing behaviors from toddler temperament, conflict, and maternal negativity. *Developmental Psychology, 39*(1), 164–176.

Wang, M. & Liu, L. (2018). Reciprocal Relations Between Harsh Discipline and Children's Externalizing Behavior in China: A 5-Year Longitudinal Study. Child Development, 89, 174–187.

Xing, X., Zhang, H., Shao, S., & Wang, M. (2017). Child negative emotionality and parental harsh discipline in Chinese preschoolers: The different mediating roles of maternal and paternal anxiety. *Frontiers in Psychology, 8*, 339.

Xu, Y., Zhang, Z., & Farver, J. A. M. (2009). Temperament, harsh and indulgent parenting, and Chinese children's proactive and reactive aggression. *Child Development, 80*(1), 244–258.

# 16

# PARENTAL RESPONSES, TODDLER TEMPERAMENT, AND BEHAVIOR PROBLEMS

*Ibrahim Acar, Amanda Prokasky, Maria Beatriz Martins Linhares, Felipe Lecannelier, and Samuel P. Putnam*

Parents from different cultural backgrounds tend to view their children's temperamental characteristics from somewhat different perspectives. Super et al. (2008) described pathways to these cross-cultural differences, noting that how parents respond to their children's temperament reflects cultural influences on demands and expectations associated with child attributes.

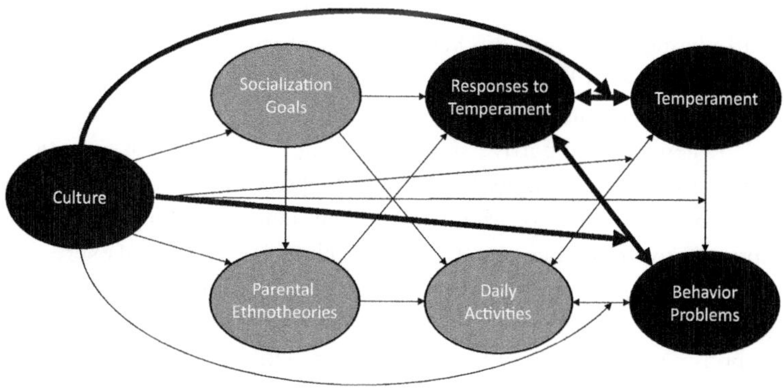


**FIGURE 16.1** Parent responses and child outcomes in the JETTC Conceptual Model

The current study examines parental responses to child temperament, and the extent to which parental responses shape individual differences in reactivity and regulation, as well as behavior problems. These links will be considered both within and between cultures, enabling us to examine whether parental reactions to child manifestations of temperament are culture-specific or more universal in nature (see Figure 16.1).

Parents' responses to children's temperament play an important role in children's development (Roberts, 1999). Existing research and theory suggest that how parents respond to children's emotional expression is related to their social competence, peer acceptance, and modulation of negative affectivity (e.g., anger; Eisenberg, Fabes, & Murphy, 1996; Roberts, 1999). Whereas parents from individualistic cultures emphasize autonomy, self-sufficiency, and assertiveness in their children's expression of emotions, using supportive approaches, parents with collectivistic cultural backgrounds tend to prioritize self-restraint of emotions that may be disruptive to the social context, using obedience-demanding approaches (Corapci et al., 2017; Raval & Martini, 2009). Wang (2001) found that Chinese mothers used an "emotion-criticizing style," installing proper behavior, whereas United States (US) mothers used an "emotion-explaining style"—causal explanations for antecedents of emotions. Chen et al. (1998) also reported that more punishment-oriented child-rearing attitudes were expressed by Chinese–Canadian mothers, relative to their Canadian counterparts of European descent, and that this orientation was linked with higher toddler behavioral inhibition. In addition, Corapci et al. (2017) reported that European American mothers engaged in "behaviorally oriented discipline" (e.g., time out, privilege withdrawal) to help their children cope with anger more effectively, compared to Turkish and Romanian mothers. Thus, parental responses to children's temperament can be described as flexible, insofar as these appear to be more culturally influenced for certain domains of temperament.

In general, supportive responses (e.g., affirming of emotional expressions) were associated with more adaptive child social functioning (Eisenberg et al., 1996; McElwain, Halberstadt, & Volling, 2007), and unsupportive responses (e.g., minimizing children's emotional expression) with lower social competence and increased behavior problems (Eisenberg et al., 1996; Fabes, Leonard, Kupanoff, & Martin, 2001). Parental responses to child negativity were related to children's emotional knowledge, emotional displays, friendship quality, and social competence (Denham & Kochanoff, 2002; McElwain et al., 2007; Spinrad et al., 2007). When parents used emotion-focused responses to reduce child distress (e.g., talking about anger/frustration), children displayed less anger and demonstrated more effective coping with anger (Eisenberg & Fabes, 1994). On the contrary, when parents minimized or punished displays of Negative Affectivity (NEG), children showed higher levels of distress (Eisenberg & Fabes, 1994; Eisenberg et al., 1996).

Parents' supportive behaviors were associated with higher levels of child Surgency (SUR; Ogata, Bridgett, Putnam, & Gartstein, 2005). Further, parents of children high in Activity Level, a component of SUR, were most likely to use harsh and aggressive approaches, compared to caregivers of lower SUR children (Barkley, Cunningham, & Karlsson, 1983; Woodward, Taylor, & Dowdney, 1998).

For Effortful Control (EFF), when parents showed emotional support, acceptance, and sensitivity, children displayed more advanced regulation (Kochanska, Murray, & Harlan, 2000). On the contrary, when parents punitively responded to children's failures in EFF, children demonstrated dysregulation (Ogata et al., 2005).

Parental responses to manifestations of temperament have long been thought to play an important role in children's development (Roberts, 1999); however, the manner in which parental approaches to child SUR, NEG and EFF impact the development of temperament, and related internalizing (INT) and externalizing behavior problems (EXT) has not been sufficiently investigated. We considered associations between parental responses to temperament displays and child temperament and behavior problems, both within and between JETTC member cultures.

## Results

Correlations calculated using the entire sample of individual families, so conflating within-country and between-country differences, revealed several modest, but significant, associations (Table 16.1). Encouraging NEG was associated with high EFF, encouraging SUR with high SUR, punishing low EFF with high NEG and low EFF, and rewarding high EFF was associated with high EFF. Encouraging NEG was linked to low INT, EXT, and total problems, whereas punishing low EFF was associated with all behavior problems.

Between-country correlations, shown in Table 16.2, suggest that cultural differences in parental reactions to temperament were not reliably associated with cross-cultural effects for child temperament or behavior problems.

The average within-culture correlations are shown in Table 16.3 and demonstrate limited support for links between temperament and parental

**TABLE 16.1** Correlations between temperament/behavior problems and parental responses to temperament displays for the entire sample

| | *Encourage NEG* | *Encourage SUR* | *Punish Low EFF* | *Reward High EFF* |
|---|---|---|---|---|
| Negative Affectivity | –0.03 | –0.05 | 0.19** | 0.03 |
| Surgency | 0.02 | 0.07* | 0.03 | 0.04 |
| Effortful Control | 0.10** | 0.06# | –0.11** | 0.09** |
| Internalizing | –0.10** | –0.07 | 0.17** | 0.02 |
| Externalizing | –0.12** | –0.04 | 0.16** | 0.01 |
| Total problems | –0.11** | –0.04 | 0.17** | 0.00 |

Note: $n_s$ = 834 for temperament, and 829 for behavior problems. $^{**}p < 0.10$, $^{*}p < 0.05$, $^{\#}p < 0.10$

**TABLE 16.2** Between-country correlations between countries' marginal means of temperament/behavior problems and parental responses to temperament displays

| | *Encourage NEG* | *Encourage SUR* | *Punish Low EFF* | *Reward High EFF* |
|---|---|---|---|---|
| Negative Affectivity | –0.02 | –0.24 | 0.35 | 0.13 |
| Surgency | 0.01 | 0.35 | –0.06 | –0.14 |
| Effortful Control | 0.23 | 0.13 | 0.09 | –0.31 |
| Internalizing | –0.41 | –0.23 | 0.06 | 0.13 |
| Externalizing | –0.42 | 0.24 | 0.07 | –0.02 |
| Total problems | –0.41 | 0.03 | 0.07 | 0.01 |

Note: $N$ = 14

**TABLE 16.3** Average within-country correlations between temperament/behavior problems and parental responses to temperament displays

| | *Encourage NEG* | *Encourage SUR* | *Punish Low EFF* | *Reward High EFF* |
|---|---|---|---|---|
| Negative Affectivity | $-0.03^{0}$ | $-0.02^{1}$ | $0.18^{2}$ | $0.01^{1}$ |
| Surgency | $0.03^{1}$ | $0.04^{1}$ | $0.05^{1}$ | $0.06^{2}$ |
| Effortful Control | $0.10^{2}$ | $0.05^{1}$ | $-0.14^{3}$ | $0.12^{3}$ |
| Internalizing | $-0.05^{2}$ | $-0.04^{0}$ | $0.20^{4}$ | $0.02^{0}$ |
| Externalizing | $-0.07^{1}$ | $-0.07^{1}$ | $0.18^{5}$ | $0.03^{1}$ |
| Total problems | $-0.06^{1}$ | $0.05^{0}$ | $0.20^{5}$ | $0.02^{1}$ |

Note: Superscripts indicate the number of countries (out of 14) for which the correlation was significant to $p < 0.05$

responses. Among relations significant in three or more countries, Punish Low EFF failures was associated with low EFF and high levels of all types of behavior problems (Figure 16.2). In addition, Reward High EFF was linked to high EFF in three sites.

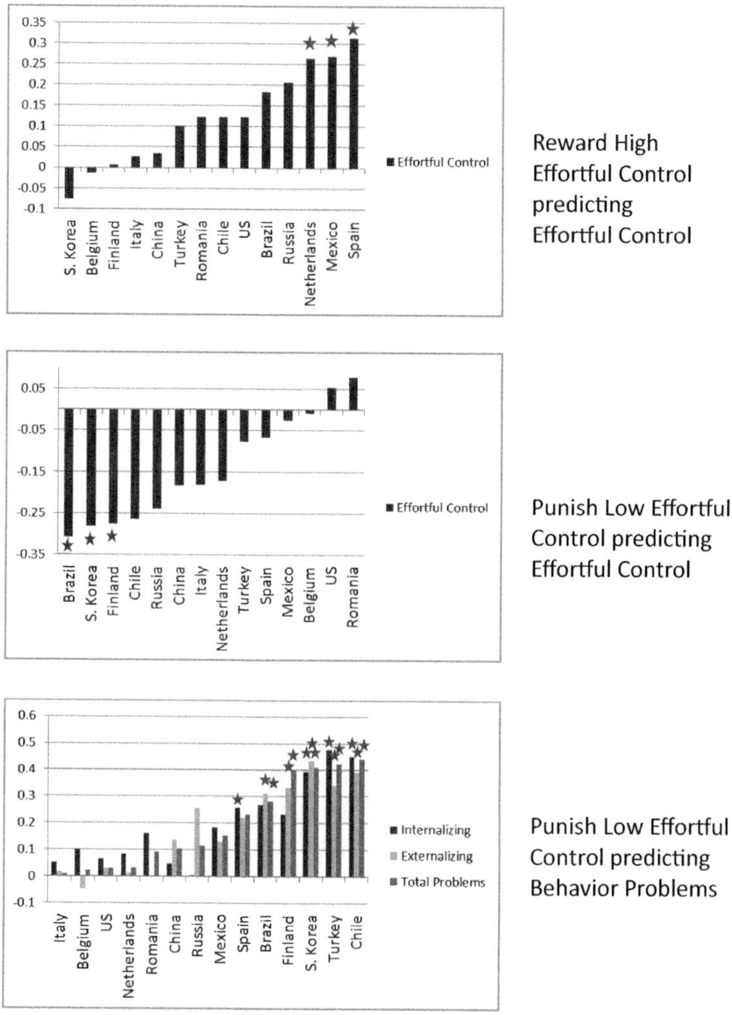


**FIGURE 16.2** Parent responses–Effortful Control correlations for JETTC countries

⋆ indicates significant correlation

## Discussion

Several noteworthy findings emerged. First, with the whole sample, discouraging NEG and punishing low EFF were associated with higher levels of behavior problems and low EFF, with the latter also linked to high NEG. These findings are commensurate with prior research (Dunsmore, Booker, & Ollendick, 2013; Eisenberg et al., 2001) wherein authoritarian parenting behaviors aimed at exercising control over children's negative emotions were associated with more significant adjustment/behavior problems and self-regulation deficits.

There was a lack of significant findings for between-country analyses addressing associations between Parental Responses to Temperament Displays (PRTD) and child temperament, as well as behavior problems. This pattern of results indicates that cultures on average higher or lower on the different dimensions of PRTD do not present with a clear pattern of child temperament or behavior problems outcomes. Average within-culture correlations demonstrated limited support for links between temperament and parent's response to these temperamental characteristics. Some consistency was apparent, as punishing low EFF was associated with low EFF in three countries and rewarding high EFF linked to high EFF in three others. The cultural mechanisms behind these effects cannot be fully discerned on the basis of this study. It is of interest that Brazil is in the top three cultures in terms of punishing low EFF, as reported in Chapter 10, and the Netherlands is second in rewarding high EFF. It is possible that, in some cultures, punishing low EFF translated into toddlers feeling scorned for their low EFF, which could contribute to power struggles that further disrupt fragile child self-regulation. In a similar fashion, rewarding high EFF may be associated with particularly salient culturally supported practices in the Netherlands, Mexico, and Spain.

The most consistent effects for parental responses to manifestations of temperament were for punishing EFF, predicting EXT, and total behavior problems, observed in five countries. At the same time, this association was only significant for a third of our sample. Thus, although parental punishment of children's failures to demonstrate control may exacerbate children's behavioral difficulties, this association is specific to culture.

## References

Barkley, R. A., Cunningham, C. E., & Karlsson, J. (1983). The speech of hyperactive children and their mothers: Comparisons with normal children and stimulant drug effects. *Journal of Learning Disabilities, 16*, 105–110.

Chen, X., Hastings, P. D., Rubin, K. H., Chen, H., Cen, G., & Stewart, S. L. (1998). Child rearing attitudes and behavioral inhibition in Chinese and Canadian toddlers: A cross-cultural study. *Developmental Psychology, 34*(4), 677–686.

Corapci, F., Friedlmeier, W., Benga, O., Strauss, C., Pitica, I., & Susa, G. (2017). Cultural socialization of toddlers in emotionally charged situations. *Social Development, 27*, 262–278.

Denham, S. A., & Kochanoff, A. T. (2002). Parental contributions to preschoolers' understanding of emotion. *Marriage and Family Review, 3*, 311–343.

Dunsmore, J. C., Booker, J. A., & Ollendick, T. H. (2013). Parental emotion coaching and child emotion regulation as protective factors for children with oppositional defiant disorder. *Social Development, 22*(3), 444–466.

Eisenberg, N., Cumberland, A., Spinrad, T. L., Fabes, R. A., Shepard, S. A., Reiser, M., . . . Guthrie, I. K. (2001). The relations of regulation and emotionality to children's externalizing and internalizing problem behavior. *Child Development, 72*(4), 1112–1134.

Eisenberg, N., & Fabes, R. A. (1994). Mothers' reactions to children's negative emotions: Relations to children's temperament and anger behavior. *Merrill-Palmer Quarterly, 40*, 138–156.

Eisenberg, N., Fabes, R. A., & Murphy, B. C. (1996). Parents' reactions to children's negative emotions: Relations to children's social competence and comforting behavior. *Child Development, 67*, 2227–2247.

Fabes, R. A., Leonard, S. A., Kupanoff, K., & Martin, C. L. (2001). Parental coping with children's negative emotions: Relations with children's emotional and social responding. *Child Development, 72*, 907–920.

Gartstein, M. A., Putnam, S. P., & Rothbart, M. K. (2012). Etiology of preschool behavior problems: Contributions of temperament attributes in early childhood. *Infant Mental Health Journal, 33*, 197–211.

Kochanska, G., Murray, K. T., & Harlan, E. T. (2000). Effortful control in early childhood: Continuity and change, antecedents, and implications for social development. *Developmental Psychology, 36*, 220–232.

McElwain, N. L., Halberstadt, A. G., & Volling, B. L. (2007). Mother- and father-reported reactions to children's negative emotions: Relations to young children's emotional understanding and friendship quality. *Child Development, 78*, 1407–1425.

Ogata, A. K., Bridgett, D., Putnam, S. P., & Gartstein, M. A. (2005, April). *Parental responses to temperament displays: Structure, stability through toddlerhood and relations with Big 3*. Presentation at the biennial convention of the Society for Research in Child Development, Atlanta, GA.

Raval, V. V., & Martini, T. S. (2009). Maternal socialization of children's anger, sadness, and physical pain in two communities in Gujarat, India. *International Journal of Behavioral Development, 33*, 215–219.

Roberts, W. (1999). The socialization of emotional expression: Relations with prosocial behaviour and competence in five samples. *Canadian Journal of Behavioural Science, 31*, 72–85.

Spinrad, T. L., Eisenberg, N., Gaertner, B., Popp, T., Smith, C. L., Kupfer, A., . . . Hofer, C. (2007). Relations of maternal socialization and toddlers' effortful control to children's adjustment and social competence. *Developmental Psychology, 43*, 1170–1186.Super, C. M., & Harkness, S. (1986). The developmental niche: A conceptualization at the interface of child and culture. *International Journal Behavior Development, 9*, 545–569.

Super, C., Axia, G., Harkness, S., Welles-Nystrom, B., Zylicz, P. O., Parmar, P., McGurk, H. (2008). Culture, temperament, and the "Difficult Child": A study in seven western cultures. *European Journal of Developmental Science, 2*(1/2), 136–157.

Wang, Q. (2001). "Did you have fun?" American and Chinese Mother–Child conversations about shared emotional experiences. *Cognitive Development, 16*, 693–715.

Woodward, L., Taylor, E., & Dowdney, L. (1998). The parenting and family functioning of children with hyperactivity. *Journal of Child Psychology and Psychiatry, 39*, 161–169.

# 17

# BRINGING IT ALL TOGETHER

## Mediational Models

*Maria A. Gartstein, Samuel P. Putnam, Mirjana Majdandžić, Soile Tuovinen, and Eric Desmarais*

To recap, the JETTC project set out to integrate the psychobiological theory of temperament with broad elements of culture, through the framework of the developmental niche which captures contextual elements contributing to temperament development, and by extension, symptoms of psychopathology. In this chapter, all variables mentioned thus far were reconsidered, examining associations across different levels of influence (see Figure 17.1). That is, Hofstede's cultural orientation dimensions were deemed most distal relative to child outcomes, and thus designated as Level 1. Next, caregiver psychology variables (socialization

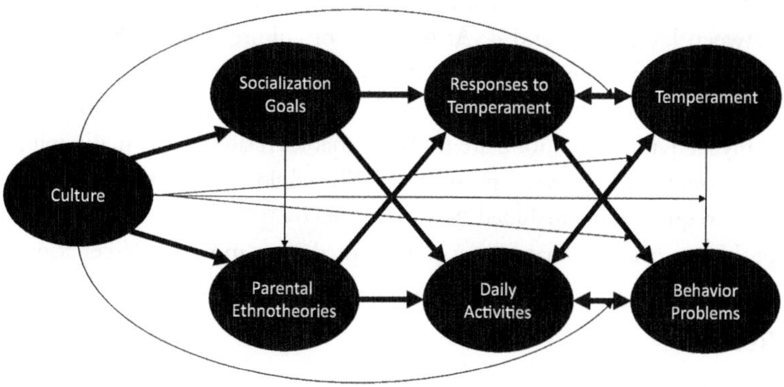


FIGURE 17.1 Mediation paths in the JETTC Conceptual Model

goals and parental ethnotheories), were designated as Level 2 variables, with Level 3 reserved for family environment factors including aspects of the daily routine and parental responses to manifestations of temperament. Child outcomes, including temperament factors and behavior problems, were designated as Level 4 constructs.

Analyses that follow are aimed at identifying potential mediators, which are defined as intermediaries that convey effects of other independent variables on the outcomes of interest (Baron & Kenny, 1986), enabling researchers to answer questions related to the "how" of developmental processes. To illustrate, in Chapter 4, we learned that Internalizing problems (INT) were higher in collectivist societies. We subsequently reported a less frequent reliance on gentle sleeping strategies in collectivist cultures (Chapter 8), and that cultures reporting greater use of these strategies also saw lower levels of INT (Chapter 14). Together, these findings invite a test of the proposal that culturally influenced bedtime routines may partially explain the tendency for higher INT in collectivist cultures and will be explored in this chapter along with other mediation possibilities.

For mediation to be considered, all variables involved must demonstrate significant correlations with one another. That is, the mediator (bedtime routine, in our example above), must be linked to the independent variable (e.g., Collectivism) as well as the outcome (e.g., child INT), and the independent variable and outcome must themselves be related. A preliminary step, therefore, was to identify all such combinations across different levels of variables in the JETTC data. Because bivariate correlations revealed very few connections between parental psychology and other variables, no mediation models involving Level 2 variables were tested. A total of 16 possible mediation models were indicated by correlations between levels 1, 3, and 4. At the level of culture, only Individualism/Collectivism and Power Distance demonstrated patterns of correlations for which mediation could be tested. At the parenting level, models involving Daily Activities Questionnaire (DAQ) variables related to sleep, discipline, and computer use were possible. Finally, child characteristics meeting these requirements included Negative Affectivity (NEG), INT, and total problems. Analyses that follow explore mediation in these 16 scenarios.

## Results

The classic regression approach to mediation outlined in the seminal paper by Baron and Kenny (1986) was deemed optimal given the nature of our analyses and sample size, which did not allow for the use of more modern analytic techniques, such as structural equation modeling. To test mediation, an initial regression equation is calculated with the independent variable as a sole predictor of the dependent variable; followed by a second equation with both the independent variable and mediator as predictors. Mediation is supported when (A) there is a significant relation of the independent variable to the dependent variable in the initial equation, and (B) the mediator is significantly related to the dependent variable when both the independent and mediating variables are in the equation. Traditionally, a third requirement is that the coefficient relating the independent to the dependent variable becomes nonsignificant in the second equation. Due to our small sample of cultures; however, this criterion is quite liberal, such that even small reductions in the variance associated with the independent variable would lead to nonsignificant results. Furthermore, even the most sensitive tests designed to quantify mediation (e.g., bootstrapping, Sobel's test) are not able to detect expected effects in samples containing fewer than 35 cases (Fritz & MacKinnon, 2007). To allow exploration of mediation-like patterns in the 14 JETTC cultures, we adapted a "rule of thumb," considering a beta reduction of > 0.20 in the independent variable to be meaningful.

Table 17.1 presents standardized coefficients for regression equations containing only the independent variable (Model 1) and the independent variable and mediator (Model 2) for the 16 mediation possibilities. Because testing mediation requires that the effects are in the same direction, two variables were reversed: Individualism/Collectivism was reversed, so that high scores represent Collectivism, and the Gentle Sleep technique scores in these equations represent low use of these techniques.

Of the 16 models tested, six followed the pattern suggesting mediation outlined above. The Individualism—"Think about It" discipline—INT, as well as the closely related Individualism—"Think about It" discipline—total problems, and Power Distance—"Think about It" discipline—INT models were consistent with this pattern of results. Three other equations with Power Distance as the independent variable and INT problems as the dependent variable presented with a mediation-type pattern: Power Distance—Gentle Sleep techniques—INT; Power Distance—late bed times—INT; and Power Distance—late wake times—INT. For the other 10 models, the independent variable beta dropped, but the effect of the mediator did not reach < 0.10, and in other cases the independent variable beta change with the entry of the mediator was negligible.

**TABLE 17.1** Regressions testing parenting as mediator of associations between cultural orientation and child outcomes

| | *Model 1* | | *Model 2* | |
|---|---|---|---|---|
| | *Beta* | *p* | *Beta* | *p* |
| Predicting Internalizing | | | | |
| Individualism/Collectivism | 0.70 | 0.01 | 0.44 | 0.06 |
| Think about It | | | 0.48 | 0.04 |
| Power Distance | 0.74 | 0.01 | 0.48 | 0.06 |
| Think about It | | | 0.42 | 0.09 |
| Power Distance | 0.74 | 0.01 | 0.53 | 0.02 |
| Gentle Sleep | | | 0.40 | 0.08 |
| Power Distance | 0.74 | 0.01 | 0.49 | 0.05 |
| Bed time | | | 0.42 | 0.08 |
| Power Distance | 0.74 | 0.01 | 0.54 | 0.05 |
| Wake time | | | 0.38 | 0.09 |
| Individualism/Collectivism | 0.70 | 0.01 | 0.37 | 0.22 |
| Bed time | | | 0.44 | 0.16 |
| Individualism/Collectivism | 0.70 | 0.01 | 0.46 | 0.11 |
| Wake time | | | 0.37 | 0.19 |
| Individualism/Collectivism | 0.70 | 0.01 | 0.43 | 0.17 |
| Gentle Sleep | | | 0.37 | 0.23 |
| Predicting total problems | | | | |
| Individualism/Collectivism | 0.60 | 0.05 | 0.35 | 0.19 |
| Think about It | | | 0.46 | 0.09 |
| Power Distance | 0.60 | 0.05 | 0.32 | 0.28 |
| Think about It | | | 0.45 | 0.13 |
| Power Distance | 0.60 | 0.05 | 0.44 | 0.14 |
| Wake time | | | 0.30 | 0.30 |
| Individualism/Collectivism | 0.60 | 0.01 | 0.43 | 0.19 |
| Wake time | | | 0.25 | 0.45 |
| Predicting Negative Affectivity | | | | |
| Individualism/Collectivism | 0.77 | 0.01 | 0.50 | 0.08 |
| Gentle Sleep | | | 0.37 | 0.17 |
| Individualism/Collectivism | 0.77 | 0.01 | 0.66 | 0.01 |
| Naps | | | 0.18 | 0.43 |
| Individualism/Collectivism | 0.77 | 0.01 | 0.72 | 0.01 |
| Wake time | | | 0.07 | 0.78 |
| Individualism/Collectivism | 0.77 | 0.01 | 0.80 | 0.01 |
| Bed time | | | −0.05 | 0.86 |

Note: N = 14.

## Discussion

The six models reflective of mediation comprise two sets: one involving "Think about It" discipline as the mediator between Individualism/Power Distance and behavior problems, and another in which Power Distance was linked to INT through aspects of parenting involving sleep.

The "Think about It" discipline technique was conceived to be reflective of an inductive approach, wherein the parent directs the child to consider her actions and the negative impact on others, with the expectation that the child will experience guilt, subsequently avoiding future rule violations (Hoffman, 1975). Our findings suggest that the frequent use of this technique provides a partial explanation for elevated levels of INT and other problems in more collectivist cultures. It is perhaps not surprising to observe parenting techniques emphasizing guilt in cultures that have strong expectations of obedience, viewed as promoting group harmony and maintaining existing hierarchies. For children raised in such cultures, however, the guilt associated with these expectations may manifest as behavioral/emotional difficulties.

Cultures with greater Power Distance (i.e., more accepting of a hierarchical social structure) had toddlers with higher INT, explained in part by later average bedtimes and wake times, as well as less frequent use of gentle techniques in facilitation of transition to sleep. Similar to earlier studies (Super et al., 1996), our results suggest that even a biological function like sleep can be shaped by cultural influences, conferring effects onto child behavior/emotions. One possibility is that parents in more hierarchically minded cultures expect their children to be active along with them later, following the parents' lead in terms of staying awake. This pattern likely translates into later awakenings, and our data suggest has a dysregulating effect on toddlers, contributing to INT.

Of the six cultural dimensions examined, only Individualism/Collectivism and Power Distance were associated with both parent behaviors and child outcomes. Both dimensions speak to negotiating relationships between the individual and her social group, and appear to translate into elements of the family environment that are important in establishing risk, primarily for INT. A somewhat similar pattern of results emerged in a recent meta-analytic effort wherein these cultural orientation dimensions were linked to NEG (Putnam & Gartstein, 2017). Of note, these regression models did not provide evidence that parenting explained relations between culture and temperament.

It is notable that Level 2 Caregiver Psychology variables were neither robust predictors of child outcomes, nor other independent variables, despite observed cross-cultural differences in parental socialization goals and ethnotheories (Chapter 6). The latter have been emphasized in several models of cultural effects (e.g., Harkness et al., 2011; Keller et al., 2006), yet our results do not reflect this important role. Cultural differences in caregiver psychology may be more critical in the infancy period, when the majority of existing studies were conducted (Keller, 2007; Keller et al., 2006), than during toddlerhood. Decisions concerning proximity to the infant and frequency of contact and/or feeding may reflect cultural values embedded in parents' thinking in ways that factors operating in the toddler period do not.

Clinical implications should be noted, as the toddler period signals a transition in terms of increased expectations for self-regulation and is marked by the emergence of behavioral/emotional concerns. Results of this study provide preliminary information concerning potential targets for preventative efforts, which could be implemented prior to onset of full-blown disorders.

## References

Baron, R. M., & Kenny, D. A. (1986). The moderator-mediator variable distinction in social psychological research: Conceptual, strategic, and statistical considerations. *Journal of Personality and Social Psychology*, *51*, 1173–1182.

Chen, X., Hastings, P.D., Rubin, K.H., Chen, H., Cen, G., & Stewart, S. L. (1998). Child-rearing attitudes and behavioral inhibition in Chinese and Canadian toddlers: A cross-cultural study. Developmental Psychology, 34, 677.

Fritz, M. S., & Mackinnon, D. P. (2007). Required sample size to detect the mediated effect. *Psychological Science*, *18*, 233–239.

Harkness, S., Zylicz, P. O., Super, C., Welles-Nystrom, B., Bermudez, M. R., Bonichini, S., Mavridis, C. J. (2011). Children's activities and their meanings for parents: A mixed-methods study in six Western cultures. *Journal of Family Psychology*, *25*, 799–813.

Hoffman, M. (1975). Moral internalization, parental power, and the nature of parent-child interaction. *Developmental Psychology*, *11*, 228–239.

Hofstede, G. (1980). *Culture's Consequences: International Differences in Work-Related Values*. Beverly Hills, CA: Sage.

Keller, H. (2007). *Cultures of infancy*. Mahwah, NJ: Lawrence Erlbaum Associates.

Keller, H., Lamm, B., Abels, M., Yovsi, R., Borke, J., Jensen, H., . . . Chaudhary, N. (2006). Cultural models, socialization goals, and parenting ethnotheories: A multicultural analysis. *Journal of Cross-Cultural Psychology*, *37*, 155–172.

Krassner, A., Gartstein, M. A., Park, C., Dragan, W. L., Lecannelier, F., & Putnam, S. P. (2017). East-West, Collectivist-Individualist: A Cross-Cultural Examination of Temperament in Toddlers from Chile, Poland, South Korea, and the U.S. *European Journal of Developmental Psychology, 14*, 449–464.

McKinney, C., & Brown, K. (2017). Parenting and emerging adult internalizing problems: Regional differences suggest Southern parenting factor. *Journal of Child and Family Studies, 26*, 3156–3166.

Putnam, S. P., & Gartstein, M. A. (2017). Aggregate temperament scores from multiple countries: Associations with aggregate personality traits, cultural dimensions, and allelic frequency. *Journal of Research in Personality, 67*, 157–170.

Rentfrow, P. J., Gosling, S. D., Jokela, M., Stillwell, D. J., Kosinski, M., & Potter, J. (2013). Divided we stand: Three psychological regions of the United States and their political, economic, social, and health correlates. *Journal of Personality and Social Psychology, 105*, 996–1012.

Super, C. M., Harkness, S., van Tijen, N., van der Vlugt, E., Dykstra, J., & Fintelman, M. (1996). The three R's of Dutch child rearing and the socialization of infant arousal. In S. Harkness & C. M. Super (Eds.), *Parents' cultural belief systems: Their origins, expressions, and consequences* (pp. 447–466). New York, NY: Guilford.

# 18

# SUMMARY AND FUTURE DIRECTIONS

*Samuel P. Putnam, Maria A. Gartstein, Rosario Montirosso, Livio Provenzi, and Zhengyan Wang*

The Joint Effort Toddler Temperament Consortium (JETTC) work outlined in this book has taken us from considering basic differences between our 14 cultures with respect to child temperament and behavior problems, as well as the developmental niche, to examining interrelations among different aspects of the niche, and putting it all together. The final chapter provides a summary of this journey, noting limitations of the JETTC dataset and pointing to some future directions. We have argued that cross-cultural research is essential for outlining those aspects of child development and socialization that appear to be universal and those that are culture specific. Although additional research is required to fully understand the implications of these distinctions, JETTC provides ample evidence that culture-specific effects are non-trivial in understanding social–emotional development, as cross-cultural differences were pervasive across all comparative analyses. The effect of culture was statistically significant in each of the 37 Analyses of Variance (ANOVAS) calculated, with effect sizes generally in the moderate to large range.

Another critical take-home point concerns the importance of broad cultural orientation factors in modulating links between aspects of the developmental niche, child temperament, and behavior problems. This conclusion is afforded by the relatively large number of countries represented, which allowed us to investigate overarching aspects of culture in relation to parent and child characteristics. Previous studies involving comparisons of very few (i.e., two to four) cultures have often invoked cultural dimensions, typically Individualism/Collectivism (e.g., Chen et al., 1998; Gartstein, Slobodskaya, & Kinsht, 2003; Krassner et al.,

2017) as potential reasons for the cross-cultural differences obtained. Such small numbers of countries, however, have not permitted statistical tests of associations, rendering these interpretations questionable. In contrast, inclusion of 14 countries permitted an empirical evaluation of cultural orientation as an influence on individual and family functioning—an advance of the JETTC. At the same time, the JETTC sample still represents a very limited proportion of the world's population. A related shortcoming of the JETTC is the reliance on single sites for most countries. Substantial variability within cultures has been observed for adult personality (e.g., Rentfrow et al., 2013), and parental discipline strategies (e.g., McKinney & Brown, 2017), and requires an expanded investigation of the JETTC variables with larger and more diverse samples, both within and across nations.

The number and variety of cultures comprising the JETTC is complemented by a focus on aspects of culture that are often overlooked in developmental research. Although several studies have implicated concepts of Individualism/Collectivism as influential for shaping the values imparted by parents, few have moved beyond this cultural dimension to explore how children's experiences and behaviors are related to other macrosystem attributes. Critiques of Hofstede's cultural orientation scores (e.g., Blodgett, Bakir, & Rose, 2008; McSweeney, 2002) have questioned their meaning, as these scores and factors were derived largely from select samples (e.g., IBM employees; Hofstede, 1980). We argue, however, the fact that variables assessed on the basis of one segment of a culture (business professionals) were associated in meaningful ways with discrete behaviors in a very different segment (parents and children), speaks to the robustness of their relations. Our enthusiasm regarding these findings is tempered by the possibility that some may be spurious, due to the multiple tests conducted. We hope that future studies attempt replication, using this perspective on culture to extend our understanding of family functioning and child development.

The overarching conceptual model viewed parent psychology as a critical mechanism for the maintenance of cultural values across generations. Our findings provided support for this notion, as cultures broadly endorsing indulgent pursuit of gratification expressed this cultural orientation through parenting theories and associated socialization goals that promote child autonomy. Furthermore, the broad goals parents have for their children related meaningfully to the environments they provide, with (for example) cultures valuing autonomy promoting sleep and refraining from raising their voice to discipline children.

Surprisingly, our measure of parental ethnotheories was scarcely related to other variables measured in this study. The instrument was adapted from a measure originally intended for infants (e.g., Keller et al., 2006), and the resulting scales demonstrated poor psychometric qualities and questionable applicability to toddlers. Similarly, a new measure designed to directly assess parental responses to children's demonstrations of temperament was only modestly related to cultural orientation or child outcomes. Both of these instruments are relatively vague, asking parents whether certain practices are appropriate or whether they would encourage or discourage broad categories of child behaviors. Such general perspectives appear to be of limited utility in quantifying aspects of the developmental niche that shape child behavior.

In contrast, our newly developed Daily Activities Questionnaire (DAQ), which measured more specific parenting behaviors and structuring of the child's world, demonstrated varied and robust connections to child behavior and cultural dimensions. In addition, our evaluations of the structure and psychometric properties of this instrument revealed meaningful dimensions of daily settings/activities. Additional research with different samples is required to provide further support for its reliability and validity, and we anticipate that the DAQ will receive substantial use in the field, given the limited choices available for measuring components of the developmental niche.

Analyses linking the DAQ and other instruments to child outcomes; and of associations between temperament and behavior problems; reveal both universal and specific connections. Associations between Negative Affectivity (NEG), Effortful Control (EFF), and behavior problems represent an example of consistent or universal connections. Specifically, within-culture correlations relating high NEG to elevated Internalizing and total problems, and low EFF to high Externalizing and total problems, were significant across all 14 JETTC countries (Chapter 5). On the parenting side, links between caregiver shouting/swearing and toddler behavior problems also appeared relatively uniform. This power-assertive strategy was associated with higher levels of Externalizing problems for all JETTC sites, significantly so in 11 of the 14 (Chapter 15). These more universally observed associations suggest fundamental connections, which in the case of the NEG temperament–behavior problem link could be interpreted as supportive of the spectrum model invoked in developmental psychopathology, wherein disorders are framed as extremes of temperament (e.g., Martel, Gremillion, Roberts, Zastrow, & Tackett, 2014).

On the other hand, variable patterns of association across countries were observed for surgencey (SUR) and behavior problems. That is, SUR was significantly associated with high Externalizing in 5 of the 14 JETTC cultures, but largely nonrelated to Externalizing in several others, suggesting moderation of this link by contextual factors. More dramatic inconsistency was observed in relations between the discipline technique of telling the child to think about misbehavior and behavior problems. This parental behavior was linked to low Externalizing and/or total behavior problems in some cultures (i.e., Finland, Mexico), but high levels of behavior problems in others (i.e., Russia, Romania, Italy, and South Korea). This pattern of results indicates that similar behaviors may be used for divergent purposes in different cultural contexts. We noted earlier (Chapter 15) that Power Distance/Collectivism cultural values may play a role in moderating these relations, and the strategy of telling the child to think about misbehavior was related to greater behavior problems primarily in cultures identifying with the importance of social hierarchy and prioritizing the needs of the social group (i.e., Russia, Romania, and South Korea). These findings support the importance considering function along with form of parenting behaviors. As suggested by Bornstein (1995), different parenting behaviors could serve the same purpose with respect to socialization, and interpretations of the same actions vary across different cultures. Identifying the rationale underlying parents' use of inductive techniques, as well as how they are perceived by children, could clarify the reasons why these are linked to adaptive child characteristics in some cultures, but to problems in others.

The cognitive, motivational, and emotional processes operating on within-culture relations between parenting and child behavior may differ from those operating at a between-culture level. Our findings suggested that patterns of linkage were often not congruent with one another at these different levels of analyses. For example, between-culture tests indicated high SUR, low NEG, and low Internalizing in countries in which parents frequently used gentle soothing techniques at bedtime, but within-culture analyses suggested small and inconsistent associations between these bedtime practices and reactive temperament traits or problems. Between-culture associations can be viewed as a conduit for shaping children's development in culturally accepted ways, and gentle soothing techniques may reflect a cultural tendency to promote high positive affectivity and diminish expressions of negative emotions. Within a given culture, however, individual differences in children's emotionality do not appear to be strongly influenced by the degree to which individual parents use these practices. Both levels of analysis appear informative in elucidating contextual contributors to child social-emotional development.

Although biological variables were not gathered in the JETTC, the results of this study have implications for biological mechanisms relevant to child temperament and developmental psychopathology. At the most distal level, genetic factors may be implicated. The role of genes in the etiology of temperament has been long established (e.g., Saudino & Wang, 2012), with individual differences in temperament, considered, at least partially, under genetic control (Papageorgiou & Ronald, 2013). For example, BDNF*val66met* polymorphism was linked to infants' temperament, as met-carriers had lower regulatory capacities compared to val-homozygotes (Giusti, Provenzi, Tavian, Missaglia, & Montirosso, 2017). The role of genes in the etiology of temperament has rarely been applied to population-level differences. Recently, Putnam and Gartstein (2017) related aggregate scores on EFF, NEG, and SUR from multiple cultures to the proportion of neuro-behaviorally relevant alleles in these countries, interpreting their findings in light of the gene-culture co-evolution theory (e.g., Boyd & Richerson, 1985; Gintis, 2011). This concept refers to the dynamic relation between individuals and societies, in which biologically distinct populations develop cultural values and practices that reflect intrinsic tendencies of individuals to react to their environment; with these cultural forces affecting evolutionary fitness of those who behave in ways counter to, or consistent with, societal expectations. Both parenting behavior and child outcomes may be viewed as mediators of the bidirectional connections between allelic distributions and cultural value systems, ensuring transmission across generations.

The impact of genes on individual functioning is dependent on epigenetic processes taking place from the moment of conception forward. Recently, environmental alterations of epigenetic functioning related to a variety of prenatal exposures were described as contributing to temperament development across species (Gartstein & Skinner, 2017). Furthermore, postnatal experiences can have an impact via epigenetic mechanisms, shaping individual differences. For example, DNA methylation, one of the most studied epigenetic mechanisms in humans, is highly susceptible to environmental conditions and associated with reduced transcriptional activity of specific genes (Hyman, 2009). DNA methylation occurring at specific behavior- and stress-related genes (e.g., glucocorticoid receptor gene, *NR3C1*, Griffiths & Hunter, 2014; serotonin transporter gene, *SLC6A4*, Provenzi, Giorda, Beri, & Montirosso, 2016) was shown to affect infant behavior. Methylation status of these target genes is sensitive to early adversity, including maternal depression (Devlin, Brain, Austin, & Oberlander, 2010) and pain exposure (Provenzi et al., 2015). Emerging research suggests that epigenetic mechanisms could be involved in setting the stage for less-than-optimal temperament under specific at-risk conditions, including preterm birth (Montirosso et al., 2016) and prenatal exposure to antidepressant drugs (Gartstein et al., 2016). Importantly, epigenetic processes were shown to be involved in the inter-generational transmission of trauma, including the holocaust (Yehuda et al., 2014).

Results of this study also have implications for more proximal, contemporaneous physiological process. Biomarkers such as Hypothalamic-Pituitary-Adrenal (HPA) axis response, electroencephalography (EEG) frontal asymmetry, and Respiratory Sinus Arrhythmia (RSA), are thought to underlie individual differences in temperament (Gartstein et al., 2016), and require examination in future cross-cultural developmental research. For example, considering whether or not SUR is accompanied by a neurophysiological signature of dysregulated approach (i.e., left frontal EEG asymmetry) in cultures for which higher levels were linked with more significant behavior problems could be important, as existing studies suggest that coordination between behavioral and neurophysiological approach-related activity increases risk for externalizing (Degnan et al., 2011). Additional biomarkers may be particularly relevant to cross-cultural research. For example, microbiota can be expected to differ among cultural groups with variability in diet and other relevant practices, and microbiome composition has been linked to toddler temperament (Christian et al., 2015), albeit in the US only thus far.

The lessons of the JETTC are limited in multiple ways that suggest promising directions for future research. Extending our framework downward in age to infancy, and even gestation, would allow insight on very early differences between populations, with prenatal evaluations essential to discerning epigenetic effects. Likewise, extending study to older ages would allow consideration of children's perspectives and the ways that families negotiate more complex interactions with the social world. Longitudinal investigation is needed to enhance inference regarding the degree to which parents and children change one another in a cultural context. Consideration of other aspects of the developmental niche will also prove important. In particular, including fathers, grandparents, siblings, teachers, and other members of children's worlds, in data collection efforts is crucial for understanding the way in which culture shapes their behavior.

Perhaps the most important shortcoming of the JETTC is our reliance exclusively on parent report. One implication of this circumstance concerns source variance, or the likelihood of inflated or spurious associations among examined variables caused by their originating from the same source. More specific concerns have been raised with respect to parent report of temperament, with questions regarding caregivers' ability to provide meaningful temperament-related information for their offspring because of their considerable investment in their outcomes, and thus, an inherent lack of objectivity (e.g., Kagan, 1998; Rothbart & Bates, 2006). Similarly, parent reports of their own behavior may be compromised by social desirability, such that they reflect cultural ideals as well as indication of their true actions. Despite potential limitations, however, parent report offers an effective developmentally appropriate approach, and at least with respect to temperament assessment, often demonstrates reliability and predictive validity superior to other methods, including structured observations (Hart, Field, & Roitfarb, 1999; Pauli-Pott, Mertesacker, Bade, Haverkock, & Beckmann, 2003).

Additional future directions do not require more data and involve further analyses of the JETTC and related datasets. One important task is continuing to hone measures of temperament and other constructs for the purposes of cross-cultural investigations. Specifically, measurement invariance has only been rarely considered (Ahadi, Rothbart, & Ye, 1993; Porter et al., 2005; Zhou, Lengua, & Wang, 2009) in measures of children or their developmental niche. Measurement invariance reflects the degree to which instruments operate equivalently between groups. Without evidence of invariance, there is a possibility that observed differences between groups are a function of measurement (e.g., differential item functioning), rather than differences in the underlying constructs themselves. Existing datasets, including, but not limited to JETTC, because of the considerable requirement for the number of participants, could be leveraged to examine measurement invariance, improving our instruments as a result.

Temperament and behavior problem domains captured by JETTC should be analyzed at the fine-grained level. Previous studies indicated important differences among fine-grained temperament attributes associated with the same overarching factor (e.g., Gartstein et al., 2017), and differentiation among domains of symptoms/behavior problems would be informative with respect to treatment and prevention targets. Further consideration of sex differences may also be valuable, despite the relative dearth of effects in the presented analyses.

The JETTC message seems particularly resonant in the current climate, with cooling of friendships at best, and escalation of tensions at worst, becoming the norm in international relations. Our findings underscore the fact that often there is not one typical or healthy pattern of relations among influential variables, and that contextual factors can moderate links between the developmental niche and child outcomes. Perhaps most importantly, JETTC serves as an illustration of what can be accomplished by embracing international collaboration and supporting cooperative efforts. Funding provided to one of the editors (MAG) supported data collection only, with investigators and research assistants across sites contributing without compensation to further our common understanding of social-emotional development. Similar joint effort around the globe is required more than ever to address critical challenges facing all of us and our planet.

## References


Ahadi, S. A., Rothbart, M. K., & Ye, R. M. (1993). Child temperament in the U.S. and China: Similarities and differences. *European Journal of Personality, 7*, 359–378.

Blodgett, J. G., Bakir, A., & Rose, G. M. (2008). A test of the validity of Hofstede's cultural framework. *Journal of Consumer Marketing, 25*, 339–349.

Bornstein, M. H. (1995). Form and function: Implications for studies of culture and human development. *Culture and Psychology, 1*, 123–137.

Boyd, R., & Richerson, P. J. (1985). *Culture and the evolutionary process*. Chicago, IL: The University of Chicago Press.

Chen, X., Hastings, P. D., Rubin, K. H., Chen, H., Cen, G., & Stewart, S. L. (1998). Child-rearing attitudes and behavioral inhibition in Chinese and Canadian toddlers: A cross-cultural study. Developmental Psychology, 34, 677.

Christian, L. M., Galley, J. D., Hade, E. M., Schoppe-Sullivan, S., Kamp Dush, C., & Bailey, M. T. (2015). Gut microbiome composition is associated with temperament during early childhood. *Brain, Behavior, and Immunity, 45*, 118–127.

Degnan, K. A., Hane, A. A., Henderson, H. A., Moas, O. L., Reeb-Sutherland, B. C., & Fox, N. A. (2011). Longitudinal stability of temperamental exuberance and social-emotional outcomes in early childhood. *Developmental Psychology, 47*, 765–780.

Devlin, A. M., Brain, U., Austin, J., & Oberlander, T. F. (2010). Prenatal exposure to maternal depressed mood and the MTHFR C677T variant affect SLC6A4 methylation in infants at birth. *PLoS ONE, 5*(8), e12201.

Gartstein, M. A., Hookenson, K. V., Brain, U., Devlin, A. M., Grunau, R. E., & Oberlander, T. F. (2016). Sculpting infant soothability: The role of prenatal

SSRI antidepressant exposure and neonatal SLC6A4 methylation status. *Developmental Psychobiology, 58*(6), 745–758.

Gartstein, M. A., Prokasky, A., Bell, M. A., Calkins, S., Bridgett, D. J., Braungart-Rieker, J., . . . Seamon, E. (2017). Latent profile and cluster analysis of infant temperament: Comparisons across person-centered approaches. *Developmental Psychology, 53*, 1811–1825.

Gartstein, M. A. & Skinner, M. K. (2017). Prenatal influences on temperamental development: The role of environmental epigenetics. *Development and Psychopathology, 12*, 1–35. [Epub ahead of print]

Gartstein, M. A., Slobodskaya, H. R., & Kinsht, I. A. (2003). Cross-cultural differences in the first year of life: United States of America (U.S.) and Russian. *International Journal of Behavioral Development, 27*, 316–328.

Gintis, H. (2011). Gene-culture coevolution and the nature of human sociality. *Philosophical Transactions of the Royal Society B, 366*, 878–888.

Giusti, L., Provenzi, L., Tavian, D., Missaglia, S., & Montirosso, R. (2017). The BDNFval66met polymorphism and individual differences in temperament in 4-month-old infants: A pilot study. *Infant Behavior and Development, 47*, 22–26.

Griffiths, B. B., & Hunter, R. G. (2014). Neuroepigenetics of stress. *Neuroscience, 275*, 420–435.

Hart, S., Field, T., & Roitfarb, M. (1999). Depressed mothers' assessments of their neo nates' behaviors. *Infant Mental Health Journal, 20*, 200–210.

Hofstede, G. (1980). *Culture's Consequences: International Differences in Work-Related Values*. Beverly Hills, CA: Sage.

Hyman, S. E. (2009). How adversity gets under the skin. *Nature Neuroscience, 12*(3), 241.

Kagan, J. (1998). Biology and the child. In W. Damon & N. Eisenberg (Eds.), *Handbook of child psychology: Social, emotional and personality development* (5th ed., Vol. 3, pp. 177–235). New York, NY: Wiley.

Krassner, A., Gartstein, M. A., Park, C., Dragan, W. L., Lecannelier, F., & Putnam, S. P. (2017). East-West, Collectivist-Individualist: A Cross-Cultural Examination of Temperament in Toddlers from Chile, Poland, South Korea, and the U.S. *European Journal of Developmental Psychology, 14*, 449–464.

Keller, H., Lamm, B., Abels, M., Yovsi, R., Borke, J., Jensen, H., . . . (2006). Cultural models, socialization goals, and parenting ethnotheories: A multicultural analysis. *Journal of Cross-Cultural Psychology, 37*, 155–172.

McKinney, C., & Brown, K. (2017). Parenting and emerging adult internalizing problems: Regional differences suggest Southern parenting factor. *Journal of Child and Family Studies, 26*, 3156–3166.

McSweeney, B. (2002). Hofstede's model of national cultural differences and their consequences: A triumph of faith – A failure of analysis. *Human Relations, 55*, 89–118.

Papageorgiou, K., & Ronald, A. A. (2013). He who sees things grow from the beginning will have the finest view of them: A systematic review of genetic studies on psychological traits in infancy. *Neuroscience and Biobehavioral Reviews, 37*, 1500–1517.

Martel, M. M., Gremillion, M. L., Roberts, B. A., Zastrow, B. L., & Tackett, J. L. (2014). Longitudinal prediction of the one-year course of preschool ADHD symptoms: Implications for models of temperament-ADHD associations. *Personality and Individual Differences, 64*, 58–61.

Montirosso, R., Provenzi, L., Fumagalli, M., Sirgiovanni, I., Giorda, R., Pozzoli, U., . . . Borgatti, R. (2016). Serotonin transporter gene (SLC6A4) methylation associates with Neonatal Intensive Care Unit stay and 3-month-old temperament in preterm infants. *Child Development, 87*(1), 38–48.

Pauli-Pott, U., Mertesacker, B., Bade, U., Haverkock, A., & Beckmann, D. (2003). Parental perceptions and infant temperament development. *Infant Behavior & Development, 26*, 27–48.

Porter, C., Hart, C., Yang, C., Robinson, C., Frost Olsen, S., Zeng, Q., Jin, S. (2005). A comparative study of child temperament and parenting in Beijing, China and the western United States. *International Journal of Behavioral Development, 29*, 541–551.

Provenzi, L., Fumagalli, M., Sirgiovanni, I., Giorda, R., Pozzoli, U., Morandi, F., Montirosso, R. (2015). Pain-related stress during the Neonatal Intensive Care Unit stay and SLC6A4 methylation in very preterm infants. *Frontiers in Behavioral Neuroscience, 9*, 99.

Provenzi, L., Giorda, R., Beri, S., & Montirosso, R. (2016). SLC6A4 methylation as an epigenetic marker of life adversity exposures in humans: A systematic review of literature. *Neuroscience & Biobehavioral Reviews, 71*, 7–20.

Putnam, S. P., & Gartstein, M. A. (2017). Aggregate temperament scores from multiple countries: Associations with aggregate personality traits, cultural dimensions, and allelic frequency. *Journal of Research in Personality, 67*, 157–170.

Rentfrow, P. J., Gosling, S. D., Jokela, M., Stillwell, D. J., Kosinski, M., & Potter, J. (2013). Divided we stand: Three psychological regions of the United States and their political, economic, social, and health correlates. *Journal of Personality and Social Psychology, 105*, 996–1012.

Rothbart, M. K., & Bates, J. E. (2006). Temperament. In W. Damon, R. Lerner, & N. Eisenberg (Eds.), *Handbook of child psychology: Social, emotional, and personality development* (6th ed., Vol. 3, pp. 99–166). New York, NY: Wiley.

Saudino, K. J., & Wang, M. (2012). Quantitative and molecular genetic studies of temperament. In M. Zentner & R. Shiner (Eds.), *Handbook of temperament* (pp. 315–346). New York, NY: Guilford.

Yehuda, R., Daskalakis, N. P., Lehrner, A., Desarnaud, F., Bader, H. N., Makotkine, I., Meaney, M. J. (2014). Influences of maternal and paternal PTSD on epigenetic regulation of the glucocorticoid receptor gene in Holocaust survivor offspring. *American Journal of Psychiatry, 171*(8), 872–880.

Zhou, Q., Lengua, L. J., & Wang, Y. (2009). The relations of temperament reactivity and effortful control to children's adjustment problem in China and the United States. *Developmental Psychology, 45*, 724–739.

# INDEX

Page numbers in *italics* denote an illustration, **bold** a table